"This is a...
thought.... Its theology ...
talism and theologies which ignore the realities of political power and self-righteousness."

—Harvey Stevens,
United Church of Canada

"What a serious and loving endeavor. This will be valuable to . . . readers who, like the editor, longed for this voice."

—Rose-Hannah Gaskin,
United Church of Canada, retired

"First impressions; I like."

—Doug Flint,
United Church of Canada, retired

"Your timing is on the mark. Post-COVID-19 pandemic, a meditative and contemplative reader such as this is needed. . . . Your daily reader will deepen my tiny meditative practice—and that of others as well."

—Michele Lamont,
public health consultant

"During the COVID-19 pandemic, I felt isolated and needed connection with others and something larger than myself. Readings that are based in history and the larger Christian community bring comfort and solace. Many people don't have time to read books but would like short readings to support them in times of suffering and difficulty. Barry Morris's reflections provide this support and fill this need."

—Joanne Keelan,
retired social worker

"Invitational and wise, this Niebuhr-family meditation-contemplation reader will be a rich resource to any who seek contemplation and spiritual growth. Morris has thoughtfully woven together timeless and prophetic insights. The Niebuhr family's words and stories offer the reader a much-needed lens through which to reflect on today's personal and global challenges."

—TRACY J. TROTHEN,
Canadian Association for Spiritual Care (CASC)

"I found both the foreword and the preface very interesting. Douglas Hall's description of theology having to 'reach down deeply into the human mind and spirit and grasp the meaning for society here and now' resonated with me. . . . I looked at several entries and decided 'Yes, it would be a good book to have.' The passages I read in the book are inspiring reading."

—MARY AL LAY,
member, Trinity Grace United Church

"I think people who are interested in 'what makes Barry tick,' including me, would be interested in reading the reflections. And I sure appreciate Reinhold Niebuhr's 'public theology' and 'serenity prayer.' He and his family contributed hugely to social, public theology."

—VICKI OBEDKOFF,
United Church of Canada

"This is a beautiful work, and a great treasury of wisdom."

—ROBERT ELLSBERG,
Orbis Books

"This book presents much wisdom and as many challenges . . . the book addresses the needs of those who are serious, studious, willing to be patient, and yet open to social activism even if on the 'sidelines.'"

—SIMON APPOLLONI,
associate publishing director, Novalis Publishing

"This was a fascinating read. Barry Morris has compiled a thoughtful and thoroughly engaging daily meditation and contemplation of Niebuhr's work. . . . This book is most certainly one that belongs on the bedside table of anyone committed to living their faith out justly, as it provides daily moments of pause, taking stock, and preparing oneself to be engaged in the world around them."

—JEFFREY DALE,
United Church of Canada

"The well-selected excerpts of various writings from members of the Niebuhr clan provide windows for readers—Christian or not—into how to live with searching honesty, integrity, humbleness, and hope. Not at all a bad thing to add to one's day."

—ELEANOR (ELLIE) J. STEBNER,
Simon Fraser University, emeritus

"Here is an excellent introduction to neoorthodoxy and Christian realism for some readers and a welcome reengagement with the Niebuhrs for those already familiar with writings by and about these giants of American theology and models of pastoral discernment. Recent developments, international and domestic, confirm the timeless insight of Reinhold and H. Richard Niebuhr and underscore their conviction that Christian faith must issue in faithful living even to the broadest horizons of life."

—BRUCE TAYLOR,
author of *Love Walks on Wounded Feet*

Remembering Faithfully Forward

To Charles Anderson

For my good ol'
studious religion
teacher while @
U.B.C — 1960's —
and who sponsored
me / coaxed me to
Steely Theology beyond
UBC, where
the introduction
expresses led to
an earest encounter
and life — long
dew cotton t
the Niebuhrs.
¡ Gracias!
Aarm

Remembering Faithfully Forward

*The Daily Niebuhr Family
Meditation-Contemplation Reader*

BARRY K. MORRIS

Foreword by Douglas John Hall
Illustrations by Jim Houston

RESOURCE *Publications* • Eugene, Oregon

REMEMBERING FAITHFULLY FORWARD
The Daily Niebuhr Family Meditation-Contemplation Reader

Copyright © 2022 Barry K. Morris. All rights reserved. Except for brief quotations in critical publications or reviews, no part of this book may be reproduced in any manner without prior written permission from the publisher. Write: Permissions, Wipf and Stock Publishers, 199 W. 8th Ave., Suite 3, Eugene, OR 97401.

Resource Publications
An Imprint of Wipf and Stock Publishers
199 W. 8th Ave., Suite 3
Eugene, OR 97401

www.wipfandstock.com

PAPERBACK ISBN: 978-1-6667-3835-3
HARDCOVER ISBN: 978-1-6667-9892-0
EBOOK ISBN: 978-1-6667-9893-7

MAY 27, 2022 12:17 PM

O Lord, who has promised that all things will work together for good to those who love you, grant us patience amidst the tumults, pains and afflictions of life, and faith to discern your love within, above, and beyond impartial destinies of this great drama of life. Save us from every vain glorious pretension by which we demand favors which violate your love for all your children, and grant us grace to appropriate every fortune, both good and evil, for the triumph of the suffering, crucified, and risen Lord in our souls and life. In whose name we ask it.

NIEBUHR, R., *JUSTICE AND MERCY*, 22.

I am haunted by the phrase: "the hungry sheep look up and are not fed."

[CITING JOHN MILTON, LYCIDAS, 1638]
NIEBUHR, H.R., *RESPONSIBILITY OF THE CHURCH*, 144.

The work of the theologian is not simply to clarify the logic of faith by abstracting it from this complex human world, but rather to steady faith by sharpening its expressiveness and practical efficacy in this complex world.

NIEBUHR, R.R., IN *THE CHRISTIAN CENTURY*, 2017.
HTTPS://WWW.CHRISTIANCENTURY.ORG/ARTICLE/RICHARD-
NIEBUHR-THEOLOGIAN-AND-TEACHER-DIES-AGE-90

After a time Paul went on another missionary journey, accomplished this time with Silas. He was more certain than ever before that, through Jesus, God made it clear that there is no distinction between Jew and Greek, between slave and free, between male and female—that all are equally important.

NIEBUHR, H., *ONE STORY*, 162.

Whether we live or die, we live unto the Lord.

NIEBUHR, L., CITED IN BINGHAM, *COURAGE TO CHANGE*, 52. (CF. ROMANS 14:8).

To follow Jesus is the first commandment of the Kingdom of God, that is, we are disciples of Jesus exactly to the extent that we serve, giving our life and strength in the service of our fellow men.

NIEBUHR, G. [SR.], CITED IN CHRYSTAL, "*A MAN OF THE HOUR AND THE TIME*," 423.

Contents

Acknowledgments | ix

List of Figures | x

Foreword: The Niebuhrs by Douglas John Hall | xi

Preface | xv

JANUARY | 1
National Mentoring Month

FEBRUARY | 21
Black History Month (USA and Canada)

MARCH | 41
Women's History Month

APRIL | 62
Second Chance Month

MAY | 83
Mental Health Awareness Month

JUNE | 102
National Indigenous History Month (Canada) and National Safety Month

JULY | 120
National Fragile X Awareness Month

AUGUST | 140
National Immunization Awareness Month (Canada and USA)

SEPTEMBER | 155
Gospel Music Heritage Month

OCTOBER | 171
National Bullying Prevention Month, and Action

NOVEMBER | 187
National Family Caregivers Month (USA)

DECEMBER | 204
Month of the Advent Season

APPENDIX: Brief Profiles of the Niebuhrs Employed in This Reader | 221

INDEXES | 227

Bibliography | 233

Acknowledgments

KEN LYOTIER, FOR ORIGINAL table talks at the Cottage Deli in Gastown Vancouver, BC, and consistent encouragement on the very possibility of this Reader; Bruce Alexander, John Badertscher, Pam Cooley, Lori Gabrielson, Tim Dickau, Harvey Stevens, and many others who offered actual endorsements, for quick labors-of-love feedback; the thoughtful foreword of Douglas J. Hall and, along with a polite rejection e-mail or two from other hoped-for publishers (re: "un-marketability"), the encouragement of Professors Rebekah Miles, Ellie Stebner, Tracy Trothen, and Ray Whitehead, and, of course, the gracious sketches of Jim Houston (below as a young lad). I thank Joanie Wolfe, an intrepid editor, for her painstaking work, from scratch to finish (accompanied in and to the end by Wipf & Stock's patient typesetter). All such persons, along with the selected Niebuhrs, form that indispensable cloud of witnesses that inspire, correct, cajole, balance, and sustain one for the long haul.

Jim Houston as an early youth and budding artist/cartoonist

List of Figures

Figure 1.   Jim Houston as an early youth and budding artist/cartoonist, Acknowledgments

Figure 2.   "Barry Morris, Toronto 1970s," Preface

Figure 3.   "Hunkered down in a storm at sea," January 23

Figure 4.   "Forgiveness," March 31

Figure 5.   "Good Friday Walk for Justice," April 4

Figure 6.   "Betrayed," April 19

Figure 7.   "I have a dream . . .," December 31

Front Cover: "Grace-based Serenity Prayer Themes"

Six Niebuhrs (back row left to right: Gustav [Sr.], Lydia [matriarch];

front row left to right: Gustav [Jr.], Reinhold, Richard, and Elizabeth)

Foreword

The Niebuhrs

NORTH AMERICA HAS MANY well-known "religious" families, but none, I think, is so paramount in modern Christian history as the Niebuhr family. The patriarch of the family, Gustav [Sr.], ran away from his home in the principality of Lippe, Germany, at age eighteen, settled in the American mid-West and became a minister of his German-American denomination. Three of his children became theologians—Hulda, Richard and Reinhold. Reinhold was my teacher at Union Theological Seminary in New York City for seven years in the 1950s, and I admired him greatly. I also came to know his wife, Ursula, and their children, Elisabeth and Christopher who were both a little older than I.

What distinguishes Reinhold Niebuhr from many who teach theology today, I think, is that he was a minister before he entered the world of scholarship: for seventeen years he preached every Sunday in a growing church in Detroit. Consequently, he not only knew the Bible very well, but he knew how to teach it in an ordinary congregation. Though he became in time perhaps the best-known Protestant thinker in North America, he never lost his remarkable capacity for explaining complex theological, ethical and psychological language in the language of "ordinary people." His brother, Richard, who achieved a high reputation as a theologian never quite managed that very basic translation.

For Reinhold Niebuhr, theology was a matter of life and death. It could never be for the intellect alone, it came from deeper down, and no Christian theological concept, however complex and historically involved, could convey what it had to say until it had reached down deeply into the human mind and spirit. Moreover, it was not enough to discover the personal meaning of biblical ideas and texts, one had to grasp their

xi

xii   FOREWORD

meaning for society here and now. That is why Reinhold Niebuhr became most public theologian in North American history: He wanted not only to change individuals but to change society—or to attempt it! He used to say that he had cut his theological eye-teeth fighting Henry Ford, the largest employer of his city, who fought the unions, boasted about his five-dollar-a-day wages, and did not draw attention to the fact that his car-factory was regularly closed down for "retooling." It takes courage and patience to "change what can be changed."

Of course, Reinhold knew that many things ought, but could not, be changed. They had to be lived with. This takes serenity, assisted by and grounded in grace. Yet some of the things that could be changed were not. "It's always been like that," people would say. "For example, there have always been two political parties in this country, . . . etc." But Niebuhr wasn't satisfied with either of those political parties, so for a time he became a socialist, and a Left-ish inclination could usually be detected in his social teachings. His famous "Serenity Prayer" therefore cautions against both the arrogant assumption of mastery and the excuse of inability. We should aim for "the courage to change what can be changed" and "the serenity to accept what cannot be changed"—and perhaps above all we should covet the wisdom that can distinguish between the two." These grace-based Serenity Prayer virtues are helpfully referenced and valuably cited in Morris' edited Niebuhr Family Daily Mediation and Contemplation Reader.

From the outset of his ministry, Reinhold Niebuhr pursued theological study because that was the path to wisdom. He had no patience with intellectual laziness! But neither did he like the snobbery of many intellectuals.

Ursula Keppel-Compton, Reinhold's wife, was a bright Oxford University graduate and a scholar in her own right. She brought to the ongoing dialogue with her husband a fine English sense of language and logic and, as Reinhold himself often said publicly, his many books and speeches were always consequences of that dialogue.

Niebuhr believed that egocentrism, unwarranted and exaggerated pride, is humankind's most characteristic sin. I remember an incident at the opening of the new Huron College buildings at the University of Western Ontario half a century ago. The last question from the audience of clergy (mostly Anglican) was: "Dr Niebuhr, what precisely do you mean by pride?"

FOREWORD

Just behind the lectern there was a painting by a prominent London artist. Quick as a wink, Niebuhr spun around where he stood and pointed his finger at the large signature of the artist in the right-hand corner of the nature painting: "That's what I mean," said he. I think the artist was in the audience.

Douglas John Hall, C.M., Th.D.

Preface and Introduction

It is the recall of an anxious browsing for a book in the University of British Columbia store of the early 1960s that aroused an exploration of the Niebuhrs' and, particularly (but not only), Reinhold Niebuhr. *An Interpretation of Christian Ethics* was not his eventual masterpiece, but it was compact enough for a start and convenient for my jacket pocket. I had been cautioned not to read Niebuhr by then Young Life mentors; he was deemed too liberal, and insufficiently orthodox. This enticed me to buy the book, and many more since. On another occasion, I made use of my older brother, John's, south Vancouver apartment between summer passenger railway trips as a dining car waiter. In the quietness and light of the bathroom, I poured over the two volumes of *Human Nature* and *Human Destiny* (*The Nature and Destiny of Man, Vol. I and Vol. II*, respectively), engrossing the topics of sin and accompanying grace-based mercy. These were among many nudges to go deeper and be thankful for the accompaniment; also, a stirring to consider at least theological studies and just possibly, eventually, the ministry (which for over a decade I had "prayerfully" resisted).

On to Chicago Theological Seminary via a fortuitous fellowship, I gleaned *Human Nature* and *Human Destiny* chapters on social justice and eschatology; I also picked up Reinhold Niebuhr's *Leaves from the Notebook of Tamed Cynic* journal. Through the seminary's bookstore I also bought some of his younger brother, H. Richard Niebuhr's, books out of his long Yale Divinity School career, recalling *The Responsible Self* and *Christ and Culture*. In that period, I feasted on a course from the University of Chicago's Divinity School and, just on Reinhold's writings, focusing again on *Human Nature* and *Human Destiny*. Later still, for another post-graduate degree with Vancouver School of Theology, I took another seminar on Reinhold Niebuhr via the last teaching assistant he had had before enforced retirement, Terry (Terence R.) Anderson. His interpersonal reminiscences enriched the sessions. Each class opened with a Reinhold Niebuhr prayer. My library expanded and, fast forward, added H. Richard Niebuhr's son, Richard Reinhold Niebuhr—what a family name! He long taught and wrote via Harvard Divinity School. Then Richard's son, the last chosen Niebuhr alive, a journalist and teacher of newspaper and online journalism, Gustav Niebuhr [Jr.] ("Jr." has been employed to distinguish him from his great-grandfather). Among newspaper articles, his two books of *Beyond Tolerance: Searching for Interfaith Understanding in America* and *Lincoln's Bishop: A President, a Priest, and the Fate of 300 Dakota Sioux Warriors* are herein employed. In 2003, my late colleague and fellow United Church of Canada-traveler, Doug Graves, commended Reinhold Niebuhr's daughter, Elisabeth Sifton's, exploration and exposition of *The Serenity Prayer* with its instructive subtitle, *Faith and Politics in Times of Peace and War*. What an oft-commended morsel to those in recovery from addictions and pandemic-enhanced post-traumatic stress, including loss and grief (personal and vocational for me and, thus, this reader's existential importance). Her recent anthology of some of her father's religious and political writings, especially the presence of valuable prayers, is gratefully used. Most recently, I sought out the two Niebuhr brothers' sister, Hulda Niebuhr's, writings (*The One Story* and a discovered biography by Elizabeth Caldwell, *A Mysterious Mantle*), though scarce since she concentrated her studies and teaching primarily as an educator. Their father, Gustav (Sr.'s) ("Sr." has been added to distinguish him from his great-grandson) work is still alive thanks to meticulous research by Niebuhr family scholar, William Chrystal. Their mother, Lydia Niebuhr, makes a direct appearance in the opening quotations and elsewhere via her offspring. Finally, Reinhold Niebuhr's wife and collaborative writing partner, Ursula, is duly employed. *Justice and Mercy* (Niebuhr, R., 1974) and *Remembering Reinhold Niebuhr: Letters of Reinhold and Ursula M. Niebuhr* could not have been possible without her diligent and devoted research and editing. This is duly acknowledged in Reinhold Niebuhr's opening remarks in On Man's Nature and His Communities. It has been intentional, thus, to have included four of the Niebuhr family women.

Over decades, I have made thankful use of daily meditation books, in particular, those of/on Thomas Merton, Dietrich Bonhoeffer, and Benedictine Sister Joan Chittister. Out of their beneficence, and to collect and justify the presence of so many Niebuhr (and family) writings, why not a daily meditation and contemplation reader on/of the Niebuhrs, and

PREFACE AND INTRODUCTION

not only Reinhold? (See the Appendix for profiles on the summoned and employed Niebuhrs.) There are several biographies and anthologies of especially Reinhold's writings, and Scott Paeth's convenient *The Niebuhr Brothers for Armchair Theologians* along with Douglas J. Hall's *Remembered Voices: Reclaiming the Legacy of "Neo-Orthodoxy,"* (on Reinhold and H. Richard Niebuhr) but nothing with Reinhold and his relatives in a patient meditative—and really contemplative—process. Thus, this book of 366+ entries is herein presented and barely resisting an appendix (if only on the sources and reflections of the grace-based "Serenity Prayer"). How was it that "grace" got overlooked in its long and popular uses? Alas, what has been overlooked in this daily meditation and contemplation offering?

As a meditation reader, it is unlike many other readers where a single sentence is noted, or excerpted, and the writer quickly adds his or her own commentary and helpmate for the day to engage. Herein the texts, including supplementary or complementary entries, attest for themselves. Jim Houston's long sought suggestive sketches add a "right-brain" (creative) balance to otherwise preponderantly heavy "left-brain" (logical) statements (albeit stories and prayers complement).

It is my hope that the selections—among a vast number that could be gleaned and applied—are inspiring and encouraging. But also representatively faithful of the paradoxes, tensions, frustrations, conflicts, afflictions, and incomplete scars and sufferings of the soul—and, the scars and soul in/of society—that this family of thinkers, teachers, preachers, journalists, editors, correspondents, diary or journal writers and, not all, church planters and network activists with and for which they sought to communicate and thereby bequeath legacies. Bordering on the esoteric and somewhat dated language of their era, may these daily entries nourish. While making several inclusive changes, I also ask for the reader's understanding and forbearance in the decision to retain the authors' use of some specific gender references in some selected entries as it was written in their own time. Merci.

Overall, I have aimed for variety in the mix and possible match of the chosen entries via the nine Niebuhrs (including the patriarch, Gustav, Sr., and Lydia, the matriarch, for December 31). I often wondered if an entry was too long, perhaps too short and, in any event, not overly captivated by the authors' historical embeddedness. When is an offering timely and timeless? In the process of considering, choosing, and assiduously copying from the Niebuhrs to enrich, supplement or complement an entry, could this amount to a degree of intensity and hint of harmony of the selections' authors and the eventual title headings (via a word or phrase from the text itself and often with a question mark)? Would a series of successive entries contribute to a sustained reading of a theme over several days and in sync with the seasons of the calendar and church year and perhaps specially named days and months of the year? (With the use of the Index one can discern successive entries pertaining to the church seasons of Advent, Lent/Easter, and Pentecost; also, the topics of the grace-based "Serenity Prayer," sin and the need thus for organizing power for justice, reconciliation and, not all, mystery and meaning.) The reader is thus an exercise in contemplation as well. Variety and vitality hopefully are depicted in the savored and sundry themes (with which the Index hopefully assists) and by way of use of prayers, sermons and/or lectures, special or guest lectureships, letters, interviews, and with gratitude to Jim Houston (a long-time urban minister, originally with the Jesuits and then the Anglican Church in Canada's ministries) for his gifted sketches.

Is a rough yet meaningful integration of the various sources and themes thus evident? With the book as a whole—where Gestalt-wise, there may be a promise of the whole being greater than the sum of its parts—I hope for and entrust that in the reader, here and there, arises a contemplative nudge to read—and pray—deeper, thicker, and wider.

HELPFULLY ENGAGING THIS DAILY READER?

One may draw insight and inspiration from a first-time browse. One may file it in the imagination and read it again when the dust settles and a bit more integration occurs (even years later on) via return visits. One may well wish for a guiding question as, again, some popular daily meditation readers offer. Or you may wish for a summary mantra at the end of a daily entry and even a prayer to try to present a tidy morsel to munch on. Or you may look for your own special theme day of a year, albeit not all to everyone's satisfaction could have been found and included. Hulda Niebuhr, the educator of the family and with a focus on children and young people says:

> Sometimes a story [aka entry] is ineffective because it is a poor story, not worth the telling. Sometimes it is a good story in the wrong place. Often it is a good story in the right place, gone savorless because the teller [aka reader] is not prepared to tell [aka hear] it.

> in Caldwell, *A Mysterious Mantle*, 70.

In any case, I hope you do not feel prematurely discouraged if a daily entry is just not your immediate cup of tea or strong cup of coffee. Other daily entries' title captions, the index and within it, special marked days and months as a whole, may assist you. As my close and now, alas, late friend Ken Lyotier, has commented and commended:

> People will need to give it a serious read in order to realize the importance of it. This type of reader may be more difficult to find in a day and age when our time is torn in so many fractured directions. Ironically, it is all the more reason why such a devotional as this one could be so beneficial.[1]

"Barry Morris, Toronto 1970s," by Jim Houston

---

1. "We live in an age that is said to be ahistorical. It is difficult to remember the past —or even acknowledge it—living as we do, focused on an an 'eternal present,' driven by busy schedules and information overload, and wrapped in anxieties about careers, family, health, the environment, terrorism, the future of the world. It can be both comforting and discouraging to know that many of the issues we confront today have been with us in different forms for a long time . . . " Bernie Lucht executive producer of the CBC Massey Lectures, introduction to *The Lost Massey Lectures: Recovered Classics from Five Great Thinkers*. Toronto, ON: House of Anansi, 2007, xv-xvi.

The past is not done and it is not over. it's still in process. which is another way of saying that when it's critiqued, analyzed, it yields new information about itself.

TONI MORISON (AMERICAN NOVELIST)

There shines forth fleetingly the ever threatened truth that each and every [person], on the foundation of their own sufferings and joys, builds for all.

ALBERT CAMUS, "CREATE DANGEROUSLY,"
RESISTANCE, REBELLION, AND DEATH

JANUARY
National Mentoring Month

Revelation means for us that part of our inner history which illuminates the rest of it and which is itself intelligible. Sometimes when we read a difficult book, seeking to follow a complicated argument, we come across a luminous sentence from which we can go forward and backward and so attain some understanding of the whole. Revelation is like that.

Niebuhr, H.R., *Meaning of Revelation*, 68.

The Letter to the Hebrews calls Jesus Christ the *archegos*, that is . . . "the captain of salvation" [2:10], "the pioneer and perfecter of our faith" [12:2]. Of all the New Testament titles for Jesus, *archegos* commends itself as the most descriptive, the most elastic and the least metaphysical.

Niebuhr, R.R., in Primeaux, *Richard R. Niebuhr on Christ*, 103.

[My father] was probably more responsible than anybody else for the choice of my vocation and avocation . . . I was thrilled by my father's sermons and regarded him as the most interesting man in town. So what else should I do but be a minister in his image . . . I'm glad insofar as I have adequately exploited the vision of my father.

Niebuhr, R., in Chrystal, "Man of the Hour and the Time," 416.

JANUARY 1.   SOURCE AND THE END . . . SUSTAINED BY A VAST COMPANY?

Almighty Father, who are the source and the end of our life and the light also of our pilgrimage, grant your grace so that the good in us may prevail over the evil, so that everything in us may be brought in harmony with your will, and we may be enabled to live in charity with our neighbors and fellow workers. Keep us humble in your sight and before our fellow-men, so that neither pride nor indifference may destroy the bond which we have with our co-workers. May our love of you hallow all our relations, and our service to our fellows complete our reverent obedience.

Niebuhr, R., *Reinhold Niebuhr: Major Works*, 698.

. . . Eternal God, creator and redeemer of all, we thank you for this new day and for all your mercies which reveal the constancy of your love . . . We give thanks that we are heirs of all the ages and that our faith is sustained by a vast company of the living and the dead who have known you and proclaimed your mercy . . . and that each one may in their own way find access to the throne of grace.

Niebuhr, R., *Reinhold Niebuhr: Major Works*, 704.

I have long known myself to be singularly fortunate, blessed . . . by a virtual "cloud of witnesses" who have strengthened us on our way, a cloud that includes my father, H. Richard; my uncle, Reinhold; my aunt, Hulda; and also "Muttenchen," my remarkably strong, strong-willed, and gifted grandmother [Lydia]. How all these near ancestors strengthened and shaped one another, while also sometimes disagreeing with one another, is knowledge of which I have only intimations, and do not expect to possess. But the suspicion lingers that family legacies, while they can be intricately woven and become cherished "garments," are woven out of many lives and are of a different order from prophetic mantles.

Niebuhr, R.R., in Chrystal, *A Father's Mantle*, x.

JANUARY 2.   ULTIMATE CLUE TO THE MYSTERY OF . . . ?

The Christian faith, at least, is faith in revelation. It believes that God has made himself known. It believes that God has spoken through the prophets and finally in the Son. It accepts the revelation in Christ as the ultimate clue to the mystery of God's nature and purpose in the world, particularly the mystery of the relation of God's justice to the Holy One's mercy. But these clues to the mystery do not eliminate the periphery of mystery. God remains deus absconditus.

Niebuhr, R., *Reinhold Niebuhr: Major Works*, 155.

Insofar as God is Deus Revelatus [the revealed God] it is clear that God's righteousness is not that of rewards and punishment but of forgiveness, and in the light of revelation, history is illumined as the place where now God rules and does so with precision.

Niebuhr, H.R., *Theology, History, and Culture*, 100.

I cannot know you if you do not speak to me out of the depths of your personal unity and transcendence. I can make all kinds of guesses about your behavior, but probably they will be false. I make guesses about God's behavior in the world but they are false unless God speaks out of his freedom to my freedom. This is why history is of revelational importance in human life.

Niebuhr, R., *Justice and Mercy*, 135.

JANUARY 3.   PURSUIT OF PEACE, BUT HOW . . . ?

The human's unquiet and restless life is the fruit of his or her special freedom; and of the inevitable corruptions of that freedom by inordinate desire. But one cannot accept this anxiety and friction as normal. All creatures, including man and woman, must have peace. Harmony is the normal condition of all existence. All vitalities and centers of life in the whole creation were meant to exist in conformity with their own proper nature and in accord with all other creatures. For this reason we seek after peace just as certainly as we also seek after many ends incompatible with it. But what kind of peace is possible for humans? How are we to find a peace which will not destroy our essential freedom? Which will not rob us of the unique dignity that distinguishes us from the brute creation?

Niebuhr, R., *Discerning the Signs,* **176.**

JANUARY 4. MEANING IN MYSTERY?

The sense of both mystery and meaning is perhaps most succinctly expressed in the forty-fifth chapter of Isaiah, where, practically in the same breath, the prophet declares on the one hand, "Verily thou art a God that hidest thyself, O God of Israel, the Saviour" [Isa. 45:15] and on the other, insists that God has made himself known: "I have not spoken in secret, in a dark place of the earth: I have not unto the seed of Jacob, Seek ye me in vain: I the Lord speak righteous, I declare things that are right" [Isa. 45:19]. This double emphasis is a perfect symbolic expression both of the meaning which faith discerns and of the penumbra of mystery which it recognizes around the core of meaning. The essential character of God, in God's relations to the world, is known. God is the Creator, Judge and Saviour of [humanity]. Yet God does not fully disclose [God's self], and [God's] thoughts are too high to be comprehended by human thought.

Niebuhr, R., *Discerning the Signs,* **156.**

JANUARY 5. STAYING POWER

Meditation books occasionally draw criticism, though of a mild sort. "It's almost like looking up your horoscope," said Renita Weems, a professor of Old Testament at Vanderbilt Divinity School. "Every now and then it's on the money." ...

But Ms. Weems, who is also an ordained elder in the African Methodist Episcopal Church, added that she owns four daily devotional books, including one designed for new mothers. "They are great for people like me who after harassed, tired and don't have much time, and want one new thought for the day," she said.

Ms. Johnson-Byrne of the Hazelden Foundation says reading the books can be considered a form of prayer, but others say the books are more a form of psychological affirmation," said Dianne, the owner of Miami's 9th Chakra bookstore who, "like Cher or Madonna," does not use a last name.

Will meditation books have a staying power with their current audience?

Niebuhr, G. [Jr.], "Seeking Solace and Support," 5.

JANUARY 6. END OF CHRISTMAS SEASON/FEAST OF EPIPHANY.

This has been a wonderful Christmas season. The people have been splendid. It is fun to go into the homes and to see the laughter and joy of the children. It is rewarding to see how the people respond to our call for Christmas giving among the poor. The church was piled high yesterday with groceries and toys of every description. There is so much that is good in human nature. Of course, critics will say that it is easier to be charitable than to be just, and the astute social observers will note that what we give to the needy is but a small fraction of what we spend on ourselves. After all, the spirit of love is still pretty isolated in the family life . . . If I had a family maybe that thought would never occur to me. If I had about four children to love I might not care so much about insisting that the spirit of love shall dominate all human affairs. And there might be more value in loving the four children than in paying lip service to the spirit of love as I do.

Niebuhr, R., *Leaves from the Notebook*, 49.

The peace of God is a peace of love. There is no simple peace in love. The peace of love is the most perfect peace, because in it spirit is related to all of life. Yet it is a very imperfect peace because attachments to the pains and sorrows of others subject us, and even God, to those sorrows. That so imperfect a peace should also be the most perfect peace passes understanding. Yet is the peace of God; and it is also the only possible peace for humans. St. Paul, in the words of this [following] text, expresses the hope that this kind of peace may guard the hearts and minds of Christian people: "The Peace of God, which passeth all understanding, shall keep your hearts and minds through Christ Jesus," [Phil. 4:7]. How would our hearts be "kept" or "guarded" by such a peace?

Niebuhr, R., *Discerning the Signs*, 184.

JANUARY 7.   LOVE GIFTED AND . . . OBEYED?

Love is indeed the law of life; but it is most surely obeyed when we are not conscious of obedience to any law. It is obeyed when the sorrows of others arouse our sympathies, when their needs prompt us to forget our own needs and meet those of our friends and neighbors. We become most truly ourselves when we forget ourselves; for it is the preoccupation with self that prematurely arrests the growth of the self and confines it too narrow limits. The peace of love is thus the ultimate peace of being or becoming what we truly are: creatures who do not live in and for themselves in the life of the community, and finally in God. Obviously, however, this ultimate peace of love is filled with pain and sorrow. It is aware not only of its own pains but also of those of others. The anxious mother keeping a night-watch over the bed of a sick child has no peace within the limits of understanding. That kind of peace belongs to those who sleep soundly because they have no responsibility for any ailing creature. Yet there can be in the heart of that mother a peace which passeth understanding. Above, beyond, and yet within her anxieties and apprehensions there can be a peace which is the fruit of her complete devotion of the child and the consequence of her fulfillment of the nature and the responsibilities of motherhood. The servants of the needy who embody various ministries of mercy, doctors and visiting nurses, social workers and champions of social justice, pastors and all other ministers of need . . . have experienced the joys which are "three parts pain"; and have touched the fringes of the mystery of the peace of God.

Niebuhr, R., *Discerning the Signs*, 185–86.

JANUARY 8.   OF CROSS PURPOSES . . . ?

It is idle to assume that human society could ever be completely knit together by the perfection of love in which each carries the burden of all, and the anxieties of each are quieted by the solicitude of all. That is the vision of the Kingdom of God, of the Kingdom of perfect love, which hovers as a possibility and yet impossibility over all human life. Actually the perfect accord between life and life is constantly spoiled by the inordinate concern of each life for its own weal. So pervasive is this self-love that it is sometimes most dangerously expressed when we think we are serving the needs of others; but when really we desire to keep the affairs of others in our power. Human society is full of the friction of cross purposes. The conflict of interest and passion between races, classes, nations, and individuals can be arbitrated into a tolerable harmony by the wise statesmanship and astute methods of adjudication and arbitration; but the peace of the world is always, as St. Augustine observed, something of an armistice between opposing factions. There is no perfect social harmony in human history, no peace within the limits of understanding.

Niebuhr, R., *Discerning the Signs,* 186–87.

JANUARY 9.   PEACE OF FORGIVENESS—POSSIBLE?

The only possible peace within and between human communities is the peace of forgiveness. It is not a peace of perfect accord of life with life, but a peace which is established beyond the frictions of life. And this is a peace beyond understanding . . . Reconciliation with even the most evil foe requires forgiveness; and forgiveness is possible only to those who have some recognition of common guilt. The pain of contrition is the root of the peace of forgiveness. The forgiveness of God is the readiness of guiltlessness to bear the sin of the guilty. There is an element of this vicariousness in human forgiveness also. Yet a too conscious righteousness never achieves real forgiveness toward an enemy. It is too anxious to censure the evil in the foe; and too oblivious of its own sins. The capacity for forgiveness in humans is therefore drawn both from the highest forms of loving righteousness and from the consciousness of common guilt . . . it is a form of love which transcends all law and is an offense to makers and keepers of the law.

Niebuhr, R., *Discerning the Signs,* 187–88.

JANUARY 10.   PERFECTLY DISINTERESTED JUDGES . . . ?/DEATH OF URSULA NIEBUHR.

There are proximate standards of justice and virtue by which society judges the most explicit forms of vice and rebellion against order. But there are no perfectly disinterested judges: all of them are partially involved in the contest of life with life which their judgements seek to arbitrate. They are interested participants in the conflict which they seek to compose. Insofar as they are righteous and just but without mercy, they may repress evil but they can not induce true repentance in the evil doer.

Insofar as they are righteous, but unconscious of their own unrighteousness—that is, insofar as they pretend to a divine and impartial justice, when in fact they are men who are engaged in an interested conflict with the enemy—their pretension of virtue is a temptation to cynicism rather than repentance in the foe.

Niebuhr, R., *Discerning the Signs*, 188–89.

We give thanks that we are heirs of all the ages and that our faith is sustained by a vast company of the living and the dead who have known you and proclaim your mercy. We thank you that we are sons and daughters as well as heirs; and that each one may in his or her own way find access to the throne of grace.

Niebuhr, R., *Justice and Mercy*, 118.

JANUARY 11. A PERFECT ACCORD OF LIFE WITH LIFE?

The peace of forgiveness is . . . beyond understanding. The roots of it lie in combination of vicarious love and consciousness of sin, which is beyond the understanding of all righteous, and inevitably self-righteous, men and nations. It is possible only to those who by faith know themselves under a judgement which in its final dimension can make no distinction between the self and the enemy, or between the righteous and unrighteous man. The power and the source of this no perfectly disinterested judges. The effect of it is also beyond understanding, in the sense that it is a peace within strife, reconciliation within friction. Its highest perfection is achieved at precisely the point where no one imagines that there is a possibility within the sinful conditions of history to find a perfect accord of life with life, or to achieve a vantage point of disinterested love from which others, but not the self, could be accused of breaking the peace.

Niebuhr, R., *Discerning the Signs*, 189–90.

We pray for all who have authority in the world, for the leaders of our nation and for those who bear office in all the nations, that they may seek the peaceable fruits of justice; grant that they may know the limits of human wisdom in the perplexities of this day, and calling upon you in humility, and acknowledging your majesty, may learn the wisdom of restraint and the justice of charity.

Niebuhr, R., *Reinhold Niebuhr: Major Works*, 702.

JANUARY 12. LONGING FOR THE IMPOSSIBLE . . . ?

If the peace of God which passeth understanding keeps our hearts it will infuse them not only with the peace of forgiving but with the peace of being forgiven. All efforts to arrive at internal peace by moderating passions and desires, or by developing a rational detachment from passion and desire, are only provisionally efficacious. Man is a creature of infinite desires; and the longing for the impossible is the root of both man's greatness and his misery . . . Peace would be the fulfillment of man's infinite purposes: though such a peace would not be too simple, for how are boundless possibilities to be realized?

Niebuhr, R., *Discerning the Signs* 190–91.

JANUARY 13. INTERMINGLING LOVES.

The love of God and the love of self are curiously intermingled in life. The worship of God and the worship of the self confronts us in a multitude of different compounds. There is a taint of sin in our highest endeavors. How shall we judge the great statesperson who gives a nation its victorious courage by articulating its only partly conscious and implicit resources of fortitude; and who mixes the most obvious forms of personal and collective pride and arrogance with this heroic fortitude? If one had been a more timid person, a more cautious soul, he or she would have not have sinned so greatly, but neither would he have wrought so nobly. The perplexing mixture of good and evil in human history can not be solved by a complacent attitude toward the evil which is mixed with the good. In that case the evil would grow to intolerable proportions. Nor can evil be eliminated even by the more precise distinctions of the moralists. Every effort to do so creates forms of Christian perfectionism in which the meaningful responsibilities of life are finally disavowed. The kinship between Christian asceticism and oriental forms of life-detachment is significant. The only possible peace for humans, thus involved in the contradictions of existence, is the peace of being forgiven.

Niebuhr, R., *Discerning the Signs,* 191–92.

JANUARY 14. FATE AND SIN: INEVITABLE YET RESPONSIBLE?

The pretensions of human cultures and civilizations are the natural consequences of a profound and ineradicable difficulty in all human spirituality. We are mortal. That is our fate. We pretend not to be mortal. That is our sin. One is a creature of time and place, whose perspectives and insights are invariably conditioned by immediate circumstances. But one is not merely the prisoner of time and place. He or she touches the fringes of the eternal. One is not content to be merely an American person, or Chinese, or bourgeois . . . One wants to be a person. We are not content with his or her truth. One seeks the truth. One's memory spans ages in order that he or she may transcend one's age. The restless mind seeks to comprehend the meaning of all cultures so that one may not be caught within the limitations of his or her own.

Niebuhr, R., *Beyond Tragedy*, 28–29.

JANUARY 15. CONTRITION?

The Tower of Babel myth [of Genesis 11] is one of the first, as it is one of the most vivid, expressions of the quality of biblical religion. The characteristic distinction of biblical religion, in contrast to culture religion, is that the latter seeks to achieve the eternal and the divine by some discipline of the mind or heart, whether mystical or rational, while the former believes the gulf remains fixed between Creator and the creature which even revelation does not completely bridge. Every revelation of the divine is relativized by the finite mind which comprehends it. Consequently God, though revealed, remains veiled; [God's] thoughts are not our thoughts nor [God's] ways our ways. The worship of such a God leads to contrition; not merely to a contrite recognition of the conscious sins of pride and arrogance which the human spirit commits, but to a sense of guilt for the inevitable and inescapable pride involved in every human enterprise, even if the highest and most perfect or, more correctly, particularly in the highest and noblest human enterprise.

Niebuhr, R., *Beyond Tragedy*, 44–45.

JANUARY 16.   FRUIT OF AN INSIGHT TOO PROFOUND . . . ?

Such contrition will probably never be perfect enough to save enterprises of collective [selves] from the periodic catastrophes which overtake them, precisely because they do not know their own limits. But this contrition is possible at least for individuals. Those who understand the limits of human intelligence in the sight of God do not thereby overcome those limits. A [person] may build a Tower of Babel at the same moment in which he or she recognises the unjustified pretensions of all human spirituality. It is precisely this conviction, that one faces an inescapable dilemma in the Tower of Babel, which gives the profoundest versions of the Christian religion a supramoral quality. It imparts a sense of contrition not only for moral derelictions but for the unconscious sins involved in the most perfect moral achievements. This is what the Psalmist means when he prays "Enter not into judgment with thy servant, for in thy sight is no man living justified." . . . The primitive sense of guilt expressed in this myth is the fruit of an insight too profound for modernity's superficial intelligence.

Niebuhr, R., *Beyond Tragedy*, 45–46.

JANUARY 17.   INTIMATIONS OF A PROPHET-MARTYR.

"I hate, I despise your feasts, and I take no delight in your solemn assemblies . . . Take away from me the noise of your songs; to the melody of your harps I will not listen. But let justice roll down like waters and righteousness like an overflowing stream" [Amos 5:23–4].

Amos' last phrase was a favorite text of the late Martin Luther King. He used it in his "I Have a Dream" speech to the thousands at the March on Washington. It is unfortunate that he was murdered before he could be invited to that famous ecumenical congregation in the White House. But on second thought, the question arises: would he have been invited? Established religion with or without legal sanction, is always chary of criticism, especially if it is relevant to public policy.

Niebuhr, R., "The King's Chapel," 211.

JANUARY 18.   MARTIN LUTHER KING JR. DAY

Racial conflict has become the most vicious of all forms of social conflict in this nation. And the racial tensions will become worse long before they will become better. The church has been very busy telling the nation what to do about this. The church might better try to present the national community with a greater number of truly contrite souls, truly "emancipated" of race prejudice, who express their emancipation partly in the contrite recognition of the remnant of pride that remains in the soul of even the emancipated.

Niebuhr, R., *Love and Justice*, 129.

[In a telegram to King, Reinhold wrote:] Thank you for your invitation ... Only a severe stroke prevents me from accepting it. Hope there will be a massive demonstration of all the citizens with conscience in favour of the elemental human rights on voting and freedom of assembly in your march on Alabama's capital.

Niebuhr, R., *Reinhold Niebuhr: Major Works*, 688.

JANUARY 19.   A DEEPER SOURCE . . . ?

The church knows, or ought to know, that though humans may be incredibly stupid, the hatred and contempt that they exhibit in their lives springs from a deeper source than stupidity. It is the consequence of the corruption of a greater spiritual freedom in humans than those understand who speak of us as "rational." Both the dignity and misery of humans are greater than modern culture understands. The misery of the person is derived from his or her idolatry, from the partly conscious and partly unconscious effort to make oneself, his or her race, and his or her culture God. This idolatry is not broken until the human is confronted with the real God, and finds their pride broken by the divine judgment, and learn that from this crucifixion of the old proud self a new self may arise, and that this new self has the "fruits of the spirit," which are "love, joy, and peace."

Niebuhr, R., *Love and Justice*, 129.

Revelation means the moment in our history through which we know ourselves to be known from beginning to end, in which we are apprehended by the knower . . .

Niebuhr, H.R., *Meaning of Revelation*, 111.

JANUARY 20. PRIDE AND PRETENSIONS . . . ?

One builds towers of the spirit from which he or she may survey larger horizons than those of one's class, race and nation. This is a necessary human enterprise. Without it one could not come to his or her full estate. But it is also inevitable that these towers should be Towers of Babel, that they should pretend to reach higher than their real height; and claim a finality which they cannot possess. The truth one finds and speaks is, for all of his or her efforts to transcend one's self, still one's truth. The "good" which one discovers is, for all of the efforts to disassociate it from one's own interest and interests, still one's "good." The higher the tower is built to escape unnecessary limitations of the human imagination, the more certain it will be to defy necessary and inevitable limitations. Thus sin corrupts the highest as well as the lowest achievements of human life. Human pride is greater when it is based upon solid achievements; but the achievements are never great enough to justify its pretensions. This pride is at least one aspect of what Christian orthodoxy means by "original sin." It is not so much an inherited corruption as an inevitable taint upon the spirituality of a finite creature, always enslaved to time and place, never completely enslaved and always under the illusion that the measure of one's emancipation is greater than it really is.

Niebuhr, R., *Beyond Tragedy*, 29–30.

JANUARY 21. DISREGARDING LIMITATIONS . . . ?

The very character of a Tower of Babel, and the primary cause of its always tragic history is that its limitations, and its pretentious disregard of those limitations, are not seen from the inside, i.e., by those groups who have compounded partial insights and particular interests with eternal and universal values. Thus the landlords never discovered, and have not discovered yet, that their civilization was less than Christian. The class which discovered this and which finally brought this Tower of

Babel down was the class of merchants, business men, artisans and bankers who had been disregarded in the organisation of medieval life. The city grew up under the protection of the castle wall and, in spite of the oppression of the castle's power, finally acquired a power great enough to destroy the castle. But the lord protested to the end that he was protecting not his civilisation but civilisation as such, against the bolshevist of his day: the business man.

Niebuhr, R., *Beyond Tragedy*, 32–33.

JANUARY 22.   SOCIAL STRUGGLE . . . RATIONALISATIONS OF INTEREST?

Just as the business people discovered the dishonesties of the landed aristocrats, because they had been left out of the alleged paradise of the latter, so the industrial worker assumes the role of the rebel and critic in bourgeois society. The industrial worker's most characteristic philosophy is Marxism. The particular virtue of this philosophy is that it brings the Tower of Babel character of all civilisations into the open and makes humans conscious of it. It clearly discerns the economic basis of all culture and points a finger of scorn at the claims of impartiality made by the cultural enterprises of the ages. It sees them all as instruments of a social struggle and as rationalisations of interest, as indeed they are. The remarkable characteristic of this philosophy is that, having recognised the finite perspectives of all cultures and the sinful effort to hide and deny this finiteness, it proceeds to construct another Tower of Babel.

Niebuhr, R., *Beyond Tragedy*, 36.

JANUARY 23.   GOD'S PEACE . . . TO US.

The peace of Christian faith passes understanding because it is God's peace, transferred to us. It is the peace of having and yet not having the perfection of Christ; of having it only by grace and yet having it the more surely for not pretending that we have it as a right. This peace will offend both rationalists and moralists till the end of history, because it does not conform to the simple canons of either rationality or morality. But it alone does justice to the infinite complexities and contradictions of human existence. Within this peace all of life's creative urges may be expressed and enlarged. There is therefore no simple calm in it. It is as tumultuous as the ocean, and yet as serene as the ocean's depths, which bear the tumults and storms of the surface. It is the only peace which does not destroy but fulfills all human powers. In that peace we understand that [a person's life] in history is fragmentary and frustrated precisely because it is boundless and unlimited.

Niebuhr, R., *Discerning the Signs*, 194.

"Hunkered down in a storm at sea" by Jim Houston

JANUARY 24.   NO COMPLACENT PEACE?

[There] is no complacent peace which condones the taint of evil in us. It knows that evil costs God dearly. But neither is it a peace which prematurely arrests the creative urges of life for the sake of a tranquility, or which denies responsibilities of the self toward others for fear of becoming soiled in fulfilling our duty. It is a peace in which an uneasy conscience is curiously compounded with an easy conscience. This peace rests upon the faith that God is great enough and good enough to resolve the contradiction in which human life stands; and that God's mercy is the final resource of divine power, by which the Holy One overcomes the rebellion of creatures against the Creator . . . All forms of simple moralism, whether Christian or pagan, move between the poles of complacency and despair. They pretend to a peace which does not acknowledge the residual chaos in the human soul; or they are overcome by that chaos.

Niebuhr, R., *Discerning the Signs*, 193–94.

JANUARY 25. SEEING BUT NOT REACHING.

A businessperson is forced to earn his or her livelihood within terms of an economic system in which perfect honesty would probably lead to self-destruction. According to the sensitivity of their spirit they will find some compromise between their immoral actions to which they are tempted by the necessities of the social system in which they operate and the ideal possibilities which their consciences project. But there is no compromise at which he or she can rest complacently. Even though the highest moral possibility transcends the limits of one's imperfect freedom, there is always an immediately higher possibility which he or she might take. A general sense of religious guilt is therefore a fruitful source of a sense of moral responsibility in immediate situations . . . One, as the creature of both necessity and freedom, must like Moses, always perish outside the promised land. He or she can see what they cannot reach.

Niebuhr, R., *Interpretation of Christian Ethics (1956)*, 76.

JANUARY 26. A GENUINE FAITH . . . ?

Those who disavow all knowledge of the final mystery of life are so impressed by the fact that we see through a glass darkly that they would make no claim of seeing at all. Agnosticism sees no practical value in seeking to solve the mystery of life. A much larger number of people forget that they see through a glass darkly. They claim to know too much.

Niebuhr, R., *Discerning the Signs*, 152.

A genuine Christian faith must move between those who claim to know so much about the natural world that it ceases to point to any mystery beyond itself and those who claim to know so much about the mystery of the "unseen" world that all reverence for its secret and hidden character is dissipated. A genuine faith must recognize the fact that it is through a dark glass that we see; though by faith we do penetrate sufficiently to the heart of the mystery not to be overwhelmed by it. A genuine faith resolves the mystery of life by the mystery of God. It recognizes that no aspect of life or existence explains itself, even after all known causes and consequences have been traced. All known existence points beyond itself. To realize that it points beyond itself to God is to assert that the mystery of life does not dissolve life into meaninglessness. Faith in God is faith in some ultimate unity of life, in some final comprehensive purpose which holds all the various, and frequently contradictory, realms of coherence and meaning together.

Niebuhr, R., *Discerning the Signs*, 154.

JANUARY 27. INTERNATIONAL HOLOCAUST REMEMBRANCE DAY.

The Baltimore Holocaust Memorial . . . sculpture represents the boxcars that carried European Jews to the death camps. It is undecorated, save for a descriptive statement taken from the autobiography of Primo Levi, an Italian Jew, a chemist and writer, who described his imprisonment in Auschwitz in a 1958 memoir. "On both sides of the track rows of red and white lights as far as the eye could see . . . With the rhythm of the wheels, with every human sound now silenced, we waited to see what was to happen . . . In an instant, our women, our parents, our children disappeared. We saw them as an obscure mass at the other end of the platform. Then we saw them no more."

Niebuhr, G. [Jr.], *Beyond Tolerance*, 123.

Good is a term which not only can but which—at least in the form of one of its equivalents—must be applied to that which meets the needs, fits the capacity, which corresponds to the potentialities of an existent being. It is, in this sense, that which is "useful." Evil, on the other hand, is that which thwarts, destroys, or starves a being in its activities.

Niebuhr, H.R., *Radical Monotheism*, 103.

JANUARY 28.   EVIL AT THE JUNCTURE OF . . . ?

The most basic and fruitful conception flowing from the ancient myth [of the Fall] is the idea that evil lies at the juncture of nature and spirit. Evil is conceived as not simply the consequence of temporality nor the fruit of nature's necessities. Sin can be understood neither in terms of human reason alone, nor yet in terms of the circumscribed harmonies in which the human body is bound. Sin lies at the junction of spirit and nature, in the sense that the peculiar and the unique characteristics of human personality, in both its good and evil tendencies, can be understood only by analyzing the paradoxical relation of freedom and necessity, of finiteness and the yearning for the eternal in human life.

Niebuhr, R., *Interpretation of Christian Ethics* (1956),74–75.

JANUARY 29.   NATIONAL DAY OF REMEMBRANCE OF THE QUEBEC CITY MOSQUE ATTACK AND ACTION AGAINST ISLAMOPHOBIA (CANADA)

In a brief but impassioned essay published on Hartford Seminary's Web site, Ingrid Mattson . . . called on preachers and politicians to envision and proclaim the need for "a new heroism" that eschews violence and values life for its own sake. Mattson, a Canadian convert to Islam who teaches at the seminary, holds a unique status among Muslims in the United States: She is president of the Islamic Society of North America, perhaps the best known network of mosques in the USA and Canada and one whose mission specifically calls for fostering good relationships with people of other faiths. Until her election to the position the organization had never had a female president . . . In her essay, Mattson said she was disturbed by that particular statistic on support for a murderous tactic used against civilians. "How could those who claim to follow Muhammad reject his explicit teachings on this topic?" She also cited another Pew study . . . that found that a majority of American Catholics and white Protestants believed that the use of torture against suspected terrorists could be justified in efforts "to gain important information." "How could those who claim to worship Jesus, who was tortured by political authorities, accept the torture of human beings?" Popular culture, playing on the fear of those who feel powerless, creates a false idea of heroism, often in the form of cinematically glorious explosions, she said. "Rather, nails and screws pierce the eyes, hands, and abdomens of children and elderly women whose flesh burns and lungs gasp for a last breath." By contrast, Mattson said, "Authentic religion teaches one to imagine the other—to consider another's vulnerability and humanity. The beginning of ethics is this transcendent imagination." The message, she said, to be expounded by preacher and politician alike is that all human beings possess a God-given dignity.

Niebuhr, G. [Jr.], *Beyond Tolerance,* 100–101.

JANUARY 30. FAITH OF PROPHETIC CHRISTIANITY?

The Christian analysis of life leads to conclusions which will seem morbidly pessimistic to moderns, still steeped as they are in their evolutionary optimism. The conclusion most abhorrent to the modern mood is that the possibilities of evil grow with the possibilities of good, and that human history is therefore not so much a chronicle of the progressive victory of the good over evil, of cosmos over chaos, as the story of an ever-increasing cosmos, creating ever increasing possibilities of chaos . . .

Niebuhr, R., *Interpretation of Christian Ethics* (1956), 92.

Since the vertical dimension in human life, revealing the ultimate possibilities of good and the depth of evil in it, is a reality which naïve philosophies may obscure but cannot destroy, it will be necessary for our generation to return to the faith of prophetic Christianity to solve its problems. At the same time, it will be necessary for prophetic Christianity, with a stronger emphasis upon its prophetic and a lesser emphasis upon its nationalistic inheritance, to develop a more adequate social ethic within terms of its understanding of the total human situation. The approach of the historic Christian Church to the moral issues of life has been less helpful than it might have been, partly because a literal interpretation of its mythical basis destroyed the genius of prophetic religion, and partly because Christianity, in the effort to rationalize its myths ran upon the rocks either of the Scylla of a too optimistic pantheism or the Charybdis of a too pessimistic and otherworldly dualism.

Niebuhr, R. *Interpretation of Christian Ethics* (1956), 93.

JANUARY 31. 13TH AMENDMENT . . . ABOLISHING SLAVERY IN AMERICA?

Can war be fought without some realization that ultimately you need a vision for peace? I don't mean the initial vision that everyone has, that everything will turn out just the way the war planners expected. We might recall what Lincoln said in his second inaugural address, delivered nearly four years after the fall of Fort Sumter: "Each side had looked for an easier triumph, and a result less fundamental and astounding." Those last three words remind us of what is at stake in all-out wars. By extension, those words put me in mind of the warning once delivered by a Sri Lankan Buddhist monk, in a speech he gave to Christians and Buddhists at [Thomas] Merton's former monastery: "The only alternative to talking is the building up of resentment and anger, which in time must inevitably become open hostility and conflict."

Niebuhr, G. [Jr.], *Beyond Tolerance*, xxxvii.

. . . [W]e awaken in being acted upon and in suffering. Patio ergo sum [I suffer, endure, thus I am]. This is the original and encompassing experience that goes with all experiences, for neither thinking nor willing nor acting on the environment are appropriate or conceivable human responses unless the field of surrounding forces disposes [humans] towards thought and action by making them suffer as understanding and willing beings. Suffering, then, is also a ne plus ultra [the highest point possible] of experience, correspondingly our world appears to us a field of energies converging on us, shaping us, distending us, shattering us, and sending us on paths we have not chosen for ourselves. Suffering horizons our awareness . . . Suffering of this order as something universal is the matrix that generates the passion of believing. It is the medium in which human faithfulness forms itself and appears in determinate shapes in our radial world [arranged and dispersed like rays or radii].

Niebuhr, R.R., "The Widened Heart," 128.

FEBRUARY
Black History Month (USA and Canada)

The preaching of the ideal possibilities of brotherhood and sisterhood that is not accompanied by a careful and pitiless analysis of the motives, of the inner fears, self-accusations, and self-justifications of those who deny brotherhood is not religious. It moves on the plane of secular idealism and does not bring the terror of the judgements of the living God to bear upon the soul. Only if this is done can the mercy of God also heal the hurt that men and women have in their own heart and that prompts them to hurt each other.

Niebuhr, R., *Love and Justice,* 144.

FEBRUARY 1. BEYOND A SIMPLE IDEALISM.

In my parish duties I found that the simple idealism into which the classical faith had evaporated was as irrelevant to the crises of personal life as it was to the complex social issues of an industrial city. Two old ladies were dying shortly after I assumed charge of the [Detroit] parish. They were both respectable members of the congregation. But I soon noted that their manner of facing death was strikingly dissimilar. One lady was preoccupied with self, too aggrieved that Providence should not have taken account of her virtue in failing to protect her against a grievous illness, to be able to face death with any serenity. She was in constant hysteria of fear and resentment. While my own simple idealism would have scarcely been equal to the test of facing the ultimate issue, I found myself deeply disturbed by the fact that faith was evidently of so little account in the final test. The other old lady had brought up a healthy and wholesome family, though her husband was subject to periodic fits of insanity which forced her to be the breadwinner as well as homemaker. Just as her two splendid daughters had finished their training and were eager to give their mother a secure and quiet evening of life, she was found to be suffering from cancer. I stood weekly at her bedside while she told me what passages of Scripture, what Psalms and what prayers to read to her; most of them expressed gratitude for all the mercies of God which she had received in life. She was particularly grateful for her two daughters and their love; and she faced death with the utmost peace of soul.

Niebuhr, R., "Intellectual Autobiography" (1984), 6.

Like all human faith Christian faith is a way of accepting suffering that the world of power inflicts on [people]; it is a way of appropriating the experiences of diminution and enlargement, of distraction and motion, by interpreting them as twin moments in the ruling action of God. So the beliefs that God is and that God rules human life generate in the suffering of power around and in oneself. These beliefs and doctrines do not, of course, spring unaided from such experience; they are rather the confessions of what [people] hold dear when they become convinced that their most authoritative predecessor in such experience was and is Jesus of Nazareth, who thought of his own life and then tried to teach others to see that life as the place where the ruling of God becomes apparent. But in turn this perception of Jesus's authority opens itself only to those who are willing to come in upon themselves and find that they are [persons]

FEBRUARY 23

affected in all that they think and do, needing to be widened in their understanding of what affects them.

Niebuhr, R.R., "The Widened Heart," 154.

FEBRUARY 2.   RELEARNING THE ESSENTIALS . . . ?

I relearned the essentials of the Christian faith at the bedside of that nice old soul [see February 1, Beyond a simple idealism]. I appreciated that the ultimate problem of human existence is the peril of sin and death in the way that these two perils are so curiously compounded; for we fall into sin by trying to evade or to conquer death or our own insignificance, of which death is the ultimate symbol. The Christian faith holds out the hope that our fragmentary lives will be completed in a total and larger plan than any which we can control or comprehend, and that a part of the completion is the forgiveness of sins, that is, the forgiveness of the evils which we fall into by our frantic efforts to complete our own lives or to endow them with significance. I was conscious of the nobility which was the fruit of the simple faith of a simple woman; and that was not the only time in parish duties in which I learned the meaning of Christ's prayer: "I thank Thee, Father, that Thou has withheld these things from the wise and prudent and revealed then unto babes." As for the difference between the faith of the two old ladies, outwardly so similar until submitted to the ultimate test, we in the churches ought to admit more humbly than is our wont that there is a mystery of grace which no one can fathom. "Two women will be grinding at the mill. The one will be taken and the other left." The Church is a curiously mixed body consisting of those who have never been shaken in their self-esteem or self-righteousness and who use the forms of religion for purposes of self-aggrandizement; and of the true Christians who live by "a broken spirit and contrite heart." Whether we belong to this latter group, which makes up the true but invisible church, no one but God can know. Facing the test of death is obviously more important than I had imagined in the days of my simple "moralism" . . . Indeed, one must come to the conclusion that none of us can be certain whether we have the faith or the courage to pass any final test. "If any [person] stand let him or her take need lest [one] fall."

Niebuhr, R., "Intellectual Autobiography" (1984), 6–7.

FEBRUARY 3.   LIKE AN ANCIENT MEDICINE MAN?

Visited Miss Z, at the hospital. I like to go now since she told me that it helps to have me pray with her. I asked the doctor about her and he says her case is hopeless. Here faith seems to be functioning in lifting the soul above physical circumstance. I have been so afraid of quackery that I have leaned over backwards trying to avoid the encouragement of false hopes. Sometimes when I compare myself with these efficient doctors and nurses hustling about I feel like an ancient medicine man dumped into the twentieth century. I think they have the same feeling toward me that I have about them. I am still praying for health with Miss Z. But of course I don't leave it at that. I am trying to prepare her for the inevitable and I think I have helped her a little in that regard.

Niebuhr, R., *Leaves from the Notebook*, 24.

FEBRUARY 4.   LEARNING FROM HER QUIET COURAGE . . . ?

I think since I have stopped worrying so much about the intellectual problems of religion and have begun to explore some of its ethical problems there is more of a thrill in preaching. The real meaning of the gospel is in conflict with most of the customs and attitudes of our day at so many places that there is adventure in the Christian message . . . I think I am beginning to like the ministry also because it gives you a splendid opportunity to have all kinds of contacts with people in relationships in which they are at their best. You do get tired of human pettiness at times. But there is nevertheless something quite glorious about folks. That is particularly true when you find them bearing sorrows with real patience. Think of Mrs. ____ putting up with that drunkard of a husband for the sake of her children—and having such nice children. One can learn from her quiet courage than from many a book.

Niebuhr, R., *Leaves from the Notebook*, 27–28.

FEBRUARY 5.   SOBER OBSERVATION AND INTROSPECTIVE ANALYSIS?

It is the absurd notion of modern liberalism, both Christian and secular, that the Christian estimate of our sinfulness is determined by the Biblical account of the fall of Adam, and that it can be dismissed by anyone who does not find this primitive account credible. Actually the estimate is supported by overwhelming evidence taken both from a sober observation of human behavior and from introspective analysis. The latter evidence is important because it reveals that the self as subject, as distinguished from the self as object of thought, is not some universal and rational self but is always, even in its height of self-transcendence, a particular self; and that this self is even more inclined to be preoccupied and anxious about its position and prestige than the self which is engaged in its affections and responsibilities. On the other hand, the various forms of secularism, whether naturalistic or idealistic, have such a unanimously favorable opinion of human virtue because the naturalists regard man as an object in nature who can be manipulated to desire and seek "socially-approved" ends; while the idealists, after the manner of classical philosophy, place the root of evil in the impulses of the body, and expect "mind" to come into progressive control of the infra-rational impulses. Only the Biblical-Christian view sees that the evil in a person is at the center of the self, and that it involves all his or her unique capacities of freedom which endow one with "dignity" and make him or her, though a creature, also a creator . . . The fact is that the human self can only be understood in a dramatic historical environment. Any effort to coordinate man to some coherence, whether of nature or of reason, will falsify the facts; because the self's freedom, including its creative and destructive capacities, precludes such co-ordination.

Niebuhr, R., "Intellectual Autobiography" (1984), 11.

FEBRUARY 6. TO WHOM SHALL WE GO?

No ultimate sense of meaning of life is rationally compelling. Our apologetic task as proponents of the Christian faith must include the analysis of experience which proves alternative faiths to be mistaken. The apologetic task has the object of inducing the confession: "Lord, to whom shall we go? Thou hast the words of eternal life." But we must recognize that not only is no faith rationally compelling but that there is a special difficulty with references to the Christian faith which seem to make it quite unacceptable to persons schooled in the ethos of scientific culture. That difficulty arises from the fact that the Christian faith distinguishes itself from other forms of faith by its greater degree of explicitness. There is a difference between the implicit faith that some system of nature or reason embodies ultimate meaning, and the Christian faith which apprehends a realm of mystery above and beyond the ascertainable structures of the world. This is explicit faith because it is recognized that meaning must be discerned in the mystery above the rationally intelligible structures of existence.

Niebuhr, R., "Intellectual Autobiography" (1984), 17.

FEBRUARY 7. PERSONALITY IN DRAMATIC AND HISTORIC ENCOUNTER?

Personality, whether God's or human's, is defined only in dramatic and historic encounter. Though these dramatic and historical media of personality are not inherently "irrational," they are not subject to the ordinary "scientific" tests of rational intelligibility. Nothing in history follows as it does in nature or reason, "in a necessary manner." The personality is bound by historical destiny rather than by natural or ontological necessity. The revelation of "God in Christ," for instance, is a force of destiny for the community of faith which has been gathered by that revelation: the Christian Church. The Church does not exist to propound eternal ethical truths, though it significantly regards the "love of Christ" as normative for human existence. But the truth of Christ cannot be speculatively established. It is established as only humans encounter God, individually and collectively, after the pattern of Christ's mediation. The creative consequences of such encounters, the humility and charity of true repentance, the absence of pride and pretension, must be the proofs there has been an encounter with the only true God and not on the one hand with an idol of our imagination who is invented to establish some interest of ours; and not on the other hand with a vast ocean of fullness and nothingness which condemns our individuality and particularity in a judgment in which the whole of history is also annulled. The encounter between God and humans, as the encounters between us in history, must be by faith and love . . . It is perhaps significant that among artists, dramatists, novelists, and poets, there have always been some who understood the Christian faith, while philosophers and scientists found it difficult to respect it intellectually. The former had an artistic understanding of the dramatic and historical which was less evident among the wise people who were prompted by nature and inclination to reduce all of life to its causalities and rational coherences.

Niebuhr, R., "Intellectual Autobiography" (1984), 20–21.

FEBRUARY 8.   DISSIPATING CHRISTIAN TRUTH?

A defense of the Christian faith as ultimately true must include a more generous and humble recognition than has been the wont of the falsehoods and corruptions which may use a final truth as their instrument in actual history. The liberal church has made one admission and sought to correct one traditional error of historic Christianity: its cultural obscurantism. In fact the liberal church has been so conscious of this error that it has been in danger of dissipating Christian truth in its effort to correct it.

Niebuhr, R., "Intellectual Autobiography" (1984), 21.

FEBRUARY 9.   ADMISSION OF HUMILITY?

In addition to the obscurantist corruption, we must admit that there is no guarantee in any theology or form of worship that a community of faith, which intends to bring [people] into contact with the true God, may not be used for essentially idolatrous purposes. [Humans] may use it to claim a special allegiance with God against their foes. We must confess the significance of the long history of religious fanaticism, and must admit that a religion which has triumphed over idolatry in principle may in actual fact be made an instrument of partial and interested perspectives. Without such an admission the humility of a genuine scientist and measured common sense of the person of affairs, who knows his or her ends to be in conflict with other legitimate ends, are superior to the wisdom of Christians.

Niebuhr, R., "Intellectual Autobiography" (1984), 22.

FEBRUARY 10.   MEDIATING THE DIVINE JUDGMENT?

Christianity is, in principle, a religion of the spirit rather than of law. We are warned to "stand fast in the freedom with which Christ has set you free." St. Paul means that no meticulous obedience to specific moral standards can be a substitute for the self's encounter with God, in which the pretensions and the pride of the self are broken and it is set free of self and sin. But actually the excessive conventionality, the frantic respectability, and the devotion to the minutiae of propriety in historic Christianity stand in sharp contrast to the "love, joy, and peace" which characterize a genuine conversion. They sometimes compare unfavorably with the freedom of the best secular idealists. In short, a genuine Christian apologetic must be prepared to bring the judgment of Christ to bear as rigorously on the household of faith as upon the secular and pagan world, even as the prophets of Israel were as severe in mediating the divine judgment upon Israel as upon Babylon.

Niebuhr, R., "Intellectual Autobiography" (1984), 22.

FEBRUARY 11. SERVANT . . . RATHER THAN THE MASTER, OF THE SELF?

The faith of modern [humanity] contains two related articles: the idea of progress and the idea of the perfectibility of [one]. The latter is frequently the basis of the former article. One is regarded as indeterminately perfectible because it is not understood that every growth of human freedom may have evil as well as virtuous consequences. The root of this error is that reason is identified with freedom, and it is not seen that reason may be the servant, rather than the master, of the self. This essential religion of modernity is no less "dogmatic" for being implicit rather than explicit, and it is no more true for being arrayed in the panoply of science. Any encounter with the essential religion of a secular age must penetrate through the confusions which have been created by equating history with nature and meaning with rational intelligibility, and implicit though highly questionable dogmas with the prestige of science. The fact that the Communists should adorn their more explicit dogma with the prestige of science provides modern liberal culture with a caricature of its own beliefs.

Niebuhr, R., "Intellectual Autobiography" (1984), 15.

FEBRUARY 12. LINCOLN DAY

It would be impossible to trace the biographies of creative people to show that the push of ambition may have at least the provisional relation to the pull of their creative responsibilities because it furnishes them with an arena where these creative responsibilities take hold . . . [Abraham Lincoln's] ambition prompted him to secure an education beyond the formal limits of his family. It persuaded him to apprentice in the law, to run for Congress, and finally to debate with Douglas on the slavery issue . . . Ambition may not have been responsible for his native endowment or for his sense of style in rhetoric of which his Gettysburg Address and his Second Inaugural Address were such striking examples. It did not endow him with that unique combination of a moderate anti-slavery impulse and a strong sense of national patriotism, tinged with a sense of mission for the preservation of a unique nation "so conceived and so dedicated," which made him prevail politically against his foes . . . Nor could ambition be held responsible for his spirit of charity . . . "With malice toward none, with charity for all, let strive to do the work we are in." [Ambition] does not, of itself, create or recreate character. That original endowment, furnished by heritage and nature, may be used by the ambitious self in different ways. Both character and talent may give ambition scope and justification . . .

Niebuhr, R., *On Man's Nature and His Communities*, 113–14.

More profoundly, ambition should be regarded as the fruit of what theologians call "common grace," for ambition provided the particular niche and eminence in the social and culture structure in which they exercised their creativity.

Niebuhr, R., *On Man's Nature and His Communities*, 116–17.

FEBRUARY 13. LOVE FROM BEING LOVED.

Every experience must persuade us that our conscience is uneasy not because we are egos but because we are egoists . . . [Humans are] primarily historical creatures, our real milieu is history. The validity of Christianity is inextricably bound up with the idea of the historically character of man or woman. The preference of the "wise and prudent" for ontological religions represents the mind's abhorrence of the incredulities of history. The Christian faith asserts about God that [God] is a person and God has taken historical action to overcome the variance between humanity and God: "God was in Christ reconciling the world unto [God's] self." ... [W]e can define the structure of human personality and the freedom which rises indeterminately above structure; but we cannot find a system which will do justice which will do justice to both structure and freedom ... Biblical faith derives the injunction that we love one another from the original historical affirmation God, in Christ, loved us.

Niebuhr, R., "Intellectual Autobiography" (1984), 18-19.

FEBRUARY 14. FEAST OF ST. VALENTINE: GRANT US GRACE.

A defense of the Christian faith as ultimately true must include a more generous and humble recognition than has been the wont of the falsehoods and corruptions which use a final truth as their instrument in actual history. The liberal church has made one admission and sought to correct one traditional error of historic Christianity: its cultural obscurantism. In fact the liberal church has been so conscious of this error that has been in danger of dissipating Christian truth in its effort to correct it.

Niebuhr, R., "Intellectual Autobiography" (1984), 21.

Almighty and eternal God, creator of the world, judge and redeemer of men and women, who gives us the treasures of darkness and the hidden riches of secret places, grant that we know that you are Lord, and there is none else beside ... Grant us grace to separate the precious from the vile, that we may speak boldly and humbly to suffering and perplexed persons.

Niebuhr, R., *Justice and Mercy*, 114.

"You will love him," So Professor John Baillie charmingly had said when discussing with me which lecture courses I should attend [at Union Seminary]. Not only did I discover that I *did* love Reinhold but he had been discovering that he was in love with me.

Niebuhr, U., *Remembering Reinhold Niebuhr*, 26.

FEBRUARY 15.   BEWARE SPECIAL ALLEGIANCES' FAVOURS?

"Providence" is not an answer to Jesus' question: Why did the tower fall on these men? Nor does it prevent Augustine's protesting prayer: "How much better had it been for me to have been speedily cured . . . " If anything, as "doctrine" providence sets aside visibility of pattern and symmetry within personal experience. When, therefore, a man wrestles with the unlikeness of today to yesterday, with the randomness and disparateness of the elements of his own life-course and ambience, then looks to the doctrine of providence for a method of eliciting clarity, balance, and equity, where otherwise they do not appear, he can only end by doubting the meaning of belief itself. He doubts the belief of a providing-God, because the providence for which he looks and which he does not find is a providential ordering of his own history. But, in the mind of Jesus or Augustine, believing in God-providing expresses confidence in an order not in the history of the self but in the works of God, an order not within the time of the individual's birth [, life,] and death but an infinite order, to which the birth, life, and death of the individual belong . . . When people perceive that the life of Jesus Nazareth—as full as any life can be and also as fragmented and lacking in Emersonian symmetry and compensation as any life can—elicits from themselves the judgment, It is good! they find that statements about this messiah-prophet-servant become for them symbols expressing and reacting upon their own believing experience of their own incomplete lives and of their neighbors' lives and of their agent-world as a whole.

Niebuhr, R.R., *Experiential Religion,* 72–73.

FEBRUARY 16.   STAND FAST IN THE FREEDOM . . . ?

Justification by faith in the realm of justice means that we will not regard the pressures and counter pressures,s the tensions, the overt and covert conflicts by which justice is achieved and maintained, as normative in the absolute sense; but neither will we ease our conscience by seeking to escape from involvement in them. We will know that we cannot purge ourselves of the sin and guilt in which we are involved by the moral ambiguities of politics without also disavowing responsibility for the creative possibilities of justice.

Niebuhr, R., *Human Destiny,* Vol. II, 284.

FEBRUARY 17.   REVEALED AS FORGIVING LOVE?

I can find no way proving by any epistemological method that God, the creator, is revealed as forgiving love in the drama of Christ's life, death, and resurrection. Upon that faith the Christian Church is founded. I think that this faith may be validated in experience. It is the key which resolves the divine mystery into meaning and makes sense out of life. But I know of no way of inducing this faith by purely rational arguments . . . I know that God must be reason or have a reason of the type Aristotle ascribes to the divine. The human self also has this logos type of reason as part of its unique creative power. But the self has a freedom which cannot be equated with this reason; and God has freedom beyond the rational structure. The Bible attributes the power of creation to him or her . . . the idea of creation points to a mystery beyond any system of rational intelligibility.

Niebuhr, R., *Reinhold Niebuhr: His Religious,"* 508.

FEBRUARY 18.   MEANING OF HISTORY TRANSCENDS ITS FULFILMENTS?

The whole of modern culture tries too desperately to contain the ultimate within the fragmentary tasks and possibilities of history. I have never criticized a [statesperson] for responsibly seeking to maintain a tolerable peace or establish a tolerable justice. I have criticized the Christian perfectionist who either claimed these tasks could be accomplished more perfectly by the "love method" or who have sought to prove that their love is "perfect," even if they had to disavow responsibilities to preserve its perfection. I have never insisted on a sharp distinction between sacrificial love and mutual love, that is, between the love which is, and which is not, reciprocated and historically justified. I have only criticized the tendency to identify these two facets of love completely, so that the New Testament ethic is reduced to the limits of a prudential ethic, according to which we are counseled to forgive our foes because he or she will then cease to be our foe; and are promised that if suffering love becomes sufficiently general it will cease to be "suffering" and change society into a harmony of life in which no one need suffer. The relation between sacrificial love and mutual love contains the issue of the relation between the eschatological and the historical in a nutshell. Love, heedless of the self, must be the initiator of any reciprocal love. Otherwise the calculation of

FEBRUARY   33

mutual advantages makes love impossible. But heedless love usually wins
a response of love. That is a symbol of the moral content of history. But
this response cannot be guaranteed, as modern thought sought erroneously to guarantee it. That is symbolic of the "tragic" dimension of history
and a proof that the meaning of history always transcends the fulfilments
of meaning in history.

Niebuhr, R., Reinhold Niebuhr: His Religious, 518.

FEBRUARY 19.   WITHOUT ILLUSION/WITHOUT DESPAIR?

I have come gradually to realize that it is possible to look at the human
situation without illusion and without despair only from the standpoint
of the Christ-revelation. It has come to be more and more the ultimate
truth. If it is reduced to something other than its scriptural content, if,
for instance, Jesus is revered as an exemplary person and example, all
the confusions and sentimentalities of secular idealism are multiplied. I
have come to know with Pascal that only in "simplicity of the Gospel" is
it possible to measure the full "dignity" and the "misery" of the self. Thus
the Christological center of my thought has become more explicit and
more important . . . I have elaborated the Christological theme only in the
context of inquiries about human nature and human history.

Niebuhr, R., Niebuhr, R., "Reply to Interpretation and Criticism"
(1984), 515.

FEBRUARY 20.   WORLD DAY OF SOCIAL JUSTICE: CHURCH AS A COMMUNITY OF GRACE?

I have increasingly recognized the value of the Church as a community of
grace which, despite historic corruptions, has the "oracles of God," as St.
Paul said about Israel. The church is the one place in history where life is
kept open for the final word of God's mercy to lift up the brokenhearted
. . . But when I see how much new evil comes into life through the pretension of the religious community, through its conventional and graceless
legalism and through religious fanaticism, I am concerned that my growing appreciation of the Church should not betray me in this complacency.

Niebuhr, R., Niebuhr, R., "Reply to Interpretation and Criticism" (1984), 513.

A simple Christian moralism counsels people to be unselfish. A profounder Christian faith must encourage us to create systems of justice which will save society from their own selfishness . . . But justice arbitrates not merely between the self and the other, but between the competing claims upon the self by various "others."

Niebuhr, R., *Love and Justice*, 28.

FEBRUARY 21.   HOPE FOR YOUR/OUR FUTURE?

The human needs that the Church exists to meet are much the same at all times. Whether the stars are as near as they seemed to the Psalmist or are removed by the millions and billions of light years to which we must accustom our imagination, still the question is the same: "When I look at thy heavens, the work of thy fingers, the moon and the stars which thou hast established; what is man that thou are mindful of him and the son of man that thou dost care for him" [Ps 8]. Whether Israel is exiled by Babylon or a modern people displaced, whether Rachel or a twentieth-century mother mourns for her children they need the same assurance that "your work shall be rewarded . . . There is hope for your future . . . and your children shall come back to their own country." When the social gospel was at its height its greatest exponent in American, Walter Rauschenbusch, despite his animadversions against traditional religion, saw clearly how much the human problem would remain the same in the best of all possible worlds. He wrote: "No material comfort and plenty can satisfy the restless soul in us and give us peace with ourselves . . . In the best social order that is conceivable, men will still smolder with lust and ambition, and be lashed by hate and jealousy as with the whip of a slave driver."

Niebuhr, H.R., *Purpose of the Church*, 92.

FEBRUARY 22.   DIVERSE EXPLORATIONS.

From September to May most of the Union [Seminary] community attended the Sunday morning services at the James Chapel unless they were at work elsewhere, which many of them were. The senior professors

FEBRUARY 35

took turns in the pulpit and in leading these services, so we came to know their prayers well. [There were daily morning and afternoon services, too, in the Lampman chapel.] But we Niebuhrs were slightly disloyal to Union and varied our Sunday churchgoing; we went to the Union Chapel often enough but also to services at St. Paul's Chapel at Columbia, paid an occasional visit to Riverdale or to the rousing services at the East Harlem Protestant Parish [organized and run by Union students and faculty], and went quite frequently to the nearby Episcopal cathedral of St. John the Divine. "We" in my childhood usually meant my mother and me, since my father was often out of town on weekends preaching himself in Chicago or Philadelphia or Yale or Harvard or wherever, and my brother was in boarding school. During the boring bits of any of these services, I'd divert myself by exploring the hymn books and prayer books. Goodness me, what one could find out!

Sifton, *Serenity Prayer,* 177–78.

FEBRUARY 23. THE AUTOBIOGRAPHER'S WORK.

The church does not command priority in [the Christ-follower's] consciousness. Unlike [his or her] forbears, this [person] has not received the strongest personality from the great Catholic Christian society, what has come to take its space of primacy in one's being is very much his or her question. One cannot argue with the self, "I join in prayer, therefore I am," because the society of praying people is not antecedently real enough to one. [He or she] cannot point to any single birth moment of [his or her] self-consciousness. What has come to be first in [one's] mind is the world—not the world of which the Gospel of John speaks as the realm of darkness nor the world as the territory of men and women still unevangelized, but in the world as the age of his man- or woman-hood: the world of beings and actions that pushes against them, invades their thoughts and passions through the great telecommunications system and yet is in no obviously symmetrical relation to his or her being and action. The church becomes real to this person as a visible-invisible fellowship only as he or she becomes a person in their own eyes. But it is difficult for one to collect him or herself, to pick out the pieces of his own experience that fit each other and add up to a solid sense of being. The autobiographer's work is immense. He or she has been interwoven into the experiences and passions, the creeds and philosophies of so many other people.

How can one then recognize his or her kindred in the fellowship of the Holy Spirit, when one is so uncertain as to what of him and herself ought to re-cognize there?

Niebuhr, R.R., *Experiential Religion*, 20–21.

FEBRUARY 24. RECONSTITUTING ONESELF AND PINK SHIRT DAY/ANTI-BULLYING DAY.

[The radial-age Christian, radiating from a common center,] is a person belonging to the age as a whole, not only to its light but also to its shadowed scenes, and he or she is inhabited by its many spirits. One has not necessarily repudiated the church, but it is undeniably difficult for him or her to feel at home in it. A person may listen to the pastoral assurance that humanity's true nature disposes him or her toward life in the Body of Christ, but true human nature so often appears much less clearly than do acquired second natures. And the secular person is a being to whom a bewildering variety of second natures is possible. In order to therefore to live in the church as a communion building up a new and true humanity, one has to begin by reconstituting him or herself out of the confused materials their times afford them. One has first to collect him or herself.

Niebuhr, R.R., *Experiential Religion*, 21.

O Lord . . . Save the strong, the secure, the successful, and the wise, that they may glory not in their might nor in their wisdom. Save the weak and the debased and all who are victims of heedless and cruel persons, and reveal to them the final court of judgement where those of low degree are exalted and the disbalance of the world redressed.

Niebuhr, R.R., *Justice and Mercy*, 116–17.

FEBRUARY 25. WARMTH OF THE PRESENCE OF OTHERS.

The one who makes the [human effort to become one] with Jesus of Nazareth upon his or her mind is not a solitary, heroic artist for whom the church and his Christianized childhood are merely incumbrances upon one's shaping imagination. One is very much a person of the crowd: surrounded by other persons and mammoth institutions. One is influenced

FEBRUARY   37

by a history he or she breathes with every word they speak. One is also the same person about whom economists, psychologists, and sociologists write as a consumer, an id and ego and superego, as an other-directed person. Nor is he or she proudly lonely in their faith or lack of faith, regarding other people's professions of belief or the historical records of the Gospels and the church as unworthy props and supports that threaten to taint the purity of one's own existence by faith alone. The warmth of the presence of others is necessary to him or her. One is already far too isolated and insignificant a creature to repudiate the fellowship available, and one knows that he or she is a person in whom are reflected and refracted the faces and feelings of hundreds of others and untold past generations . . . The cloud of witnesses to which he looks and is accountable stretches far beyond the deeds and sensibilities of church-recognized martyrs . . . The images and echoes that seethe into his or her mind have come into them from the whole ecumene . . . What one requires from this fellowship is not the diagnosis doctrinal theology provides but a sense of life great enough to welcome and encompass every spirit that has entered into the making of his or her polyglottic soul. To live Christianly means to one to believe and feel the worlds of motion pictures and clover-leaf junctions, slaughter in Vietnam, and communions in the Last Supper to be coalescing in his or her own soul.

Niebuhr, R.R., *Experiential Religion*, 23.

FEBRUARY 26.   MANY PIONEERS/MANY IMAGES/ DEATH OF RICHARD REINHOLD NIEBUHR.

There have already been many pioneers, each of whom has contributed something to our awareness. Religious persons are magic-making [persons] (Malinowski), fearing-person (Hume), and one directed toward the Unconditional (Tillich); one is man or woman shuddering before manifestations of the numinous (Otto), devoting him and herself to and denying themselves for the sake of universal ideal-energies (Dewey), like loving and dealing justly and other virtues. Religious persons are man and woman feeling their absolute dependence (Schleiermacher), persons arrogantly seeking deity and deification (Barth). They are persons homesick for primeval time (Eliade), myth-making man and woman (Cassirer), and a person giving him and herself to transcendent beauty (Jonathan Edwards).

Niebuhr, R.R., *Experiential Religion*, 33.

I am less concerned with doctrinal and dogmatic definitions than with the welter of personal experience; I can as well say that the subject matter is the history of the present-day counterpart of that man Mr. Little-Faith, of whom Christian and Hopeful once talked rather charitably as they made their roundabout way toward the Celestial City.

Niebuhr, R.R., *Experiential Religion, x.*

FEBRUARY 27. TRUST AND LOYALTY.

If we say that the church of the past is present to faith we may be misunderstood to be saying that it is merely "believed" to be present. But faith as personal existence in trust and fidelity does not "believe" what it does not see—that is a negative statement. It acknowledges that which it trusts and to which it is loyal. It is in this sense we "believe" in the community of faith which belongs to all ages of the past: we trust it in its trust in God and in its loyalty to all companions. We encounter God and Christ directly but in this company, and we acknowledge God and Lord not by ourselves but in this company. We do not first trust in this church and then in God; the relations are direct but double. We trust in God as we have been led to understand the mysterious One by the church. The dialogue has always been a double one and is now a double one.

Niebuhr, H.R., *Faith on Earth,* 113.

. . .When we seek an equilibrium in the midst of the natural and moral powers that encompass and affect our being, when we look for a principle of conduct adequate to our situation as a whole, then we behave as religious beings.

Niebuhr, R.R., *"Power and a Goodness,"* 1473.

. . . Faith is the apprehension of the power that is God, of God as the Power in the field of energies and vitalities that encompass us.

. . . Faith is the sense of not only being aimed at but of being aimed, of being directed with a field of power toward an end.

Niebuhr, R.R., *"Power and a Goodness,"* 1474.

FEBRUARY

... The ultimate problem of faith and the real task of theology are one: to wrestle with what some call theodicy and I call the logic of reconciliation to divine omnipotence and divine goodness . . . Whether the question takes the form of an inquiry into the meaning of the word "good" or the form of a doctrine of atonement. . . it is the question for faith and unbelief in our day.

Niebuhr, R.R., *"Power and a Goodness,"* 1475.

FEBRUARY 28.   INCLUSIVE FAITHFULNESS.

In that community of faith which we trust as loyal to God, loyal to [humans], lyal to us, there are no distinctions. There is here no Jew nor Greek. There are no B.C. and A.D. companies. The faith of Abraham is as great as the faith of Paul, the trust of the prophets is as great a gift, their loyalty as much to be relied upon as the faith of the apostles. It is a very Catholic Church, this community of faith to which we related in memory and in personal trust. As the Hebrews who beginning with a covenant established through Moses looked backward and saw that a covenant between God and people as well as among persons had been established through Abraham and prior to that through Noah, and prior to that through sinful Cain and fallen Eve, so we looking back from the covenant established through Jesus Christ see that it the renewal, the confirmation, the elaboration and the partial fulfillment of the covenant made by God with humanity from the foundation of the earth and witnessed to by seed-time and harvest, by rainbow and by social covenants, in marriage, in political institutions, in the community of truth-seekers. It will always seem dangerous to our thought bound by the categories of sun-time and earth-time and wanting to think only of a progress forward, not one of backward in this natural world, thus to speak of the Holy Catholic Church in which we believe as one which includes Jews and Greeks as well as Christians. But faith must confess that the trust and loyalty restored by Jesus Christ puts us into personal relationships with all those who expected the redemption of God, with all who relied upon his faithfulness.

Niebuhr, H.R., *Faith on Earth*, 113–14.

FEBRUARY 29. PRAYER FOR ONE'S COMMUNITY OF FAITH.

O Lord, look with mercy upon this congregation of your people, drawn together from every part of the earth, united in the worship of our Lord, divided by diversities of gifts, differences of custom, usage, and traditions and loyalties of language and nation. Grant us grace fitly to be joined together, to be obedient to your will and to serve one another with our several gifts. Enrich our common life through our diversities, and help us to keep the unity of the spirit in the bond of peace. May we by your mercy listen to each other in humility, and learn from each other with patience and diligence, so that our love may grow in all knowledge and discernment. Give us a sense of gratitude to all who serve us, and who give us the comfort and leisure for study by their special labors, so that we may not forget to bestow the more abundant honor upon those members of our community whose work is less obvious or apparent. This we ask through him who was among us as one who served.

Niebuhr, R., *Justice and Mercy*, 112.

MARCH
Women's History Month

This praiseworthy striving of the modern woman for higher education is confronted by the sad fact that cultured, well-educated persons . . . particularly the most learned men . . . generally have an inexplicable, deeply-rooted tendency to avoid learned women and to choose instead . . . an inexperienced, uneducated, fun-orientated young girl . . .

Niebuhr, G. [Jr.], in Caldwell, *A Mysterious Mantle*, 16.

Your Aunt, your mother's younger sister, Adele, after she had done her nursing training was ordained a deaconess. Hulda, your sister, apparently went through an agonizing time as an older adolescent wondering if she ought to follow the same vocation. I wonder who it was who released her from that felt imperative? Did your mother have the wisdom and common sense, and know it was not for her?

Niebuhr, U., *Remembering Reinhold Niebuhr*, 416–17.

Certainly one of the several benefits I have derived from William Chrystal's work is a still deeper admiration for the highly innovative and imaginative Hulda, my Aunt; and if in some degree she inherited her fortitude and great abilities as an educator from the father who so strongly disapproved of her aspirations to an education, then it may be she as much as any other to whom a mysterious "mantle" fell.

Niebuhr, R.R., in Chrystal, *A Father's Mantle*, x–xi.

MARCH 1.   SELF'S TENSIONS, STRUGGLES.

One is insecure and involved in natural contingency; he or she seeks to overcome his or her insecurity by a will-to-power which overreaches the limits of human creatureliness. One is ignorant and involved in the limitations of a finite mind; but he or she pretends not to be limited. They assume that they can gradually transcend finite limitations until their minds become identical with universal mind. All of one's intellectual and cultural pursuits, therefore, become infected with the sin of pride. One's pride and will-to-power disturb the harmony of creation. The Bible defines sin in both religious and moral terms. The religious dimension of sin is humanity's rebellion against God, an effort to usurp the place of God. The moral and social dimension of sin is injustice. The ego which falsely makes itself the centre of existence in its pride and will-to-power inevitably subordinates other life to its will and thus does injustice to the life.

Niebuhr, R., *Nature and Destiny of Man* (Vol. I), 178–79.

MARCH 2.   ADDICTION VIA LOSING ONESELF, AND THEN TO THE TIMES IN THY HANDS.

Sometimes [a person] seeks to solve the problem of the contradiction of finiteness and freedom, not by seeking to hide his finiteness and comprehending the world into himself, but by seeking to hide his or her freedom and by losing themselves in some aspect of the world's vitalities. In that case [one's] sin may be defined as sensuality rather than pride. Sensuality is never the mere expression of natural impulse in a person. [Sensuality] always betrays some abortive effort to solve the problem of finiteness and freedom . . . by immersing him or herself into a "mutable good," by losing [oneself] in some natural vitality . . . Human passions are always characterized by unlimited and demonic potencies of which animal life is innocent.

Niebuhr, R., *Nature and Destiny of Man* (Vol. I), 179, 186, 179.

. . . Insofar as I have any understanding of Christ, he is not the abolition of my religion, nor does he teach me that my religiousness is my sin. Neither does he transport me above the vicissitudes and ambiguities and vanities of human history and hence of religion. Rather, he throws me back upon my sheer humanity and—to borrow a phrase from

Schleiermacher—upon my absolute dependence on God. Therefore, if he brings me peace, he brings it with a sword, but he can bring me neither except insofar as I am a religious being . . . It is not simply Christ that I see—my religion has not become a religion of Christ. He is not the center of my world and I am not a Christo-centric man. Rather, it is with and through Christ that I see, so that he has become the form, the exemplar, through which the distortions of humanity are laid bare and the destiny of man is adumbrated. My religion has become not Christo-centric now but rather Christo-morphic. And insofar as the ultimate religion of the Bible is contained in the Psalmist's words: "My times are in thy hand," I recognize that henceforth all time for me will be informed and conformed and reformed by the image of Christ.

Niebuhr, R.R., in https://bulletin.hds.harvard.edu/a-christo-morphic-view-of-religion/ [accessed August 5, 2021].

MARCH 3.   USES AND ABUSES OF POWER.

There is a pride of power in which the human ego assumes its self-sufficiency and self-mastery and imagines itself secure against all vicissitudes. It does not recognize the contingent and dependent character of its life and believes itself to be the author of its own existence, the judge of its own values and the master of its own destiny. This proud pretension is present in an inchoate form in all human life but it rises to greater heights among those individuals and classes who have more than an ordinary degree of social power . . . Closely related to the pride which seems to rest upon the possession of either the ordinary or extraordinary measure of human freedom and self-mastery, is the lust for power, which has pride as its end. The ego does not feel secure and therefore grasps for more power in order to make itself secure. It does not regard itself as sufficiently significant or respected or feared and therefore seeks to enhance its position in nature and in society. . . the lust for power is prompted by a darkly conscious realization of its insecurity . . . The will-to-power involves the ego in injustice. It seeks a security beyond the limits of human finiteness and this inordinate ambition arouses fears and enmities which the world of pure nature, with its competing impulses of survival, does not know.

Niebuhr, R., *Nature and Destiny of Man* (Vol. I), 188–89, 192.

MARCH 4. SELF-SERVING TAINTS.

All human knowledge is tainted with an "ideological" taint. It pretends to be more true than it is. Exactly analogous to the cruder pride of power, the pride of intellect is derived on the one hand from the ignorance of the finiteness of the human mind and on the other hand from an attempt to obscure the known conditioned character of human knowledge and the taint of self-interest in human truth . . . A particular significant aspect of intellectual pride is the inability of the agent to recognize the same or similar limitations of perspective in him and herself which one has detected in others . . . In the relations of majority and minority racial groups for which the negro-white relation is an example, the majority group justifies the disabilities which it imposes upon the minority group on the ground that the subject group is not capable of enjoying or profiting from the privileges of culture or civilization. Yet it can never completely hide, and it sometimes frankly expresses the fear that the grant of such privileges would eliminate the inequalities of endowment which supposedly justify the inequalities of privilege. The pretension of pride is thus a weapon against a feared competitor. Sometimes it is intended to save the self from the abyss of self-contempt which always yawns before it.

Niebuhr, R., *Nature and Destiny of Man* (Vol. I), 194, 196, 198.

MARCH 5. PRETENSIONS

Moral pride is revealed in all "self-righteous" judgments in which the other is condemned because he fails to conform to the highly arbitrary standards of the self. Since the self judges itself by its own standards it finds itself good. It judges others by its own standards and finds them evil, when their standards fail to conform to its own. This is the secret of the relationship between cruelty and self-righteousness. When the self mistakes its standards for God's standards it is naturally inclined to attribute the very essence of evil to nonconformists.

. . . Moral pride is the pretension of finite [person] that his highly conditioned virtue is the final righteousness and that his [or her] relative moral standards are absolute. Moral pride thus makes virtue the very vehicle of sin, a fact which explains why the New Testament is so critical of the righteous in comparison with "publicans and sinners . . . " The sinner who justifies him or herself does not know God as judge and does not need God a Saviour . . . [T]he sin of self-righteousness . . . is responsible for our most serious cruelties, injustices and defamations against our fellow humans. The whole history of racial, national, religious and other social struggles is a commentary on the objective wickedness and social miseries which result from self-righteousness.

Niebuhr, R., *Nature and Destiny of Man* (Vol. I), 199-200.

MARCH 6.   GRACE VIA MERCY/WORLD DAY OF PRAYER (IF 1ST MONDAY OF MARCH).

Christian education is the believing community at work helping people listen and look in order that by God's grace they may hear and see and so be helped to know the hope to which they are called by God in Jesus Christ.

Niebuhr, H., in Caldwell, *A Mysterious Mantle*, 76.

Almighty God, our Father and Mother, look with mercy upon us that we may worship you in spirit and in truth. We lift our hearts in gladness to you as we think of all the good things in life which we have from you. We come before you in humility as we remember all things we have done and left undone in defiance of your will and become conscious of all that has been remiss in our thoughts, words, and deeds.

Sanctify our prayers, purging them of all lusts and desires which separate us from you, and filling them with all good impulses which unite us to you. Give us grace to live our life this day in your presence, and to perform our duties in accordance with your will.

Niebuhr, R., *Justice and Mercy*, 117.

MARCH 7.   SELF-ASSERTION IN RELIGIOUS DISGUISE.

The ultimate sin is the religious sin of making the self-deification implied in moral pride explicit . . . The same person may in one moment regard Christ as his or her judge and in the next moment seek to prove that the figure, the standards and the righteousness of Christ bear a greater similarity to one's own righteousness than to that of the enemy. The worst form of class domination is religious class domination in which, as for instance in the Indian caste system, a dominant priestly class not only subjects subordinate classes to social disabilities but finally excludes them from participation in any universe of meaning. The worst form of intolerance is religious intolerance, in which the particular interests of the contestants hide behind religious absolutes. The worst form of self-assertion is religious self-assertion in which under the guise of contrition before God, the Holy One is claimed as the exclusive ally of our contingent self. "What goes by the name of 'religion' in the modern world," declares a modern missionary, "is to a great extent unbridled human self-assertion in religious disguise."

Niebuhr, R., *Nature and Destiny of Man* (Vol. I), 200–201.

MARCH 8. INTERNATIONAL WOMEN'S DAY AND ONE'S HELPMATE.

The Biblical analysis of sin is filled with references to the function of deception in the economy of sin . . . In moments of crisis the true situation may be vividly revealed to the self, prompting it to despairing remorse or possibly to a more creative contrition.

Niebuhr, R., *Nature and Destiny of Man* (Vol. I), 204–205, 206.

For me worship involved the emptying of the self and the offering of the self objectively expressed in the sequences of the liturgy. In this way, the sermon should lead on to some liturgical expression of the movement of the soul under the scrutiny of conscience and of the judgment as well as the mercy of God. To have a cheerful hymn and still more cheerful slapping of the back and shaking of hand outside was inappropriate, Reinhold endured this critical attitude of mine in a very tolerant way. He would cheerfully tell other people that preaching was his art form and the Lord had given him a wife who didn't like sermons . . . [But] I did like his sermons. I also believed they were his art form and also that they were done extraordinarily well, not only from the point of view of the shaping but also in substance, so that they did reach out and touch the heart and conscience as well as the mind.

Niebuhr, U., *Remembering Reinhold Niebuhr*, 6.

MARCH 47

... [I]n my old age and being conscious of the spiritual and intellectual debt I owe my wife, not to speak of the more precious debts incurred in decades of a happy marriage, I must close this autobiographical introduction with a confession. I do not know how much Ursula is responsible for modifying my various forms of provincialism and homiletical polemics. But I know she is responsible for much of my present viewpoint . . . I know that my wife is the more diligent student of biblical literature and of the relation of psychology to literature and social dynamics. I cannot, therefore, promise that this summary of my lifework is strictly my own . . . the joint authorship is not acknowledged except in this confession. I will leave the reader to judge whether male arrogance or complete mutuality is the cause of the solution.

Niebuhr, R., *On Man's Nature and His Communities*, 28–29.

MARCH 9.   DECEPTIONS AND TRUTH?

The sinful self needs deceptions because it cannot pursue its own determinate ends without paying tribute to the truth. This truth, which the self, even in its own sin, never wholly obscures, is that the self, as finite and determinate, does not deserve unconditioned devotion. But though the deceptions are needed they are never wholly convincing because the self is the only ego fully privy to the dishonesties by which it has hidden its own interests behind a façade of general interest. If others will only accept what the self cannot quite accept, the self as deceiver is given an ally against the self as deceived.

Niebuhr, R., *Nature and Destiny of Man* (Vol. I), 206–07.

MARCH 10.   FATED TO BE LOYAL, TO LIVE BY TRUST.

What shall we say of the sources of this great sense of deception so common among [people]? Who is the betrayer? Where was the first promise broken? . . . When we contemplate our human history, the network of interpersonal relations, it is not difficult to describe it as the history of treason. When one reads the story of the nations and notes how broken treaties and deceitful promises mark each page, one wonders why anyone at any time should accept another promise, write another treaty. There is no area of human conduct—not economics, not religion, not the family—which is free from the wreckage of broken words. The massive law books and the great machinery of justice give evidence of the vast extent of fraud, deceit and disloyalty among men and women. Treason begets distrust, distrust treason. The great disorder of our existence cannot be eliminated by a return to the innocence of a life in which there is no promise and no loyalty and therefore neither treason nor deceit. We are fated to be loyal and to live by trust but all our loyalty appears only in the corrupted form of broken promises, and our trust in the perverse form of the great suspicion that we are being deceived.

Niebuhr, H.R., *Faith on Earth,* 81–82.

MARCH 11.   WHOLE AND ORDERED?

We understand our human wretchedness, self-contradictoriness, and alienation as *harmartia*, the "missing of the mark," rather than as transgression of the law. Sin is not so much law- breaking as vice; it is the perverse direction of the drives in persons, or of his and her will in general, towards ends not proper to them. Though vice leads to transgression of the law, yet this transgression is not the basic evil in self-existence. The fundamental evil is conflict within and corruption of a life meant by its internal entelechy, its "native drive," to be whole and ordered within itself, whether as personal, or as social or universal.

Niebuhr, H.R., *Responsible Self,* 132.

MARCH 12.   TEMPTATION TO ASPIRE AFTER GODHEAD.

For the individual idealist the disorder in man and woman is the multiplicity of their loves, all tending toward separate ends, unordered in a complete life directed toward a single goal, unformed in accordance with a unifying image. Or it is the disorder that results when the self holds before itself an image of itself that is not in accordance with its actual constitution and when it thus moves against its own grain. For the social idealist the disorder in mankind is to be found in the contradictory ends striven after by various groups in what is yet one society. In this contradiction the individuals that are members of more than one group, as they play their various roles, with such contradictory images before them as those of the patriotic nationalist, the good European, the white person, the Christian, etc. For the universal teleologist [purpose driven], the Christian now particularly, all these contradictions in individual and society are recognizably present, but the fundamental disorder is traced to the fact that the self has set before itself an image to be realized in action which runs counter to its place as a creature. One wants to be like God, not only in the knowledge of good and evil, but being his or her own Maker . . . the tragic center [of the story of the fall] lies in our yielding to the temptation to aspire after godhead rather than in our disobedience to commandment.

Niebuhr, H.R., *Responsible Self,* 132–33.

MARCH 13. SURROUNDING WORLDS OF AGENTS.

There is a law in me or in my mind, the law of my integrity; and there are many laws in my members, the laws of response to many systems of action about me. In my responsiveness and responsibility to the many I am irresponsible to One beyond the many; I am irresponsible as a self, however responsible the natural, the political, the domestic, the biological complexes in me may be in relation to the systems of nature, church, family, or profession, or to the closed society of life itself. I become more deeply involved in conflict within myself and in my world when I protest against this inner manifoldness by turning from many systems of action upon me to myself. I undertake then to find myself within myself and to order myself and my surrounding world by beginning with my own actions, regarding all other actions as reactions only to my own primal needs. Conflict with the others who surround me and who act similarly from themselves must now become the war of all against all. Conflict within myself ensures because I am a being of many interests, of many potential actions on my surrounding worlds of agents; I cannot identify myself with one of these sets of interests without calling forth the revolt of others. Manifoldness and conflict are not banished by this effort to flee from responsibility and responsiveness into a way of existence in which I act from myself only.

Niebuhr, H.R., *Faith on Earth,* 137–38.

MARCH 14.　PRINCIPALITIES AND POWERS.

As it with the self in itself so it is with the community of selves. The story of our communal life is the story of conflict and war and uneasy truces that hold off anarchy awhile. As flesh lusts against spirit and spirit against flesh within the self, so community lusts against community, nation against nation, church against state and state against church, religion against religion. Responsive and responsible to each other in our closed societies, we are irresponsible in the larger world that includes us all. This state of sin, or of wretchedness and lostness, seems like the state to which New Testament writers refer when they speak of our subjection to principalities and powers and the rulers of the darkness of this world.

Niebuhr, H.R., *Responsible Self,* 138.

While we may not believe in a personal devil, we must certainly agree with the Apostle Paul when he said we reasoned, not with flesh and blood but with powers and principalities.

Niebuhr, H.R., in Diefenthaler, "H. Richard Niebuhr: A Fresh Look," 182.

MARCH 15.　SMALL SEED OF INTEGRITY.

We do not think of these systems as personal or anthropomorphic in character. Nevertheless they are systems, not human individuals nor atomic agencies. There is the system of nature, partly objective to us, partly historically subjective. It is the system of forces as known and interpreted by our society. It is powerful; it is heedless of our concerns; it is neither good nor evil. But we are in it and must adjust ourselves to it, be responsive to it. There are the systems of society, the customs and the mores, the large organizations of economic and cultural activities, all of which are partly objective, partly subjective. We call them by such names as feudalism, industrialism, capitalism, communism, nationalism.

There are vaguely defined ways of thinking, such as we sometimes call climates of opinion, or spirits of civilization. These also exercise dominion over us. Unquestioned, almost inaccessible assumptions in our common minds determine how we accept and react to our fellow or sister human, or, again, the manias that possess whole peoples for long periods—manias for possession or manias for poverty as in the early days of monasticism. They are not all evil powers, not devils, with which we are concerned, though we may call some of them, with Walter Rauschen-busch, superpersonal forces of evil. But they are powers not identifiable with the willed influences of human groups or individuals. And they exercise dominion over us at least in this sense that we adjust our actions to them, do what fits into their action.

In this our personal and social manifoldness we have been left with a small seed of integrity, a haunting sense of unity and of universal responsibility.

Niebuhr, H.R., *Faith on Earth*, 139.

MARCH 16.   A GODLY SORROW.

Look with mercy upon us, our Father and Mother, for the multitude of our iniquities, for the pride with which our generation sought to build a new world, and for the despair with which we behold our world in ruins;

For the complacency of all nations who were not grieved when wounded by your judgment, and did not receive correction when consumed by your anger;

For the self-righteous fury of victorious nations, and their inhumanity toward the vanquished;

For the deafness of our ears to the cries of the needy, and for the vain glory to which our power tempts us;

For the discord we create between nations and individuals by our desire of dominion over our fellow men, and your resentment of the hurts which our brothers and sisters inflict upon us, and our unconsciousness of the pains we have inflicted upon them;

For the involvement of your church in the sins of the world, for its cowardice in tempering your judgements so that people be not grieved;

For mixing the vain glorious opinions of persons with the truth of your gospel, and for all lack of charity which has brought the prejudices of Jew and Gentiles, and the chasm between bond and free, into the community of grace where [all people] should be one in Christ;

For the despair which corrupts our faith in the day of calamity, as for the complacency which shrouded your word to all in the day of ease;

O Lord, hear the prayers of our confession and grant that our sorrow may be a godly sorrow which leads to repentance and newness of life.

Niebuhr, R., *Justice and Mercy*, 121–22.

MARCH 17.   PRETENSIONS AND CLAIMS OF A SOCIAL SELF.

A distinction between group pride and the egotism of individuals is necessary because the pretensions and claims of a collective or social self exceed those of the individual ego. The group is more arrogant, hypocritical, self-centered and more ruthless in the pursuit of its ends than the individual. An inevitable moral tension between individual and group morality is therefore created . . .

Niebuhr, R., *Nature and Destiny of Man* (Vol. I), 208.

Frederick the Great the King of Prussia from 1740 until his death in 1786, was not, as statespersons go, a person of unique moral sensitivity. His confession of a sense of this tension is therefore the more significant. "I hope," said he, "that posterity will distinguish the philosopher from the monarch in me and the decent man from the politician. I must admit that when drawn into the vortex of European politics it is difficult to preserve decency and integrity. One feels oneself in constant danger of being betrayed by one's allies and abandoned by one's friends, of being suffocated by envy and jealousy, and is thus finally driven to the terrible alternative of being false either to one's country or to one's word." . . . Sinful pride and idolatrous pretension are thus an inevitable concomitant of the cohesion of large political groups.

Niebuhr, R., *Nature and Destiny of Man* (Vol. I), 209-10.

MARCH 18.   IN MEMORY OF OVERDOSE VICTIMS
(as with Eli Cooley-Morris, January 15, 2020).

Is sin merely a form of selfishness? Or a consequence of selfishness? Or does it betray characteristics which must prompt the conclusion that sensuality is a distinctive form of sin, to be sharply distinguished from self-love? . . . If selfishness is the destruction of life's harmony by the self's attempt to centre life around itself, sensuality would seem to be the destruction of harmony within the self, by the self's undue identification with and devotion to particular impulses and desires within itself. The sins of sensuality, as expressed for instance in sexual license, gluttony, extravagance, drunkenness and abandonment to various forms of physical

MARCH   53

desire, have always been subject to a sharper and readier social disap-
proval than the more basic sin of self-love . . . Sensuality is, in effect, the
inordinate love for all creaturely and mutable values, which results from
the primal love of self, rather than love of God.

Niebuhr, R., *Nature and Destiny of Man* (Vol. I), 228, 232.

MARCH 19.   A PROPHETIC MINORITY?

The fact that human pride insinuated itself into the struggle of the Christian religion against the pride and self-will of nations merely proves how
easily the pride of persons can avail itself of the very instruments intended to mitigate it. The church, as well as the state, can become the vehicle
of collective egoism. Every truth can become the servant of sinful arrogance, including the prophetic truth that all people fall short of the truth
. . . It is important to recognize that there are "Christian" nations, who
prove themselves so because they are still receptive to prophetic words
of judgement spoken against the nation. It may be that only a prophetic
minority feels this judgement keenly.

Niebuhr, R., *Nature and Destiny of Man* (Vol. I), 217, 219.

MARCH 20.   INTERNATIONAL DAY OF HAPPINESS.

God had joy in his creation. When he looked at it all, the ancient story
says, "Behold, it was very good." But man and woman, made in God's
image, was not content to take the place God had given him or her in the
world. One wanted to be free to go his or her own way and do as he or
she pleased, apart from God. The sin of man or woman changed the joy
of the Creator, God, to sorrow. Man, together with the woman, made to
be his helpmate, was driven out of the garden God had given them. An
angel with a flaming sword guarded it against their return. Their children
and their children's children also chose an evil way, and a great flood was
sent to punish them. Noah, who was obedient to God, was saved from
the flood, together with his family. When it was over they saw a great
rainbow in the clouds and knew it was a sign that God still loved them.

Again and again man and woman rebelled against God. Their pride
was great, and they thought the way to be truly happy was to do just as

they pleased. So God set about winning man and woman to God's self. The story of how God did it is the one great story of the Bible.

Niebuhr, H., One Story, 12.

MARCH 21. INTERNATIONAL DAY FOR THE ELIMINATION OF RACIAL DISCRIMINATION.

. . . [D]espite all democratic pretensions, there is no democracy that has fully transcended racial prejudices . . . no democracy ever will transcend them completely, though of course no one can place limits upon the possibilities of surmounting them. Which is to say that race pride is one the many aspects of man's collective life that have been obscured by our contemporary culture. This culture has assumed that pride of race is no more than a vestigial remnant of barbarism and that increasing education would overcome it . . . Race bigotry is, in short, one form of original sin . . . something darker and more terrible than mere stupidity and is therefore not eradicated by enlightenment alone . . . We do not finally come to terms with race pride until the soul knows itself to be under final judgment ceases to veil its hidden fears and prides, honestly prays: "Search me, O God, and know my faults; try me and know my thoughts—see if there is any wicked way in me and lead me to the way everlasting." [Psalm 139:23–4] Race bigotry, in other words, must be broken by repentance and not merely by enlightenment. [However] racial prejudice, as every form of group prejudice, is a concomitant of the collective life of earthlings. Group pride is the sinful corruption of group consciousness. Contempt of another group is the pathetic form that respect for our group frequently takes. We must not condone these sinful corruptions . . .

Niebuhr, R., Love and Justice, 129–30, 128.

Almighty and eternal God, creator of the world, judge and redeemer of men and women, who gives us the treasures of darkness and the hidden riches of secret places, grant that we know that you are Lord, and there is none else beside . . . Grant us grace to separate the precious from the vile, that we may speak boldly and humbly to suffering and perplexed persons.

Niebuhr, R., Justice and Mercy, 114.

MARCH 22. SEEKING FOR ANOTHER GOD/ WORLD WATER DAY.

The human, having lost the true centre of one's life, is no longer able to maintain his or her own will as the centre of the self . . . The question is: does the drunkard or the glutton merely press self-love to the limit and lose all control over him and herself by the effort to gratify a particular physical desire so unreservedly that its gratification comes into conflict with other desires? Or is lack of moderation an effort to escape from the self? And does sexual license mean merely the subordination of another person to the ego's self-love, expressed in this case in an inordinate physical desire; or does undisciplined sex life represent an effort on the part of a disquieted and disorganized self to escape from itself? Is sensuality in other words a form of idolatry which makes the self god; or is it an alternative idolatry in which the self, conscious of the inadequacy of its self-worship, seeks escape by finding some other god? . . . The probable reason for the ambiguous and equivocal answers to [these questions] in the whole course of Christian theology is that there is a little of both in sensuality . . . The self is seeking to escape from itself and throws itself into any pursuit which will allow it to forget for a moment the inner tension of an uneasy conscience. The self, finding itself to be inadequate as the centre of its existence, seeks for another god amidst the various forces, processes and impulses of nature over which it ostensibly presides.

Niebuhr, R., *Nature and Destiny of Man* (Vol. I), 233–34.

We feel within ourselves the tremor and the awe that intimate the presence of beings different in power and character from those we meet in too familiar surroundings. When nature, become too familiar, can no long cast the spell of the numinous on us, when the pageantry and power of societies has revealed itself as hollow show or as destructive demonry, we seek emancipation from the sense of the barren waste of life in music and in color . . .

Niebuhr, H.R., *Meaning of Revelation*, 130.

Yours, O Lord, is the kingdom and the power and the glory. We praise you for the creation of this world, for the wonder of all living things, for the order and harmony in which your creation moves, for seedtime and harvest, summer and winter, day and night . . . We bless you for everything which supports our life and for your providence which maintains and preserves the world in order.

Niebuhr, R., Justice and Mercy, 119.

MARCH 23. STRENGTH AND LURES OF PASSION.

Sexual passion may, by the very power it develops in the spiritual confusion of human sin, serve exactly the same purpose as drunkenness. It may serve as an [soothing] anodyne. The ego, having found the worship both of self and of the other abortive, may use the passion of sex without reference to self and the other, as a form of escape from the tension of life. The most corrupt forms of sensuality, as for instance in commercialized vice, have exactly this characteristic, that personal considerations are excluded from the satisfaction of the sexual impulse. It is a flight not to a false god but to nothingness. The strength of the passion which makes this momentary escape possible is itself a consequence of sin primarily and of an uneasy conscience consequent upon sin secondarily . . .

Niebuhr, R., Nature and Destiny of Man (Vol. I), 237.

The real situation is that man and woman, granted their "fallen" nature, sins in his or her sex life but not because sex is essentially sinful. Or, in other words, man and woman, having lost the true centre of their life in God, falls into sensuality; and sex is the most obvious occasion for the expression of sensuality and the most vivid expression of it. Thus sex reveals sensuality to be first another and final form of self-love, secondly an effort to escape self-love by the deification of another and finally as an escape from the futilities of both forms of idolatry by a plunge into unconsciousness.

Niebuhr, R., Nature and Destiny of Man (Vol. I), 239.

MARCH 24. FEAST OF [ARCHBISHOP] SAINT OSCAR ROMERO.

Its face turned toward the glittery, new casino-hotels on the southern end of Las Vegas Boulevard, a life-sized statue of Jesus spreads its arms wide, as if to embrace the throngs of tourists milling about the towering Sphinx

MARCH 57

outside the Luxor, the fairy-tale castle at the Excalibur, the make-believe skyscrapers at New York New York.

And, as if responding to the invitation, many do make their way from the boulevard, the famous Strip, to the beige stone church behind the statue, the Roman Catholic Shrine of the Most Holy Redeemer, where people have been known to toss casino chips into the offering plates.

A strange juxtaposition of symbols can be found here. Within sight of the shrine stand billboards advertising magic shows, a marquee advertising a dance revue ("sexier than ever") and a big screen flashing images of Cher in a silver wig. But inside the shrine, visitors can gaze on sculptures of the Last Supper and the Crucifixion and on a mural portraying such servants of the poor as Dorothy Day and Archbishop Oscar Romero of El Salvador.

Niebuhr, G. [Jr.], "Las Vegas Journal," p. 14.

Whether Jesus conceived that the Kingdom was to be established here or beyond is a question beside the point . . . The righteousness of the gospel [is] the righteousness of community conduct.

Niebuhr, H.R., in Diefenthaler, "H. Richard Niebuhr: A Fresh Look," 179.

We praise you for the glory shining through the sad and yet majestic history of our race; for saints and seers, made perfect through suffering; for people of stout hearts who have defied malignant power; for all who have been tender toward the hurt and the maimed; for prophets who have discerned your judgments and your mercy in the events of people's history, and have proclaimed of your will to their brothers and sisters; we thank you above all for Jesus Christ, who has set before us the meaning of your righteousness and your love.

Niebuhr, R., *Justice and Mercy*, 119–20.

MARCH 25. NO BLINKING THE FACT.

The Gospels represent Jesus as a God-shaped human, as a locus in which the ruling action of God appears. It appears in him as Jesus acquires friends and disciples and takes the leadership of a new movement in history—in a word, as Jesus grows large; and it also appears as Jesus loses his friends and disciples, sees his cause meeting defeat, and finds himself taken prisoner and condemned—in a word, as Jesus grows small . . . we may take Jesus' actions and words together as a persona of God-ruling . . . the actions and words the reader learns about refer to God, and since actions and words belong to conduct and conduct makes up by what we mean by the word person, we may accept this God-shapedness as constituent of Jesus' persona . . . As a figure who attracts or fends [people] off, Jesus' relation to God is part and parcel of his effect on others. He befriends and alienates other persons as one who refers himself to God and so refers the interpreter also to the God dominating and shaping his persona. No demythologizing or modernization of Jesus can blink that fact.

Niebuhr, R.R., *Experiential Religion*, 130.

MARCH 26. TO GREAT TO BEAR.

It would not be inaccurate to define the first purpose of intoxication as the sinful ego-assertion which is rooted in anxiety and unduly compensates for the sense of inferiority and insecurity; while the second purpose of intoxication springs from the sense of guilt, or a state of perplexity in which a sense of guilt has been compounded with the previous sense of insecurity. The tension of this perplexity is too great to bear and results in an effort to escape consciousness completely . . . Anxiety tempts the self to sin; the sin increases the insecurity which it was intended to alleviate until some escape from the whole tension of life is sought . . . Whether in drunkenness, gluttony, sexual license, love of luxury or any inordinate devotion to a mutable good, sensuality is always: 1) an extension of self-love to the point where it defeats its own ends; 2) an effort to escape the prison house of self by finding a god in a process or person outside of the self; and 3) finally an effort to escape from the confusion which sin has created into some form of subconscious existence.

Niebuhr, R., *Nature and Destiny of Man (Vol. I)*, 234-35, 239–40.

MARCH 27. APPRECIATION OF THE TRAGEDY OF LIFE.

We had a communion service tonight [Good Friday] and I preached on the text "We preach Christ crucified, to the Jews a stumbling block and to the Gentiles foolishness, but to them that are called the power of God

MARCH   59

and the wisdom of God. "I don't think I ever felt greater joy in preaching a sermon. How experience and life which change our perspectives! It was only a few years ago that I did not know what to make of the cross; at least I made no more of it than to recognize it as a historic fact which proved the necessity of paying a high price for our ideals. Now I see it as a symbol of ultimate reality. Liberalism has too little appreciation of the tragedy of life to understand the cross and orthodoxy insists too much upon the uniqueness of the sacrifice of Christ to make the preaching of the cross effective. How can anything be uniquely potent if it is absolutely unique. It is because the cross of Christ symbolizes something in the very heart of reality, something in universal experience that it has its central place in history.

Niebuhr, R., *Leaves from the Notebook,* **85.**

MARCH 28.   REDEMPTIVE TRAGEDY.

Life is tragic and the most perfect type of moral beauty inevitably has at least a touch of the tragic in it. Why? That is not so easy to explain. But love pays such a high price for its objectives and sets its objectives so high that they can never be attained. There is therefore always a foolish and futile aspect to love's quest which give it the note of tragedy. What makes this tragedy redemptive is that the foolishness of love is revealed as wisdom in the end and its futility becomes the occasion for new moral striving. About heroes, saints, and saviors it must always remain true "that they, without us should not be made perfect" (Heb. 11:40).

Niebuhr, R., *Leaves from the Notebook,* **85–86.**

MARCH 29.   CLOSELY RELATED CREATION AND REDEMPTION.

The history of every nation and every people makes the crucifixion a perennial and a universal historical fact. That is the very reason why Christians can no more afford to eliminate the cross than they can ascribe it to fortunately extinct Romans. Anyone who incarnates the strategy of love as Jesus did meets the resistance and incites the passions of human society. The respectabilities of any human society are based upon moral compromises and every community is as anxious to defend these compromises against the prophet who presents some higher moral logic as against the criminal who imperils the structure from below. The cross is central in the Christian religion, moreover, because it symbolizes a cosmic as well as an historic truth. Love conquers the world, but its victory is not an easy one. The price of all creativity and redemption is pain. Most modern religionists who understand the God of creation and not the God of redemption fail in understanding the latter precisely because they do not see how closely related creation and redemption are. Which simply means that they don't understand that creation is a painful process in which the old does not give way to the new without trying to overcome it.

Niebuhr, R., *Leaves from the Notebook*, 101–102.

MARCH 30. GOD'S SUFFERING SERVANT.

To the minds of Jews, the Messiah was certain to be a consequence against whom no enemies could stand. One prophet in Old Testament times saw clearly that to serve God faithfully and to speak his truth unswervingly among [people] always meant suffering for the one who did it, and that God used this suffering to win [persons] to him. But no one ever took this to mean that the Messiah would have to suffer. Jesus, however, understood what was written, and knew that if he was to triumph as God's Servant he would have to be despised and rejected of humans. The way to victory was the way of the cross.

Niebuhr, H., *One Story*, 132.

MARCH 31. CROSS CANNOT BE SACRIFICED.

The disciples, who had waited for God's Kingdom to come in glory, were mourning over their crucified Master, all their hopes defeated. Then something happened to make them feel that God was saying to them: "I am back of all that Jesus said and did. My power is in him who was obedient in all things. His death on the cross was not defeat but . . . ."

Niebuhr, H., *One Story*, 144.

The cross of Jesus is truly the most adequate symbol of both the strategy and the destiny of love not only in history but in the universe. We may grant our Jewish brethren that it is not the only possible symbol of eternal verities, but it is a true one, and it cannot therefore be sacrificed.

Niebuhr, R., *Leaves from the Notebook,* **102.**

O Lord, hear our prayers not according to the poverty of our asking, but according to the richness of your grace, so that our lives may conform to those desires which accord with your will.

Niebuhr, R., *Reinhold Niebuhr: Major Works,* **697.**

"Forgiveness" by Jim Houston

APRIL
Second Chance Month

[Hulda Niebuhr's] The One Story was to show "again and again humans rebelled against God . . . so God set about winning [humankind] to himself. The story of how God did it is the one great story of the Bible."

Niebuhr, H., in Caldwell, *The Mysterious Mantle*, 117.

[The self] cannot be saved merely by being enlightened. It is a unity and therefore cannot be drawn out of itself merely by extending its perspective upon interests beyond itself. If it remains self-centered, it merely uses its wider perspective to bring more lives and interests under the dominion of its will-to-power. The necessity of its being shattered at the very centre of its being gives perennial validity to the strategy of evangelistic sects, which seek to induce the crisis of conversion . . . The self in this state of preoccupation with itself must be "broken" and "shattered" or, in the Pauline phrase, "crucified."

Niebuhr, R., *Nature and Destiny of Man* (Vol. II), 109.

Through Christ we become immigrants into the empire of God which extends over all the world and learn to remember the history of that empire, that is of men and women in all time and places, as our history . . . there is nothing that is alien to us.

Niebuhr, H.R., *Meaning of Revelation*, 85.

APRIL 1. JESUS' GOD-RULING WORLD.

Without God, Jesus vanishes as a concrete personality. Two aspects of his persona, as the Gospels present him, exhibit this shaping action in him. First of all, is his awareness—expressed in parable and epigram—that the world in which he moves is the ruling conduct of God. And second, there is his consciousness—expressed in counselling with his disciples about his course of action—that the intentions which inwardly determine his conduct are intended by God. Outwardly that which is objective to him is God-Ruling and inwardly that which is objective to him is God-Intending. Hence he moves and acts in the action of the Kingdom, and the Kingdom moves and acts in the action of Jesus . . . Whoever wishes to explore Jesus' humanity to understand the example of his conduct to comprehend his stature as a pioneer of faithfulness, must begin by exploring Jesus' world, which is God-Ruling. But whoever would explore Jesus' world can enter it only by beginning where his own world intersects it, at the points where it diminishes and enlarges him, giving him opportunity to recognize the unattended geneses of human faithfulness in himself. For the radial person the interpretation of Jesus begins as an interpretation of the same encompassing reality under two aspects and two names: the ruling action of which Jesus is the voice and the "finger" and the enworlding field of action that presses the interpreter.

Niebuhr, R.R., *Experiential Religion,* 134.

APRIL 2. FIVE DAYS OF DIFFERENCE.

The crowd which hailed Jesus as a triumphant Messiah probably consisted of sympathizers, rather than disciples. They did not know, in any event, that Jesus had himself renounced the role of a triumphant Messiah who would bring victory to the righteous over the unrighteous, and had chosen instead the role of a suffering servant, as suggested by the prophecies in the writings of Isaiah. He had predicted his own death and insisted that the Son of Man or the Human One had come "not to be saved but to serve, and to give his life as a ransom for many." The difference in those five days of Holy Week represents the difference between the old and new Hebraic religions. They are both creative in making the hazardous assertion that the drama of human history has meaning. The old religion tried to solve the problem of the moral ambiguity of the historical process by projecting a Messianic age in which all ambiguity would be eliminated by the triumph of justice over injustice. The new religion, despite the idea of a suffering Messiah rather than a triumphant one, also had many Messianic moods and movements.

Niebuhr, R., *Justice and Mercy*, 86–87.

APRIL 3. JEWS AND CHRISTIANS' CREATIVE TENSIONS.

Let us not observe Palm Sunday by a polemical attitude toward the old Messianism and a congratulation for Christians that Christianity is superior to Judaism. The distinguished Jewish philosopher [and biblical scholar], Martin Buber, accurately defined the differences between the two religions in this way: "To the Christian, the Jew is a stubborn fellow, who in an unredeemed world still is waiting for the Messiah. To the Jews, the Christian is the heedless fellow who, in an unredeemed world, affirms that redemption has somehow or other taken place." It is difficult to renounce the idea that mixtures of good and evil in [people] and nations, which give the drama of history such pathos and an infinite variety of themes, will be eliminated by a final triumph of good over evil; even though the clear meaning of the suffering servant, as Jesus interpreted it, was that history reached its climax of meaning, not in the triumph of good over evil, but in the contrite awareness that all persons, good and evil, must be reconciled to God. Let us leave with the Jews the problem of what it means to be "still waiting for the Messiah"; and whether, translated in modern terms, this could mean any more than a perennial utopianism, which has played such a creative but also confusing role in the history of mankind. Let Christians be concerned with their own problem . . .

Niebuhr, R., *Justice and Mercy*, 87.

APRIL 4. CROSS'S IMPACT AND IMPORT.

That "somehow or other" [via Martin Buber] is obviously related to the death of Christ on the cross. This symbol has had a mysterious power in all ages of Christianity. It evidently touches deep springs of mystery and meaning in the life of [humankind]. On the one hand, the death on the cross means an heroic effort of self-regarding people, whose inveterate self-love is the root of all historical evil, to transmute self-regard into self-forgetfulness, into "sacrificial love" or love of the neighbor. This interpretation is rooted in Christ's own words, "If anyone wishes to be a follower of mine, he must leave self behind, he must take up his cross and come with me"; or in the exhortation: "There must be no limit to your goodness, as your heavenly Father's goodness knows no bounds." It is expressed by Paul: "Having that bearing toward one another which also was found in Christ Jesus . . . who assuming the nature of a slave . . . in obedience accepted even death on a cross." It is also expressed in all the ethical teachings, of which the Sermon on the Mount is an example, which challenge the Christian disciple to a conduct heedless of any self-interest. On the other hand, the cross is a symbol of quite different meaning.

Niebuhr, R., *Justice and Mercy*, 88.

A strange thing has happened in our history and in our personal life; our faith has been attached to that great void, to that enemy of all our causes, to that opponent of all our gods. The strange thing has happened that we have been enabled to say of this reality, this last power in which we live and move and have our being, 'Though it slay us yet will we trust it (Job 13:15).' We have been allowed to attach our confidence to it and put our reliance in it which is the one reality beyond all the many, which is the last power, the infinite source of all particular beings as well as their end. And insofar as our faith, our reliance for meaning and worth, has been attached to this source and enemy of all of our gods, we have been enabled to call this reality God.

Niebuhr, H.R., *Radical Monotheism*, 122–23.

"Good Friday Walk for Justice" by Jim Houston

APRIL 5.   INFINITE PITY AND INFINITE PATHOS.

The cross emphasizes that the life of good and evil of persons is inextricably involved in a mixture of noble and petty impulses, of concern for the self and concern for the other, and that this mixture of good and evil cannot be overcome by taking thought, or by one more heroic effort to secure the triumph of good over evil; but that humankind must look to the cross of Christ, not as triumph in defeat of a noble person, but as a symbol of the merciful action of a forgiving God, "who knows our frame and remembers we are dust [Psalm 103]." Jesus expressed this meaning in his interpretation of his Messianic mission: he spoke of the Son of Man who "did not come to be served, but to give his life as a ransom for many [Mark 10:45]" . . . The thesis on which the Christian faith was founded was that reconciliation between all persons and God had taken place in the suffering and death of the Messiah; and that this event challenged good and evil people to become aware in contrition of the variance between their mixed motives and ultimate demands of love. They could be charitable and compassionate toward their sisters and brothers only against the background of a faith which knew, in the words of [Joseph

APRIL   67

Henry] Shorthouse's 18th Century novel, "John Inglesant," that "only the infinite pity is adequate for the infinite pathos of human existence."

Niebuhr, R., Justice and Mercy, 88–89.

APRIL 6.   FORCED OPTION.

Pilate offered the choice of Jesus or Barabbas, whom they knew as a rebel against Rome. The crowd that the high priests and their party had collected, with the citizens whose disappointment had turned into hate, heard Pilate's proposal and question, "Shall it be Jesus or Barabbas?" They cried out: "Give us Barabbas! Give us Barabbas!" Pilate asked, "What shall we do with Jesus, who is called King of the Jews?" They called: "Crucify him, crucify him! We have no king but Caesar!" With a guilty conscience, but in fear of offending the Jewish leaders, Pilate turned Jesus over to the military authorities to be crucified. The soldiers took off his garments and lashed him with cruel whip. Informed that he was being put to death for saying he was "King of the Jews," they put a scarlet cloak about his shoulders and placed on his head a circle of thorny briers in imitation of the Emperor's crown of laurel leaves. Then they bowed before him in mockery, saying, "Hail, King of the Jews." They struck him in the face and spat upon him. Then they put his own garments back upon him and led him to Calvary to be crucified, bearing his cross upon his shoulders.

Niebuhr, H., One Story, 142.

APRIL 7.   SATAN'S MOUTHPIECE.

"You are the Christ," answered Peter to Jesus' question. "That confession of faith," said Jesus, "is more true that you could realise. You are the mouthpiece of God in making it. But even now I doubt whether you understand what it means to be the Messiah. We will go to Jerusalem where I must suffer and die." "Lord," said Peter, "you must not allow that to happen. Certainly it is not the destiny of God's messenger to suffer but to triumph." "Now you are the mouthpiece of Satan," said Jesus, probably leaving Peter a little confused and embarrassed to be regarded in the course of a few moments as both God's and Satan's tool. Peter was the mouthpiece of Satan for being only half wrong and yet very wrong. The Messiah would triumph in the end. First the Messiah must suffer and die and be raised up and then he would come again "in all his glory." Peter understands the triumph but not the relation of suffering to it.

Niebuhr, R., *Beyond Tragedy*, 175.

APRIL 8.   POWERLESS GOODNESS?

Jesus arrived at his definition of the Messianic reign, which he was about to initiate by rejecting the political hope of a Messiah who would be a powerful and yet perfectly good king. Instead he believed that it would have to be ushered in by pure goodness which had no power. But pure goodness, without power, cannot maintain itself in the world. It ends on the cross. Yet that is not where it finally ends. The Messiah will finally transmute the whole world order. The contradictions of human existence which prevent power from ever being good enough to belong to the Kingdom and which equally prevent pure love from ever being powerful enough to establish itself in the world, must finally be overcome; but they can only be overcome by divine action. No human action, proceeding from these contradictions, is equal to it. Here is the simple thesis of the Lord's messianism.

Niebuhr, R., *Beyond Tragedy*, 177–78.

APRIL 9.   ANNIVERSARY OF DIETRICH BONHOEFFER'S EXECUTION?

There are many things I could say about Dietrich Bonhoeffer when he was a student here [Union Seminary, NY] particularly about the combination of his sophisticated theology and simple piety. We became very warm friends and I corresponded with him all the time until his imprisonment.

When I was in Britain in April before the war broke out, I was visited by Bonhoeffer and his brother-in-law in a little village . . . He told me that he had definite information through the Army that war would break out in September, and that he couldn't support the war, and that some of the members of the Brethren's Council had suggested to him it would be well for him to go to America if this were possible. I immediately cabled to America and he received an invitation from our seminary to lecture during the summer semester. I remained in England . . . to give my Gifford lectures and did not see him. Shortly after the outbreak of the war I received a letter from him, written in the garden of our seminary president, Dr. Coffin, in which he said that it was a mistake for him to come to America, that the Christians of Germany would have to make a decision between wanting the victory of their nation and the death of a Christian civilization, or the defeat of their nation and the survival of a Christian civilization. You cannot, he said, remain out of a country where your brother and sister Christians face such a momentous issue. He hoped therefore, that I would understand why he was going back. I report this because I think it is remarkably symbolic of the spirit of his life.

Niebuhr, R., "To America and Back," 165.

APRIL 10. GOODNESS WITHOUT POWER.

Politics is always a contest of power. At its best it arrives at a tentative equilibrium of power. "The peace of the world," said Augustine, "is based on strife." There may be long periods of covert rather than overt struggle. But this is not the love and harmony of the Kingdom of God. Perhaps Jesus regarded the political aspect of messianism as such a terrible temptation because illusions about politics lead to be most baneful consequences. They lead to the religious sanctification of the inevitable injustices of a particular power. Thus Russia, in spite of its achievements, is a partial return to the political strategy of Babylonian and Egyptian priest kings who claimed unqualified religious sanctity for the very relative justice of their rule. It does not follow that, because the balances of power, by which justice is achieved in the collective life of humans, do not belong to the Kingdom of God., we are therefore to have nothing to do with them. We live in a world in which the Kingdom is not established, in which the fate of the King of love is crucifixion. In large areas of life our concern must therefore be to prevent life from destroying life. This problem of elementary justice can be solved neither by returning to the ideal of the good king nor by trying to introduce pure goodness without power into the world.

Niebuhr, R., *Justice and Mercy*, 180–81.

APRIL 11. SUFFERING SERVANT IMPLICATIONS/ WORLD PARKINSON'S DAY.

No sinful person, even when he or she understands the law of life is love can be trusted completely to be just, if his egotism does not meet resistance. We are still living in a world which falls short of the Kingdom of God even though the law of the Kingdom has been revealed to it. In order to understand that fact more fully it is necessary to analyse the implications of the idea of the suffering servant. The suffering servant does not impose goodness upon the world by his power. Rather he suffers, being powerless, from the injustices of the powerful. He suffers most particularly from the sins of the righteous who do not understand how full of unrighteousness is all human righteousness. The Saviour of the world is not crucified by criminals or obviously evil people; he is crucified with criminals by the "princes of this world," to use the Pauline phrase. Love is the law of life; but when it enters the world of relative justice and balanced egotism it is destroyed in it. The suffering servant dies on the cross . . . Thus when the Kingdom of God enters the world it is judged by the world and found to be dangerous to all of its tentative harmonies and relative justice. But it also judges the world in the very moment in which the world is condemning it.

Niebuhr, R., *Justice and Mercy*, 181–82, 183.

Everyone with any experience of life is aware of the extent to which the characters of people one has known have been given their particular forms by the sufferings through which they have passed . . . their responses to what has happened to them have been of even greater importance, and these responses have been shaped by their interpretations of what they suffered . . . Because suffering is the exhibition of the presence in our existence of that which is not under our control, or of the intrusion into our self-legislating existence of an activity operating under another law than ours . . . it is in the response to suffering that many and perhaps all persons, individually and in their groups, define themselves, take on character, develop their ethos.

Niebuhr, H.R., *Responsible Self*, 59–60.

APRIL 12. FINAL MEANING/FINAL MYSTERY.

The Christian story is that, whatever the inadequacies of forgiveness and love may be in the operations of human justice, we ultimately face divine forgiveness as well as divine wrath. The Christ upon the cross is the point of illumination where the ultimate mercy is apprehended. It is not a mercy which cancels out divine justice; nor does it prove the divine justice to be merely love. There is a hard and terrible facet to justice which stands in contradiction to love. It is not for that reason evil. Justice is good and punishment is necessary. Yet justice alone does not move humans to repentance. The inner core of their rebellion is not touched until they behold the executor of judgment suffering with and for the victim of punishment. This is the meaning of "atonement" as apprehended by faith. It is the final meaning and the final mystery of the relation of God to man.

Niebuhr, R., *Discerning the Signs*, 146–47.

APRIL 13. FATHOMING MYSTERY.

It is meaning and not pure mystery faith must explicate. Since it is mystery it cannot be fully explicated; which is why all theories of the atonement are less illuminating (and sometimes positively confusing) than the apprehension of the mystery and the meaning by faith. Faith rises above all philosophies and theologies in sensing that the weakness of God is His final power. It is the weakness of love which touches the heart of the offender. The mystery lies in the fact that this mercy is partly the fulfillment and partly the contradiction to the justice which punishes. The fact that justice and mercy are one is symbolically expressed in the idea of the unity of God-as-Father and Son. The fact that justice and mercy stand in contradiction is symbolically expressed in the distinction between the Holy One and Son and in the idea that the Son bears wrath of the Redeemer. In less metaphysical and more historic-symbolic terms the unity of mercy and justice are expressed in the biblical idea that "God so love the world that the Holy One gave the only begotten Son." The distinction between justice and mercy is expressed by the idea that the Son bears the sufferings which the wrath of the Father exacts.

Niebuhr, R., *Discerning the Signs*, 147–48.

APRIL 14.   HARD SCHOOL/SOFT SCHOOL.

The moralists of every age and faith, including the Christian faith, regard these insights as meaningless subtleties of theologians or as incredible biblical myths which can impress only the ignorant and credulous. They make these disparaging judgments because they have never plumbed the problem of justice and mercy to its final depth . . . The hard school would seek to persuade a fallen foe to repentance by the rigor of the punishment of the victors. And the soft school would remit punishment and substitute mercy for judgement. The power which maintains the order of the world is good and not evil; but its virtue does not reach into the secret of the human heart. The justice which checks and punishes evil is also good and not evil; but its force is negative and the persuasive power of repentance and redemption is not in it. Thus the final majesty of God is the majesty of His mercy. It is both the completion and the contradiction of His power. This is the truth apprehended in the cross, which resolves the mystery of the relation of justice to mercy, and gives it meaning.

Niebuhr, R., *Discerning the Signs,* **148.**

APRIL 15.   FINAL PARADOXES OF FAITH.

. . . [T]he final paradoxes of faith are always in peril of disintegration, inside the Christian community as well as outside. Thus there have been Christian heresies . . . which make an absolute distinction between the God of power who is not good and the God of mercy who is good but not powerful. Some very persuasive forms of the Christian faith drift to the very edge of this heresy. In the first world war the most famous of English chaplains, Studdert-Kennedy, allowed his tragic sense of life to be elaborated into a homiletical theology which resolved the Christian paradox and denied every form of the divine majesty and power except the power of love.

Niebuhr, R., *Discerning the Signs,* **148–49.**

. . . H. G. Wells' *God, the Invisible King,* arrived at somewhat the same picture of a kind but not very powerful divine ruler who suffered with humanity in fighting against a recalcitrance of something in the universe more powerful than himself. Some Christian philosophers have sought to present the same doctrine in Christian form.

APRIL 73

But all these efforts . . . manage to obscure the sublimity of the paradox which the revelation of God in Christ contains. They are provisionally plausible because they are philosophically more consistent than the
Christian doctrine. But they are not true to all of the facts of existence
and they fail to illumine the final mystery of justice and mercy, or power
and goodness, which is revealed in the cross.

Niebuhr, R., *Discerning the Signs,* 150.

APRIL 16.   CLUE TO THE MYSTERY.

Faith, by a wisdom touches sublimities beyond the ken of philosophies,
will thus continue to cherish the scandal of the cross and accept the
mockery and derision of the various crowd of Calvary as a kind of tribute
to the truth which transcends and fulfills the highest insights of reason.
The words of derision: "He saved others, himself he cannot save," gives
us a clue to the innermost character of a man, a person, in history who
perished upon the cross. It also gives us a clue to the mystery of the very
character of God.

Niebuhr, R., *Discerning the Signs,* 150–51.

APRIL 17.   REMEMBER ME.

Hour after hour went by while men scoffed, saying, "He saved others,
He cannot save himself." One of the thieves joined the crowd in mock-
ing Jesus, but the other thief recognized in Jesus a dignity and a majesty
that made him different. Himself bitter at heart, he had noticed how in
all the terrible suffering Jesus had shown no trace of bitterness. Then he
heard him pray, "Father, forgive them; for the know not what they do."
Repentant, the thief begged of Jesus, "Remember me when you come into
your Kingdom," and heard Jesus answer, "Today you shall be with me in
paradise."

Niebuhr, H., *One Story,* 142.

APRIL 18.   GRAND AND AWFUL DRAMA OF LIFE.

It may be too optimistic to expect the awful chasm of a nuclear age to be
bridged by the ultimate in religious and moral experience. But even if it

should not be, it still remains true that there is no way of observing and participating in the grand and awful drama of life without despair unless we can analyze ourselves without deception or illusion.

O God, in whose sight no person is justified, pity our vanities and deceptions, our consequent cruelties and false judgments. Grant us the grace of honest self-knowledge. That we may not think of ourselves more highly than we ought to think. Knowing our frailty, we may, in compassion, join our brothers and sisters in the awesome pilgrimage of life.

Niebuhr, R., *Justice and Mercy*, 95.

APRIL 19. WHOLE GENIUS OF THE CHRISTIAN FAITH.

There is no part of the Apostolic creed which, in our present opinion, expresses the whole genius of the Christian faith more neatly than just this despised phrase: "I believe in the resurrection of the body" . . . The prejudice that the conception of the immortality of the soul is more believable than that of the resurrection of the body is merely an inheritance from Greek thought in the life of the church . . . Whatever may be the truth about the degree of Greek thought in either the Pauline Epistles or the Johannine literature, there can be no question that the dominant idea of the Bible in regard to the ultimate fulfillment of life is expressed in the conception of the resurrection.

Niebuhr, R., *Beyond Tragedy*, 290–91.

Believing is not simply asserting to propositions. Cardinal Newman long ago called such belief "notional assent," as distinguished from "real assent." By imperceptible degrees believing shades or transmutes into caring, into loving; "cherishing love" . . .

Niebuhr, R.R., "Creation of Belief," 111.

"Betrayed" by Jim Houston

APRIL 20. SEEMS MOST STRANGE.

In consequence of the coming of this Jesus Christ to us we are able to say in the midst of our vast distrust, our betraying and being betrayed, our certainty of death and our temptations to curse our birth: "Abba, our Father." And this we say to the Ground of our Being, to the mystery out of which we come, to the power over our life and death. "Our Father, who art in heaven, hallowed be thy name" (Matt. 6:9–12; Luke 11:2–4). "I believe, help thou mine unbelief" (Mark 9:24). It seems most strange that by that recollection which we have of the betrayal and the disastrous end of the one who trusted in the Power of Being as utterly faithful to him, we should have had introduced into our lives a little ability to trust. It seems most strange that when the one who had heard and believed the promise of life given to him—"Thou art my beloved Son"—that when this one had the promise of life canceled—that when we should in our recollection of this one believe that his God is indeed our Father, that his Father is the Determiner of our Destiny. This is the resurrection of Christ which we experience. In and through his betrayal, denial and forsakenness, we are given the assurance that God keeps God's promises. In and through and despite this we hear him, we read him, we accept him as God's word to us that God is faithful and true, that the Holy One does not desire the death of the sinner, that God-in-Christ is leading the kingdom to victory over all evil, that we shall not die but live, that the last word to us is not death without ending, but life everlasting.

Niebuhr, H.R., *Faith on Earth*, 96–97.

APRIL 21. AT THE JUNCTURE: GUSTAV NIEBUHR'S [SR.] DEATH DATE, AND SO BE IT.

Let . . . no doubt come up that our message has for its object the reconciliation of all people with God and the true brotherhood and sisterhood of all, and the result not only be fear, but love and respect.

Niebuhr, G. [Sr.], in Chrystal, *"Man of the Hour and the Time,"* 427.

The consequence of the fact of Christ's humanity is that the Easter morning sermon is prohibited from dwelling exclusively on the narrative of the empty tomb or the post resurrection encounters; the present reality of Christ's resurrection has also to be acknowledged in the midst of the humanity that gathers on Easter morning in some kind of hope. Otherwise it is certainly impossible to preach on that occasion without silently echoing the conclusion of Paul's syllogism: "Then our preaching is in vain and your faith is in vain." In point of fact, it is a relatively easy thing to muse on the story of the first Easter, for it is not Easter as such that is a scandal, even to the modern person. The difficulty arises at the juncture in which the humanity of Christ and our own humanity are equated or not equated, at the juncture in which we either do or do not recognize ourselves in him and him in ourselves.

Niebuhr, R.R., *"Problem of Preaching at Easter,"* 410.

This Easter has been full of deaths and dyings. The Easter story does help, I think, with words of comfort. We went to a funeral on Easter eve. Another friend died suddenly on Easter Sunday . . . The eternity of love. It is easier to think of that than of the immortality of the soul. Whatever things be good and true and beautiful—they remain. So, perhaps it was the instinct that people who express the good, as the human life and human words of Jesus did, do remain and last and are pointers toward the realm of the mysterious transcendent. So in that sense, we can sing, "Alleluia," He is Risen."

Niebuhr, U., *Remembering Reinhold Niebuhr*, 423.

APRIL   77

APRIL 22.   INTERNATIONAL MOTHER EARTH DAY: PREGNANT WITH POTENTIALITIES.

Our interpretations of present actions are made with references to the future as well as to the past. This present other being that challenges me or aids me or otherwise acts upon me is one that I expect or do not expect to meet in my future. I may interpret its action as casual, requiring no answer, because I shall never meet it again . . . On the other hand, it may be pregnant with potentialities that will culminate in some near or far future. Or otherwise, my reaction to the beings I encounter in the present is one that disvalues them as unimportant, because I am preparing to meet more valued or more significant beings in my future. I pass on by on the other side of the road, as I meet my appointments in earthly or heavenly Jerusalem, in mundane or otherworldly Gehennas. Regarding my action as directed toward future encounter, I fail frequently to note that it is also an action of response to beings I encounter in the present, though it is an action of ignoring.

Niebuhr, H.R., *Responsible Self,* 97.

Reverence for life is the expression of a loyalty that goes out to the whole realm of the living and every member of it. The one who has consciously found his ground in the unconscious will-to-live "feels compulsion," writes (Albert) Schweitzer, "to give to every will-to-live the same reverence for life that he gives to his own. He accepts as being good: to preserve life, to raise to its highest value life which is capable of development and as being evil: to destroy life, to injure life, to repress life which is capable of development. This is the absolute, fundamental principle of the moral."

Niebuhr, H.R., *Radical Monotheism,* 36–37 (and note 9).

APRIL 23.   FITTINGNESS OR UNFITTINGNESS.

Our responsive actions have the character of fittingness or unfittingness. We seek to make them fit into a process of interaction. The questions we raise about them are not only those of their rightness or wrongness, their goodness or badness, but of their fittingness or unfittingness in the total movement, the whole conversation. We seek to have them fit into the whole as a sentence fits into a paragraph in a book, a note into the chord in a movement in a symphony, as the act of eating a common meal fits into the lifelong companionship of a family, as the decision of a statesman fits into the ongoing movement of his nation's life with other nations, or as the discovery of a scientific verifact fits into the history of a science. But whether they fit into the actual process, that is another story . . . Deep in our minds is the myth, the interpretative pattern of the metahistory, within which all our histories and biographies are enacted.

Niebuhr, H.R., *Responsible Self,* 97, 106.

APRIL 24.   ITS COMPLETION IS OUR HOPE.

For we who call ourselves by Christ's name recognize the presence in ourselves of the responses of distrust, of the ethics of death, as well as the movement toward life. In our biographies as in our human history the process of reconciliation has begun; at no point is it complete. Its completion is our hope and in this way our telos and our eschaton . . . Though we speak of our reconciliation to God, we share so much of the defensive, anxious, distrustful attitude toward being that we cannot put the common human ethics of unbelief in life on one side, as though it was something apart from us, as though its theory were unknown to us. And on the other hand we do not fail to note that among our companions who refuse to take the name of Christian responses to action are made that seem to be informed by the trust, the love of all being, the hope in the open future, that have become possible to us only in our life with Jesus Christ and the presence of the One whom he encountered in all his encounters and to whom he gave fitting answer in all his answers to his companions . . . The responsible self we see in Christ and which we believe is being elicited in all our race is a universally and eternally responsive I, answering in universal society and time without end, in all action upon it, to the action of the One who heals all our diseases, forgives all our iniquities, saves our lives from destruction, and crowns us with everlasting mercy.

Niebuhr, H.R., *Responsible Self,* 144–45.

APRIL 79

APRIL 25. DOUBLE RECONCILIATION/WORLD DAY OF PRAYER FOR VOCATIONS.

How Jesus Christ in history, and the symbolic Christ within, reconciles persons to God, or God to people, or accomplished the double reconciliation of each to each, Christians cannot easily say. Few of them are satisfied with the theories of the atonement current in the churches dependent as these are on questionable images of the ultimate rightness of God, or of the source of human estrangement. To some of us it seems that in the cross of Jesus Christ, in the death of such a man who trusts God and is responsible to him as a son, we face the great negative instance or the negation of the premise that God is love, that unless this great negative instance—summarizing and symbolizing all the negative instances—is faced, faith in the universal power as God must rest on quicksand; in facing it, however, we have the demonstration in this very instance of a life-power that is not conquered, not destroyed. Reality maintains and makes powerful such life as this. The ultimate power does manifest itself as the Father of Jesus Christ through the resurrection from death. Then resurrection is not manifest to us in its physical signs but in his continuing Lordship—his session at the right hand of power, as the old creeds put it. So we apprehend the way of God as manifested not in creation and destruction but in these and resurrection, in the raising of the temporal to the eternal plane.

Niebuhr, H.R., *Responsible Self,* 176–77.

Unless, on the one hand, we obey the biblical injunction to be like Christ, and on the other hand, know that we can never be like Christ, we have not mastered the difficulty of the Christian life.

Niebuhr, R., *Justice and Mercy,* 131.

APRIL 26. INDEBTED.

Christians cannot boast that they have an excellent way of life for they have little to point to when they boast. They only confess—we were blind in our distrust of being, now we begin to see; we were aliens and alienated in a strange, empty world, now we begin sometimes to feel at home; we were in love with ourselves and all our little cities, now we are falling in love, we think, with being itself, with the city of God, the universal community of which God is the source and governor. And for all this, we are indebted to Jesus Christ, in our history, and in that depth of the spirit in which we grope with our theologies and theories of symbols. Could it have so happened otherwise; could the same results have been achieved through other means? Are they being produced elsewhere through other means? That seems possible; nevertheless this one is our physician, this one is our reconciler to the Determiner of our Destiny. To whom else shall we go for words of eternal life, to whom else for the franchised in the universal community?

Niebuhr, H.R., *Responsible Self,* 177–78.

APRIL 27. WITH THE GOODNESS OF INTEGRITY?

"Providence" is not an answer to Jesus' question: Why did the tower fall on these men? Nor does it prevent Augustine's protesting prayer: "How much better had it been for me to have been speedily cured . . . " If anything, as "doctrine" providence sets aside visibility of pattern and symmetry within personal experience. When, therefore, a man wrestles with the unlikeness of today to yesterday, with the randomness and disparateness of the elements of his own life-course and ambience, then looks to the doctrine of providence for a method of eliciting clarity, balance, and equity, where otherwise they do not appear, he can only end by doubting the meaning of belief itself. He doubts the belief of a providing-God, because the providence for which he looks and which he does not find is a providential ordering of his own history. But, in the mind of Jesus or Augustine, believing in God-providing expresses confidence in an order not in the history of the self but in the works of God, an order not within the time of the individual's birth, life, and death but an infinite order, to which the birth, life, and death of the individual belong . . . When people perceive that the life of Jesus Nazareth—as full as any life can be and also as fragmented and lacking in Emersonian symmetry and compensation as any life can—elicits from themselves the judgment, It is good! they find that statements about this messiah-prophet-servant become for them symbols expressing and reacting upon their own believing experience of their own incomplete lives and of their neighbors' lives and of their agent-world as a whole.

Niebuhr, R.R., *Experiential Religion,* 72–73.

APRIL   81

APRIL 28.   WORLD DAY FOR SAFETY AND HEALTH AT WORK. NATIONAL DAY OF MOURNING FOR WORK DEATHS

Soul and body are one. Man or woman is in nature. They are, for that reason, not of nature. It is important to emphasize both points. A human is the creature of necessity and the child of freedom. His or her life is determined by natural contingencies; yet one's character develops by rising above nature's necessities and accidents . . . whether one dominates or submits to nature, he or she is never merely an element in nature. The simple proof is that their life is not wholly determined but is partly self-determining. This is a very obvious fact of experience which is easily obscured by philosophies, which either lift one wholly out of nature or make him or her completely into a consistent scheme of analysis.

Niebuhr, R., *Beyond Tragedy*, 292–93.

Hear us as we pray:

For those who have been worsted in the struggle of life, whether by the inhumanity of their brothers and sisters, their own limitations, or by those hazards of life which beset all people, that they may contend against injustice without bitterness, overcome their own weakness with diligence, and learn to accept with patience that which cannot be altered.

Niebuhr, R., *Justice and Mercy*, 70.

APRIL 29.   A JUSTIFIED HOPE.

The possibilities of the fulfillment of this life transcend our experience not because the soul is immortal and the body is mortal but because this human life, soul and body, is both immersed in flux and above it, and because it involves itself in sin in this unique position from which there is no escape by its own powers. The fulfillment of life beyond the possibilities of this existence is a justified hope, because of our human situation, that is, because of a life which knows the flux in which it stands cannot be completely a part of that flux. On the other hand this hope is not one which fulfills itself by human's own powers. God must complete what remains incomplete in human existence. This is true both because there is no simple division in human life between what is mortal and what is immortal so that the latter could slough off the former; and because the incompleteness of human life is not only finiteness but sin.

Niebuhr, R., *Beyond Tragedy*, 297.

cf. *Nature and Destiny of Man* (Vol. II), 295.

APRIL 30.   UNITY OF BODY AND SOUL.

The idea of the resurrection of the body is a profound expression of an essential element in the Christian world-view, first of all because it expresses and implies the unity of the body and the soul. Through all the ages Christianity has been forced to combat, and has at times capitulated to, the notion, that the significance of history lies in the banishment of the good soul in an evil body and in the general emancipation of the soul from the body . . . Salvation is thought as release from physical life and temporal existence. Such conceptions have been related to modern individualism and made to yield the ideas of personal survival . . .

Niebuhr, R., *Beyond Tragedy*, 292.

In contrast to such forms of dualism it must be recorded that the facts of human experience point to the organic unity of soul and body, and do not substantiate the conclusion, suggested by a superficial analysis, that the evil in human life arises from the impulses of the flesh . . . Whatever the relation of sensuality and selfishness in the realm of human evil, whether one is derived from the other, it is obvious that both are the fruits of the spirit and not of the flesh.

Niebuhr, R., *Beyond Tragedy*, 295.

MAY

Mental Health Awareness Month

We are experiencing our isolation and our division not only as a separa-
tion of individual from individual, human group from human group, but
as an alienation of the person from his or her world. Humans feel alone in
an empty or inimical world over which chance or blind will presides. One
has no sense of being at home under the sky and upon the good earth;
the earth is not his or her mother and there is no father in the heavens.
Orphaned, anxious and alone one finds the self with brothers and sisters
wandering through time on paths that lead to no home. Yet he . . . she is
filled with a great nostalgia and envies with a certain wistfulness those
generations that believed themselves to be living in a Father's or Mother's
house or, at least, to be engaged in a pilgrimage that led daily nearer to the
quiet hearth at the center of the world.

Niebuhr, H.R., *Responsibility of the Church*, 119.

Anxiety, as the permanent concomitant of freedom, is both source of
creativity and temptation to sin. It is the condition of the sailor, climbing
the mast [to use a simile], with the abyss of waves beneath him or her
and the "crow's nest" above. One is anxious about both the end toward
which he or she strives and the abyss of nothingness into which one may
fall . . . [T]he destructive aspect of anxiety is so intimately involved in the
creative aspects that there is no possibility of making a simple separa-
tion between them. The two are inextricably bound together by reason
of humankind being anxious both to realize their unlimited possibilities
and to overcome and to hide the dependent and contingent character of
their existence.

Niebuhr, R., *Nature and Destiny of Man* (Vol. I), 185–86.

MAY 1.   INTERNATIONAL WORKERS' DAY.

Who is better able to understand the true character of a civilisation that those who suffer most from its limitations? Who is better able to state the social ideal in unqualified terms that those who have experienced the bankruptcy of old social realities in their own lives? Who will have more creative vigor in destroying the old and building the new than those in whose lives hunger, vengeance and holy dreams have compounded a tempestuous passion?

Niebuhr, R., *Moral Man and Immoral Society*, 157.

... "From each according to his ability, to each according to his needs" is indeed an ideal, which is as impossible of consistent application in the complexities of society as the Christian ideal of love. But it is an ideal toward which a rational society must move, and the religious overtone may be regarded as a guarantee against the dilution of the ideal.

Niebuhr, R., *Moral Man and Immoral Society*, 159–60.

MAY 2.   NOT DEFRAUDED OF RIGHTFUL DUE.

O God, who made your people a royal priesthood that might offer intercession and pray for all people, hear us we pray:

For all who toil in the burden and heat of the day in forest and farm, in mine and factory, on land and sea, that may enjoy the fruits of their industry, that they may not be defrauded of their rightful due, and that we may never cease to be mindful of our debt to them, remembering with gratitude the multitude of services which must be performed to make our life tolerable.

Niebuhr, R., *Justice and Mercy*, 70.

MAY 3.   HOPE OF FULFILLMENT.

It is significant that there is no religion, or for that matter no philosophy of life whether explicit or implicit, which does not hold out hope of the fulfillment of life in some form or other. Since it is human nature to be emancipated of the tyranny of the immediate present and to transcend the processes of nature in which he or she is involved, one cannot exist without having his or her eyes upon the future. The future is a symbol of his freedom.

The Christian view of the future is complicated by the realization of the fact that the very freedom which brings the future into view has been the occasion for the corruption of the present in the heart of man. Mere development of what one now is cannot save humankind, for development will heighten all the contradictions in which he or she stands. Nor will emancipation from the law of development and the march of time through entrance into a timeless and motionless eternity save oneself. That could only annihilate a person . . . hope consequently lies in a forgiveness which will overcome not one's finiteness but his or her sin, and a divine omnipotence which will complete their life without destroying its essential nature.

Hence the final expression of hope in the Apostolic Creed: "I believe in the forgiveness of sins, the resurrection of the body and life everlasting" is a much more sophisticated expression of hope in ultimate fulfillment than all of its modern substitutes. It grows out of a realization of the total situation which the modern mind has not fathomed. The symbols by which this hope is expressed are, to be sure, difficult. The modern mind imagines that it has rejected the hope because of this difficulty. But the real cause of the rejection lies in its failure to understand the problem of human existence in all its complexity.

Niebuhr, R., *Beyond Tragedy*, 305–306.

MAY 4. WHOLENESS OF THE PERSON IN HIS FINITENESS AND FREEDOM.

The idea of the resurrection clearly implies the finiteness of historical man and the wholeness of the person in [human] finiteness and freedom. That there should be a transmutation of that person "in the resurrection" can clearly only be held "by faith." On the other hand, it is supposedly more rational to believe that an immortal soul flees from a mortal body upon death. It may seem a more rational belief, but it rests upon a very dubious distinction between an immortal "mind" and a mortal body.

Niebuhr, R., *Self and the Dramas of History*, 78.

Our beliefs do not endow us with the power to manage: to manage either the present or the future. No beliefs are encompassing enough to illuminate the whole of the terrain into which we are moving. The fact that each year thousands of species and subspecies of life are passing into extinction, even before we have the means to identify them, is an emblematic fact, a symbolic fact, a hard fact that chills us. And as species of aquatic life and of arboreal life, in regions into which we have not ventured, are vanishing so too are human cultures and languages vanishing at a nearly equal rate. Our actions create not only waste that is visible to us but immeasurable waste invisible to us. The homeless we see on our streets are representatives of the countless homeless we do not see. But nonetheless our beliefs do matter, and they matter profoundly, because we not only see by them but by them we also cherish.

Niebuhr, R.R., "Creation of Belief," 210–11.

MAY 5. HOPE GROUNDED.

The Christian hope is derived from the Christian revelation of the meaning in the divine mystery. That revelation is centered in the crucifixion and resurrection of Christ. Confidence that the crucified Savior was "raised again" is the very basis of the faith which gathered the first believing community . . . it is significant for the very quality of the Christian faith in boldly asserting that there is a realm of meaning, transcending nature-history and defined by purposes of the God who has a freedom beyond the coherences of nature, in which the crucified Savior is alive and "sitteth at the right hand of God." This One is apprehended not only as a specific individual whose life has power beyond the grace, but as the key to the ultimate mystery of God and history. Naturally this whole revelatory drama presupposes, and would not be thinkable without, the Hebraic-Messianic hope of the resurrection in the Messianic age.

Niebuhr, R., *Self and the Dramas of History*, 236–37.

MAY 6. SELF-CLARIFIED AND COMPLETED/ NATIONAL DAY OF PRAYER. INTERNATIONAL DAY OF MIDWIFE

The understanding of the antinomies of the human self are: A) The self in its final freedom transcends the conditions of nature-time can not be fulfilled within them. B) The self has a unity between this freedom of the spirit and the organism of its body and soul, which makes the emancipation of an immortal soul from a mortal body unthinkable. Therefore the ultimate hope is expressed in the idea of a transfigured body. "It is sown a natural body, it is raised a spiritual body," declares St. Paul [I Cor. 15:44] . . . C) The freedom of the self is not merely a dignity which must be asserted in defiance of death . . . Completion of the human story without the forgiveness of sin would be unthinkable. The Gospel, in short, both guards the dignity of the self which transcends death and recognizes the misery of the self [if not forgiven], which faces the problem of sin, as well as the fact of death. D) The resurrection of the individual is incredibly related to a "general" resurrection which completes the whole human story, and which is associated with the "coming again" of the suffering Savior in triumph "with power and glory" . . . this incredible hope for the end of history is more in accord with actual experience than the alternative hopes which have beguiled, and then disappointed, past generations.

Niebuhr, R., *Self and the Dramas of History,* 237–38.

Teach us each day to ask what you would have us do, and help us to perform our tasks with diligence and humility. Give us grace . . . to be helpful to each other in our several responsibilities. Save us from seeking to impress our brothers and sisters, or from being afraid of their judgments . . . to learn from the prophets and sages of every age . . . Give us above all, the spirit to bear each other's burdens, and so fulfill the law of love.

Niebuhr, R., *Reinhold Niebuhr: Major Works,* 703.

MAY 7. HEIGHTS AND DEPTHS OF HUMAN SELFHOOD.

How can we bring the whole human story, including all the relevant and irrelevant dramas, into some scheme of intelligibility without obscuring and denying the richness and variety of the drama? The hope of the forgiveness of sins and life everlasting is thus a fitting climax of the faith that there is a meaning to the story beyond our understanding of its meaning because it is grounded in a power and purpose beyond our comprehension, though not irrelevant to all our fragmentary meanings. It is the final venture in modesty for the mysterious human self, which understands itself more completely if it understands that there are heights and depths of human selfhood which are beyond any system of rational intelligibility, but not beyond the comprehension of faith and hope.

Niebuhr, R., *Self and the Dramas of History*, 239.

MAY 8.   IMPOSSIBLE POSSIBILITY.

Every facet of the Christian revelation, whether of the relation of God to history, or of the relation of one to the eternal, points to the impossibility of a human fulfilling the true meaning of his or her life and reveals sin to be primarily derived from their abortive efforts to do so. The Christian gospel nevertheless enters the world with the proclamation that in Christ both "wisdom" and "power" are available to humankind; which is to say that not only has the true meaning of life been disclosed but also that resources have been made available to fulfill that meaning. In the Christ the faithful find not only "truth" but "grace."

Niebuhr, R., *Nature and Destiny of Man* (Vol. II), 98.

MAY 9.   PRIMARILY AND FINALLY, GRACE.

Grace represents on the one hand the mercy and forgiveness of God by which God completes what a human cannot complete and overcomes the sinful elements in which all of human's achievements. Grace is the power of God in us; it represents an accession of resources, which we do not have of ourselves, enabling one to become what he or she truly ought to be. It is synonymous with the gift of the "Holy Spirit." The Spirit is not merely, as in idealistic and mystical thought, the highest development of the human spirit . . . [S]he is not identical with the most universal and transcendent levels of the human mind and consciousness. The Holy Spirit is the spirit of God indwelling in humans. But this indwelling Spirit never means a destruction of human self-hood. There is therefore a degree of compatibility and continuity between human self-hood and the

Holy Spirit. Yet the Holy Spirit is never a mere extension of one's spirit identical with its purity and unity in the deepest or highest levels of consciousness. In that sense all Christian doctrines of "grace" and "Spirit" contradict mystical and idealistic theories of fulfillment.

Niebuhr, R., *Nature and Destiny of Man* (Vol. II), 98–99.

Grant us grace, O Lord, to learn of your judgments which overtake us when we set human against human and nation against nation; give us wisdom and strength to fashion better instruments for our common life, so that we may dwell in concord under your providence. May your kingdom come among us through Jesus Christ our Lord.

Niebuhr, R., *Justice and Mercy*, 72.

MAY 10. WISDOM AND POWER.

If it is possible to become aware of the limits of human possibilities by a faith which apprehends the revelation of God from beyond those limits, it must be possible to lay hold of the resources of God, beyond human limits, by faith. And this is certainly reinforced by the character of human revelation, according to which God is not a supernal perfection to which a person aspires, but has resources of love, wisdom and power, which come down to humans. The very apprehension of the "wisdom of God," the complement of that structure of meaning by faith, must have connotations of "power" in it. For if we understand the possibilities and limits of life beyond ourselves, this understanding has some potentialities of fulfilling the meaning of life. It breaks the egoistic and self-centered forms of fulfillment, by which the wholesome development of a human is always arrested and corrupted . . . the shattering of the self by a power from beyond ourself. If a man or woman does not know the truth about God, who is more than an extension of his self [a truth to be known only by faith], he or she cannot repent of the premature and self-centered completion of their life around a partial and inadequate centre. But it can be, and has been, argued with equal cogency, that without repentance, that is, without the shattering of the self-centered self, one is too much his or her own god to feel the need of, or to have the capacity for, knowing the true God. The invasion of the self from beyond the self is therefore an invasion of both "wisdom" and "power," of both "truth" and "grace."

... The peace which follows conversion is never purely the content-
ment of achievement. It is always, in part, the peace which comes from
the knowledge of forgiveness.

Niebuhr, R., *Nature and Destiny of Man* (Vol. II), 99–100.

MAY 11.   PARADOX OF SELF.

The self is so created in freedom that it cannot realize itself within itself.
It can only realize itself in loving relation to its brothers and sisters. Love
is the law of its being. But in practice it is always betrayed into self-love. It
comprehends the world and human relations from itself as the centre. It
cannot, by willing to do so, strengthen the will to do good . . . partly due
to finiteness. It is also spiritual. The self never follows its "natural" self-
interest without pretending to be obedient to obligations beyond itself. It
transcends its own interests too much to be able to serve them without
distinguishing them in loftier pretensions. This is the covert dishonesty
and spiritual confusion which is always involved in the self's undue devotion to itself.

Niebuhr, R., *Nature and Destiny of Man* (Vol. II), 108–109.

MAY 12.   HEALING VIA BROKENNESS.

The self in this state of preoccupation with itself must be "broken" and
"shattered" or, in the Pauline phrase, "crucified." It cannot be saved merely by being enlightened. It is a unity and therefore cannot be drawn out of
itself merely be extending its perspective upon interests beyond itself. If it
remains self-centered, it merely uses its wider perspective to bring more
lives and interests under the dominion of its will-to-power. The necessity
of its being shattered at the very centre of its being gives perennial validity to the strategy of evangelical sects, which seek to induce the crisis of
conversion. (Footnoted with: There is of course no absolute necessity for
a single crisis. The shattering of the self is a perennial process and occurs
in every spiritual experience in which the self is confronted by the claims
of God, and becomes conscious of its sinful self-centered state.)

This self is shattered whenever it is confronted by the power and
holiness of God and becomes genuinely conscious of the real source and
centre of all life. In Christian faith Christ mediates the confrontation of
the self by God; for it is in Christ that the vague sense of the divine, which
human life never loses, is crystallized into a revelation of a divine mercy

MAY 91

and judgment. In that revelation fear of judgment and hope of mercy are so mingled that despair induces repentance and repentance hope. (Footnoted with: A "hidden Christ" operates in history. And there is always the possibility that those who do not know the historical revelation may achieve a more genuine repentance and humility than those who do.)

Niebuhr, R., *Nature and Destiny of Man (Vol. II)*, 109–10 and notes 5 and 6.

MAY 13.   PARTLY FULFILLED AND PARTLY DESTROYED.

. . . [C]urrent and contemporary ideas of salvation by knowledge . . . rest upon a dualistic interpretation of human personality which separates mind from body, and spirit from nature. They obscure the unity of the selfhood in all its vital and rational processes. Wherever this dualism prevails "spirit" is devitalized and physical life is despiritualized. The possession of the self by something less than the "Holy Spirit" means that it possible for the self to be partly fulfilled and partly destroyed by its submission to a power and spirit which is greater than the self in its empiric reality but not great enough to do justice to the self in its ultimate freedom. Such spirit can be most simply defined as demonic. This absolute claim for something which is not absolute identifies the possessing spirit as "demonic"; for in it the nature of demons to make pretensions of divinity. The invasion and possession of the self by spirit, which is not the Holy Spirit, produces a spurious sense of transfiguration. The self is no longer the little and narrow self, but the larger collective self of race or nation. But the real self is destroyed. The real self has a height of spiritual freedom which reaches beyond race and nation and which is closer to the eternal that the more earthbound collective entities of man's history. (Footnoted with: It goes without saying that loyalty to nation and other historical communities is not destructive of freedom when these do not make final and absolute claims upon the human spirit.)

Niebuhr, R., *Nature and Destiny of Man (Vol. II)*, 110–11.

MAY 14.   TWO ASPECTS OF GRACE.

"I am crucified with Christ: nevertheless, I live; yet not I; but Christ Liveth in Me" [St. Paul, Galatians 2:20].

The "yet not I," could be intended to assert merely the "priority of grace," to be a confession by the converted self that its new life is the fruit, not of its own power and volition, but of an accretion of power and an infusion of grace. It could also be intended as an affirmation that the new self is never an accomplished reality; that in every historic concretion there is an element of sinful self-realization, or premature completion of the self with itself at the centre that, therefore, the new self is the Christ of intention rather than an actual achievement.

Is it not fundamental to Pauline thought that these two aspects of grace are always involved, in varying degrees of emphasis in the various interpretations of the life of the spirit? And is it not the testimony of human experience that in the final experience of "love, joy and peace," it is not possible to distinguish between the consciousness of possessing something which we could not have possessed of ourselves and the consciousness of not possessing it finally but having it only by faith?

Niebuhr, R., *Nature and Destiny of Man* (Vol. II), 114–15.

MAY 15.   GRACE AS THE POWER NOT OUR OWN.

Just as the truth of God which breaks the vicious circle of false truth, apprehended from the self as the false centre, can never be other than "foolishness" to the self-centered self until it has been imparted by "grace" and received by faith; so also the power which breaks the self-centered will must be perceived as power from beyond the self; and even when it has become incorporated into the new will, its source is recognized in the confession: "I, yet not, I."

Niebuhr, R., *Nature and Destiny of Man* (Vol. II), 115.

St. Paul [also] writes: "Work out your own salvation with fear and trembling; for it is God which worketh in you both to will and to do of his good pleasure" [Phil. 2:12–13]. This statement of the relation of divine grace to human freedom and responsibility does more justice to the complex facts involved than either purely deterministic or purely moralistic interpretations of conversion. (Footnoted with: A word of the Book of Revelation contains the same double emphasis: "Behold, I stand at the door and knock; if any person hears my voice and opens the door, I will come in to him or her, and will sup with them, and be with me" [Rev. 3:20].)

Niebuhr, R., *Nature and Destiny of Man* (Vol. II), **116.**

The real situation is that both affirmations—that only God in Christ can break and reconstruct the sinful self, and that the self must "open the door" and is capable of doing so—are equally true; that they are both unqualifiedly true, each on its own level. Yet either affirmation becomes false if it is made without reference to the other.

Niebuhr, R., *Nature and Destiny of Man* (Vol. II), **118.**

MAY 16.   GRACE AS THE FORGIVENESS OF OUR SINS.

The question is whether in the development of the new life some contradiction between human self-will and the divine purpose remains. The issue is whether the basic character of human history as it is apprehended in the Christian faith, is overcome in the lives of those who have thus apprehended it . . . Repentance does initiate a new life. But the experience of the Christian ages refutes those who follow this logic and without qualification . . . The sad experiences of Christian history show how human pride and spiritual arrogance rise to new heights precisely at the point where the claims of sanctity are made without due qualification.

Niebuhr, R., *Nature and Destiny of Man* (Vol. II), **121–22.**

MAY 17.   INFINITE POSSIBILITIES/

International Day Against Homophobia, Transphobia, and Biphobia.

If we examine any individual life, or any social achievement in history, it becomes apparent that there are infinite possibilities of organizing life from beyond the center of the self; and equally infinite possibilities of drawing the self back into the center of organization. The former possibilities are always fruits of grace [though frequently it is the "hidden Christ" and grace which is not fully know which initiates the miracle].

They are always the gifts of grace because any life which cannot "forget" itself and which merely makes brotherhood and sisterhood the instrument of its happiness or its perfection cannot really escape the vicious circle of egocentricity. Yet the possibilities of new evil cannot be avoided by grace; for as long as the self, individual or collective, remains within the tensions of history and is subject to the twofold condition of involvement in process and transcendence and of compounding its interests with those which are more inclusive.

Niebuhr, R., *Nature and Destiny of Man* (Vol. II), 123.

MAY 18. INTERIM OF DISCLOSURE AND FULFILLMENT.

If the Christian conception of grace be true then all history remains an "interim" between the disclosure and the fulfillment of its meaning. This interim is characterized by positive corruptions, as well as by partial realizations and approximations of the meaning of life. Redemption does not guarantee elimination of the sinful corruptions, which are fact increased whenever the redeemed claim to be completely emancipated from them. But the taint of sin upon all historical achievements does not destroy the possibility of such achievements nor the obligation to realize truth and goodness in history. The fulfillments of meaning in history will be the more untainted in fact, if purity is not prematurely claimed for them. All historical activities stand under this paradox of grace.

Niebuhr, R., *Nature and Destiny of Man* (Vol. II), 213.

MAY 19. ACTED UPON.

". . . [w]e awaken in being acted upon and in suffering. Patio ergo sum {I suffer, endure, thus I am]. This is the original and encompassing experience that goes with all experiences, for neither thinking nor willing nor acting on the environment are appropriate or conceivable human responses unless the field of surrounding forces disposes [humans] towards thought and action by making them suffer as understanding and willing beings. Suffering, then, is also a ne plus ultra [the highest point possible] of experience, correspondingly our world appears to us a field of energies converging on us, shaping us, distending us, shattering us, and sending us on paths we have not chosen for ourselves. Suffering horizons our awareness . . . Suffering of this order as something universal is the matrix that generates the passion of believing. It is the medium in which human faithfulness forms itself and appears in determinate shapes in our radial world [arranged like rays or radii].

Niebuhr, R.R., "The Widened Heart," 128.

MAY 20.   OUR TRUTH AND *THE* TRUTH.

The quest for truth and the achievement of just and brotherly relations with our fellowmen comprise the cultural and sociomoral problems of history . . . We know that the freedom of the human spirit over the flux of nature and history makes it impossible to accept our truth as the truth. The capacity for self-transcendence opens up constantly new and higher points of vantage for judging our finite perspectives in the light of a more inclusive truth. On the other hand our involvement in natural and historical flux sets final limits upon our quest for the truth and insures the partial and particular character of even the highest cultural vantage point. Thus human culture is under the tension of finiteness and freedom, of the limited and the unlimited.

Niebuhr, R., *Nature and Destiny of Man* (Vol. II), 214.

MAY 21.   TRUE CHRIST.

The denial of the finiteness of our knowledge and the false claim of finality is always partly the ignorance of our ignorance [and] failure in our capacity for self-transcendence . . . The Christian answer to this problem is the apprehension of the truth "in Christ."

This is a truth about life and history which fulfills what is valid and negates what is sinful in our knowledge of the truth. It fulfills what is valid, because our self-transcendence enables us to hope for and desire the disclosure of a meaning which has a center and source beyond [one's] self. It negates what is sinful because it disappoints that element in all human hopes and expectations, which seeks to complete the meaning of life around the self, individual or collective, as the inadequate center of the realm of meaning. Thus the true Christ is both expected and rejected . . . the believer is lifted in principle above the egoistic corruptions of the truth in history: "as many as received him, to them gave the Holy One the right to become children of God" [John 1:12].

Niebuhr, R., *Nature and Destiny of Man* (Vol. II), 215.

MAY 22. TRUTH'S PARADOX OF GRACE.

[There] is the paradox of grace applied to the truth. The truth, as it is contained in the Christian revelation, includes the recognition that it is neither possible for one to know the truth fully or to avoid error of pretending that he or she does. It is recognized that "grace" always remains in partial contradiction to "nature," and is not merely its fulfillment . . . [I]t is not possible to remain fully conscious of the egoistic corruption in the truth, while we seek to advance it in our thought and action. But is possible in moments of prayerful transcendence over the sphere of interested thought and action to be conscious of the corruption; and it is also possible to carry this insight into our interested thoughts and actions so that it creates some sense of pity and forgiveness for those who contend against our truth and oppose our action. But "grace" enters and purifies our thought and action fully only if the contradiction between it and corrupted truth is understood. Here lies the secret of forgiveness. Mercy to the foe is possible only to those who know themselves to be sinners. [Spirit] has the capacity to recognize its finiteness. But when it refuses to do so its self-glorification must be broken by the power of "grace."

Niebuhr, R. *Nature and Destiny of Man* (Vol. II),
217–18 and note 4.

MAY 23. REAL TEST OF TOLERATION.

It is significant that so much of modern toleration applies merely to the field of religion; and that the very champions of toleration in this field may be exponents of political fanaticism. It is simple enough to be tolerant on issues which are not believed to be vital. The real test of toleration is our attitude towards people who oppose truths which seem important to us, and who challenge realms of life and meaning towards which we have a responsible relation . . . [No] toleration is possible without a measure of provisional skepticism about the truth we hold. (Footnoted with: Oliver Cromwell, facing the peril to the state of conflicting religious absolutes, expressed ". . . By the bowels of Christ, remember that you may be mistaken.") The Christian position of contrition in regard to "our" truth, the humble recognition that it contains some egoistic corruption, degenerates into irresponsibility as soon as we disavow the obligation to purge the truth we hold of its egoistic corruption.

Niebuhr, R., *Nature and Destiny of Man* (Vol. II), 238–239 and note 25.

MAY 24.   TO MEET THE TEST.

The test of how well the Biblical paradox of grace is comprehended, and how genuinely it has entered human experience is the attitude of Christians towards those who differ from themselves in convictions which seem vital to each. The test, in other words, is to be found in the issue of toleration. To meet the test it is necessary not merely to maintain a tolerant attitude towards those who hold beliefs other than our own. The test is twofold and includes both the ability to hold vital convictions which lead to action; and also the capacity to preserve the spirit of forgiveness towards those who offend us by holding to convictions which seem untrue to us. Whatever instruments or pretensions we use, it is not possible to establish the claim that we have the truth. The truth remains subject to the paradox of grace. We may have it; and yet we do not have it . . . And we will have it the more purely in fact if we know that we have it only in principle. Our toleration of truths opposed to those which we confess is an expression of the spirit of forgiveness in the realm of culture. Like all forgiveness, it is possible only if we are not too sure of our own virtue. Loyalty to truth requires confidence in the possibility of its attainment; toleration of others requires broken confidence in the finality of our own truth. But if there is no answer for a problem to which we do not have the answer, our shattered confidence generates either defeat [which in the field of culture would be skepticism]; or an even greater measure of pretension, meant to hide our perplexities behind our certainties [which in the field of culture is fanaticism].

Niebuhr, R., *Nature and Destiny of Man* (Vol. II), 219, 243.

MAY 25.   THE PRETENSION OF HOLINESS.

The history of Christianity proves that grace as is manifested in Christian life does not lift humans above the finiteness of the mind; nor yet save them from the sin of claiming to have transcended it. The divisions in the church, caused by geographic and climatic conditions, by class distinctions and economic circumstances, by national and racial particularities and by historical qualifications of every kind, are proof of the continued finiteness of those who live by grace. The fanatic fury of religious controversies, the hatred engendered in theological disputes, the bitterness of ecclesiastical rivalries and the pretentious claims of ecclesiastical dominion all reveal the continued power of sin which makes for the pretension of holiness.

Niebuhr, R., *Nature and Destiny of Man* (Vol. II), 219–20.

The evil of denominationalism lies in the conditions which make the rise of sects desirable and necessary in the failure of the churches to transcend the social conditions which fashion them into caste-organizations, to sublimate their loyalties to standards and institutions only remotely relevant if not contrary to the Christian ideal, to resist the temptation of making their own self-preservation and extension the primary object of their endeavor . . . The ethical effectiveness of an individual depends on the integration of his or her character, on the synthesis of their values and desires into a system dominated by his highest good; the ethical failure of a group is no less dependent on its control by a morale in which all subordinate purposes are organized around a leading ideal. And the churches are ineffective because they lack such a common morale.

Niebuhr, H.R., *Responsibility of the Church*, 13.

MAY 26. CONTRASTING LOVES AND JUSTICE DESIRES.

The self we loved is not the self God loves, the neighbors we did not prize are God's treasures, the truth we ignored is the truth the Determiner maintains, the justice which we sought because it was our own is not the justice that God's love desires. The righteousness [God] demands and gives is not our righteousness but greater and different. [God] requires of us the sacrifice of all we could conserve and grants us gifts we had not dreamed of - the forgiveness of our sins rather than our justification, repentance and sorrow for our transgressions rather than forgetfulness, faith in [the Holy Being] rather than confidence in ourselves, trust in

MAY

[God's] mercy rather than sight of [God's] presence instead of an ever recurrent torment that will not let us be content, instead of the peace and joy of this world, the hope of the world to come . . . [God] ministers indeed to all our good but all our good is other than we thought.

Niebuhr, H.R., *Meaning of Revelation*, 138–39.

What appears to happen in in fellowship with Jesus Christ to our life of fa6th is that our distrust of God is turned somewhat in the direction of trust, that our hostility is tuned slightly in the direction of a desire to be loyal, that our view of society to which we are bound in loyalty begins to enlarge. The thunderclouds on the horizon of our existence are broken; the light begins to shine through. A great metanoia, a revolution of personal life, begins in us and n human interpersonal history.

Niebuhr, H.R., *Faith on Earth*, 99.

MAY 27.   NOTHING TO PREVENT COURAGE.

You can deal with children and young people and help them to set their life goals and organize their personalities around just and reasonable values. You can help the imperiled family shape the standards and the values by which the institution of family life may be saved and adjusted to the new conditions of an industrial civilization. You can awaken a complacent civilization to the injustices which modern industrialism is developing. While ministers fail most at this point there is nothing to prevent a courageous person from making a real contribution to his or her society in this field. You can soften the asperities of racial conflict and aid the various groups of a polyglot city to understand one another and themselves.

Niebuhr, R., *Leaves from the Notebook*, 173–74.

MAY 28.   HERE IS A TASK.

You can direct the thoughts and the hopes of people to those facts and those truths which mitigate the cruelty of the natural world and give us the opportunity to assert the dignity of human life in the face of contempt of nature. You can help them to shape and to direct their hopes and aspirations until their lives are determined and molded by the ideal objects of their devotion ... You may find real joy as a skilled craftsman in separating hopes from illusions so that the one need not perish with the other.

Here is a task which requires the knowledge of a social scientist and the insight and imagination of a poet, the executive talents of a business person and the mental discipline of a philosopher. Of course none of us meets all the demands made upon us. It is not easy to be all things to all persons. Perhaps that is why people are so critical of us. Our task is not specific enough to make a high degree of skill possible or to result in tangible and easily measured results. People can find fault with us easily enough and we have not statistics to overawe them and to negate their criticisms.

Niebuhr, R., *Leaves from the Notebook*, 174–75.

MAY 29. UNCONSCIOUS OF THE FACT THAT ANY TEACHING IS GOING ON.

Tradition says that in their anger at [the prophet] Jeremiah's counsel and warnings his country people stoned him. Years later his people knew that none in their history had spoken more clearly the word of the Lord than had Jeremiah ... He had dreamed of a time when they would not have to depend upon land, or law, or Temple to represent the Lord's presence to them but would have God's spirit in their hearts. "Behold, the days come ... that I will make a new covenant, I will put my law in their inward parts, and in their heart will I write it."

Niebuhr, H., *One Story*, 76.

MAY 30. RECONSTRUCTION OF FAITH.

Insofar as our religion is the central element in our existence its reconstruction is of central importance as its fall has the most disastrous consequences. But the reconstruction of faith is not something confined to the worship, the numinous feelings, the relations to the unseen world. It is something that extends into the whole of life. And so we see how the community of faith not only comes into appearance in our religious life, where it modifies, transforms, corrects our constant tendencies to fear but in our domestic and our total cultural life.

Niebuhr, H.R., in Niebuhr, R.R., *Faith on Earth*, 118 note 14.

MAY 31

[It] is not wise to trust general rules and principles too much. There is ....
no guarantee of justice in [human] reason.

There is a possibility of justice only in the self, provided it is not too
sure of itself. The heedlessness of love, which sacrifices the interests of the
self, enters into calculations of justice by becoming the spirit of contrition
which issues from the self's encounter with God. In that encounter, it
is made aware of the contingent character of all human claims and the
tainted character of all human pretensions and ideals.

This contrition is the social relevant counterpart of love. It breaks
the pride of the implacable contestants and competitors in all human
encounters and persuades them to be "kindly affectioned one with another, forgiving one another, even also as God in Christ has forgiven you"
(Ephesians 4:32). This spirit lies at the foundation of what we define as
democracy. . . . Thus the agape of forgiveness as well as the agape of sacrificial love become a leaven in the lump of the spirit of justice.

Niebuhr, R. 'Christian Faith and Social Action," 134–35.

JUNE

National Indigenous History Month (Canada) and National Safety Month

In [Bishop] Whipple's absence, would not more than thirty-eight have mounted the scaffold in Mankato, to fall in what remains the largest mass execution in American history? Or did [Abraham] Lincoln's meeting with Whipple lead him to spare other from death—five or ten or even fifty? Any number matters, profoundly . . .

Whipple should be measured by his consistency and dedication to a humanitarian cause. He looked in the face of Native Americans—the subjects of a brutal racism inbred in so many Americans—and he saw men and women as admirable as any others he had known, and very possibly more so. He knew this opened him up to all manner of unpleasant accusations of naiveté, and worse, somehow betraying the interests of white America. But he persisted. Whipple got to Lincoln before anyone else did and so was able to explain to the president in terms of the historic injustice of white -Indian relations. He rejected the spurious accusations common in Minnesota, that the Indians were naturally dangerous. Instead, he focused on their long mistreatment by a government that could, Whipple believed, reform itself and offer them protection, to the benefit of all—and to the pleasure of God.

Niebuhr, G. [Jr.], *Lincoln's Bishop,* 185, 184.

JUNE

JUNE 1. DEATH OF REINHOLD NIEBUHR.

The Lord has given, the Lord has taken, / Praised be the name of the Lord. / My flesh and my heart may fail, / But God is the strength of my heart. /

He is my portion for ever/ . . . Grace has been poured on your lips / Therefore God has blessed you forever.

Rabbi Abraham Joshua Heschel, in Fox,
Reinhold Niebuhr: A Biography, 293.

"These walks, ordered by the doctor for Reinhold's health, when in the company of Abraham, became times of exchange and refreshment . . . It was no wonder to me that these two friends found each other so congenial, not only in this shared universe of discourse, but also in their dependence upon and reference to the Hebrew prophets."

Niebuhr, U., in a 1983 speech delivered at the
College of St. Benedict, University of Minnesota.
https://www.tabletmag.com/sections/news/articles/
a-familiar-name-fights-presbyterian-divestment
[accessed February 14, 2022].

JUNE 2. HOME'S EXEMPLARS.

My sister and I grew up in a home where our parents led us in grace at meals, prayers at bedtime, and to church on Sundays. They made sure we understood that we shared the world with a great variety of religious [and non-religious] identities, all of which belonged to people who deserved as much respect as we would ourselves would want. As a child and, later as an adult, I've met people who share that perspective, people whom I would credit as possessing a genuine spaciousness with regard to others. I believe that quality works mightily to hold society together, even as prideful and angry individuals work to damage it. I have found myself often wishing such ordinary peacemakers were more publicly recognized . . . their success is never guaranteed.

Niebuhr, G. [Jr.], *Beyond Tolerance*, xi–xii.

JUNE 3. TRIVIAL PREOCCUPATIONS.

Triviality and simple moral absolutes were, to Reinhold Niebuhr, the two begetting sins of the preacher. Often he quoted a remark from an agnostic friend, who objected to the church "not because of its dogmas but because of its trivialities."

By triviality, this friend meant "the disproportionate concern with the minutiae of religious observance, ecclesiastical organizations and sectarian tradition at a time when a whole generation is passing through a world revolution greater than the Communist one . . . He meant preoccupation with trivial concerns with the world hanging on the rim of disaster." He continued, "The Church, like every other institution, sinks into triviality when it fails to deal with the 'weightier matters of the law,' . . . which are the law of love and its crown and servant, the law of justice." In this context, he would quote the words of Pope John, "Let love be the motive and justice the instrument."

Niebuhr, U., "Introduction" in Niebuhr, R., *Justice and Mercy*, 6.

JUNE 4. MEDIATOR OF JUDGMENT AND MERCY.

Reinhold did not preach from a written text. He mulled over the themes, memorizing some of his illustrations and quotations, with perhaps half a page of rough notes as a sort of outline. They were for his own sake . . . as markers on the way when he was thinking about it beforehand. His prayers he did write out, and when preaching, for instance in the chapel at Union Theological Seminary, two or three of these would be used in the service as well as for a concluding collect or prayer. He had been quite influenced by the Anglican prayers, and we assembled a fair assortment of others, ancient and modern, which also helped shape his own expression. He had a sense of style and, like Winston Churchill in his speeches, preferred to use simple words rather than ponderous, many syllabled alternatives . . . He felt that preaching was his vocation. He wrote, "For nearly forty years I preached almost every Sunday in various parts of the country. 'Making sense' out of the symbols and professions of faith has always been the responsibility of the preacher and teacher. The preacher is the mediator of God, God's judgment and also of his mercy."

Niebuhr, U., *Remembering Reinhold Niebuhr*, 6–7.

JUNE 5.   PRICE OF POSTHUMOUS FAME?/WORLD ENVIRONMENT DAY.

Dietrich Bonhoeffer is often hailed as the brave pastor who was executed for his role in the plot to kill Hitler, but . . . that is not quite the case. The greatest of his achievement in the Nazi years came not so much from his involvement in the anti-Hitler operations as from his steadfast opposition to National Socialism within the German Evangelical Church, his valorous efforts to gain international recognition for the Confessing Church, and his lived commitment to a free church and a free country. After the war, many German pastors wanted to emphasize his church work and dissociate their fallen comrade from any tyrannicidal activity, of which they strongly disapproved; others were happy to do the opposite, emphasizing his participation in the anti-Hitler plots and averting their eyes from the sorry record of their churches' collusion with the dictator. It was convenient simply to transform Bonhoeffer into an icon of heroic Germans Protestantism; that one could call him a martyr made it even better . . . But a price was paid for this posthumous fame.

Sifton and Stern, *No Ordinary Men*, 140–41.

In one vision after another [John the Seer] pictured how the powers of darkness will be overthrown in one crisis after another, until finally God will choose a new heaven and new earth . . . that God's mercy and power are great enough to bring to pass a time foretold by the prophets of old, when the 'knowledge of God will cover the earth as the waters cover the sea [Habukkah 2:14].

Niebuhr, H., *One Story*, 185–186.

JUNE 6.   ANNIVERSARY OF W.W. II'S D-DAY/ BATTLE OF NORMANDY.

The elevation of Bonhoeffer to iconic martyrdom occluded [obstructed] the larger, more significant German historical drama in which he played such an important part, and in which the man who decisively turned him from church opposition to state resistance is a major figure. In 1955, Eberhard Bethge [Bonhoeffer's friend/biographer] noted the regrettable tendency among some modern historians "to play down Hans von Dohnanyi's role in the resistance movement."

REMEMBERING FAITHFULLY FORWARD

... Inevitably—as is so common in history—the question remains: Is Bonhoeffer remembered correctly? Is the human decency he so well exemplified honored equally with his theological legacy? Is Dohnanyi's decency also honored, as well as his preservation, in an utterly corrupted state, of the highest standard of civic virtue? Both men's lives offer lasting moral instruction . . . Dohnanyi aptly summed up their work and spirit when he said they simply took "the path that a decent person inevitably takes." So few traveled that path—anywhere.

Sifton and Stern, *No Ordinary Men*, 141–42.

O Lord, good shepherd of the sheep, who wills not that any should perish, but that all should be saved and come to the knowledge of your truth, give grace to those who seek your lost sheep in the wilderness of this world's corruption.

Niebuhr, R., *Justice and Mercy*, 73.

JUNE 7. NOT BELIEVING THAT LIFE MUST BE BROKEN.

The practical difficulty of preaching the gospel is that it seems least relevant to those people and to those generations to whom it is most relevant. From the standpoint of the gospel, we must regard power, or the wisdom or the security of any person as not being as significant as one tries to make him or herself believe that it is.

The successful minister is in greater temptation, because he or she is more likely to deal with the powerful, the rich, the secure, and the wise. The gospel has a revolutionary transmutation of values: the maimed, and the halt, and the blind will enter the kingdom before all the "good" people, because they know life must be broken; while those who are secure with some form of philosophy, or power, or political sagacity, do not believe that life must be broken. They do not think that the gospel is relevant. But it is just for them that it is relevant. Part of the task of preaching the gospel is to persuade those people, who think that the gospel is for the weak, that it is for the strong as well; that a strong person is really very weak. He or she cannot complete their own life, but God has to complete it.

Niebuhr, R., *Justice and Mercy*, 132–33.

JUNE 8. THOU ART THE MAN.

Nathan, the prophet, stood before David, the king, to challenge his sin with Bathsheba. David, in his pride, could not be convicted of his sin with Bathsheba; so the prophet told a parable of a wealthy man who took a ewe lamb away from a poor man. The king was aroused to a fury of self-righteousness as he condemned the sin of another man. "The man . . . shall surely die." The prophet spoke, sticking in the stiletto, "Thou art the man." This is how one must practice guile in preaching the gospel to people who will not believe it. Our task then is to guard and to expound the uniqueness and vitality of the Christian faith. We recall what Pascal called the misery and dignity of man and woman, and we should try to relate that double dimension to our teaching and preaching . . . The philosophers, he said, "can tell me about man's and woman's dignity, and they drive me to pride, or about man's misery, and they drive me to despair. Where, in the simplicity of the gospel will I know about both the dignity and the misery of man and woman?"

Niebuhr, R., *Justice and Mercy*, 133, 136–37.

JUNE 9. DRAWN OUT OF OURSELVES.

The language of these [Newer Testament] Gospels, reading into our world as a communication, offers a connection that we do not otherwise easily see and name:

The *basilica tou theou*, God-ruling = the action defining Jesus and issuing in his conduct and speech = the commonality of all men who suffer diminution and enlargement in the polarity of power and pathos = the common third of past and present experience.

Niebuhr, R.R., *Experiential Religion*, 119.

Thank God, there are forces in life and in history that draw us out of ourselves and make us truly ourselves. That is grace . . .

Niebuhr, R., *Justice and Mercy*, 43.

Give us grace, our Father/our Mother, to measure the height of our dignity as free spirits, and the depth of our misery and the breadth of our responsibility. Judge us in our vanities and pretensions. Have pity on us for only your pity is adequate to the infinite pathos of human existence.

Niebuhr, R., *Justice and Mercy*, 111.

JUNE 10.   REVELATION.

Revelation means the moment in our history through which we know ourselves to be known from beginning to end, in which we are apprehended by the knower . . . the moment in which we find our judging selves to be judged not by ourselves or our neighbors but by one who knows the final secrets of the heart; revelation means the self-disclosure of the judge. Revelation means that we find ourselves to be valued rather than valuing and that all of our values are transvaluated by the activity of a universal valuer. When a price is put on our heads, which is not our price, when the unfairness of all the fair prices we have placed on things is shown up; when the great riches of God reduce our wealth to poverty, that is revelation. When we find out that we are no longer thinking of [God], but that [the Holy One] first thought of us, that is revelation . . . The definition of revelation as divine self-disclosure must call forth many questions in our mind . . . We acknowledge revelation by no third-person proposition, such as there is a God, but only in the direct confession of the heart, "Thou art my God." We can state the convincement given in the revelatory moment only in a prayer saying, "Our Father."

The content of revelation is not the self-disclosure of an unknown being, but the unveiling of the value of a known being . . . that it "loves us," "judges us," that it makes life worthwhile.

Niebuhr, H.R., *Meaning of Revelation*, 111–12.

JUNE 11.   TOO CAUTIOUS TO BE A CHRISTIAN.

There is a discouraging pettiness about human nature which makes me hate myself each time I make an analysis of my inner motives and springs of action. Here I am prodding and criticizing people continually because they have made too many compromises with the necessities of life and adjusted the Christian ideal until it has completely lost its original meaning. Yet I make my own compromises all the time . . . I am not really a Christian. In me, as in many others, "the native hue of resolution is sicklied o'er by a pale cast of thought." I am too cautious to be a Christian. I can justify my caution, but so can the other fellow who is more cautious than I am. The whole Christian adventure is frustrated continually not so much by malice as by cowardice and reasonableness. And perhaps everyone is justified if he or she tries to prove that there is a particular reasonableness about the type of compromise which they have reached. But one might well learn, better than I have learned, to be charitable with those who have made their adjustments to the right and to the left of his position . . . A reasonable person adjusts his or her moral goal somewhere between Christ and Aristotle, between an ethic of love and an ethic of moderation. I hope there is more of Christ than of Aristotle in my position. But I would not be too sure of it.

Niebuhr, R., *Leaves from the Notebook*, 166–67.

JUNE 12. MINISTRY . . . IMPOSSIBLE VOCATION?

A very sophisticated young man assured me in student discussion at a middle western university today that no intelligent person would enter the ministry today. He was sure that the ministry was impossible as a vocation not only because too many irrationalities were still enmeshed with religion but also because there was no real opportunity for usefulness in the church. Granted all the weakness of the church and the limitations of the ministry as a profession, where can one invest one's life where it can be made more effective in as many directions?

Niebuhr, R., *Leaves from the Notebook*, 173.

JUNE 13. OUR DIGNITY/OUR MISERY.

The self is free to defy God. The self does defy God. The Christian conception of the dignity of man and of the misery of man is all of one piece, as Pascal rightly apprehended . . . But the Christian doctrine of selfhood means that neither the life of the individual self nor the total drama of [our] existence upon earth can be conceived in strictly rational terms of coherence. Each is a drama of an engagement between the self and God and between mankind and God, in which all sorts of events may happen. The only certainty from a Christian standpoint is that evil cannot rise to the point of defeating God; that every form of egotism, self-idolatry, and defiance stands under divine judgment; that this judgment is partially executed in actual history, though not in complete conformity with the divine righteousness, so that history remains morally ambiguous to the end; and that a divine redemptive love is always initiating a reconciliation between God and humans. According to this answer, a suffering divine love is the final coherence of life. To a certain degree this answer reaches down to cover even the antinomies known as natural evil.

Niebuhr, R., *Christian Realism and Political Problems*, 183–84.

JUNE 14. INCONGRUITIES, HUMOUR, AND FAITH.

To meet the disappointments and frustrations of life, the irrationalities and contingencies with laughter, is a high form of wisdom . . .

Niebuhr, R., *Discerning the Signs*, 126.

Insofar as the sense of humour is a recognition of incongruity, it is more profound than any philosophy which seeks to devour incongruity in reason. But the sense of humour remains healthy only when it deals with immediate issues and faces the obvious and surface irrationalities. It must move toward faith or sink into despair when the ultimate issues are raised.

Niebuhr, R., *Discerning the Signs*, 130–31.

That is why there is laughter in the vestibule of the temple, the echo of laughter in the temple itself, but only faith and prayer, and no laughter, in the holy of holies . . . There is no humour in the cross because the justice and the mercy of God are fully revealed in it.

Niebuhr, R., *Discerning the Signs*, 131, 118.

JUNE 15. BEAUTY IN OUR TRAGEDY.

For what the individual conscience feels when it lifts itself above the world of nature and the system of collective relationships in which the human spirit remains under the power of nature, is not a luxury but a necessity of the soul. Yet there is beauty in our tragedy. We are, at least, rid of some our illusions. We can no longer buy the highest satisfactions

JUNE

of the individual life at the expense of social injustice. We cannot build our individual ladders to heaven and leave the total human enterprise unredeemed of its excesses and corruptions.

Niebuhr, R., *Moral Man and Immoral Society*, 276–77.

Real participation involves waiting patiently trying to see what is there and to catch what is honestly representative of it. This imperative—to see what is actually there—is a moral responsibility that belongs to the photographer.

Niebuhr, R.R., in Primeaux, *Richard R. Niebuhr on Christ*, 216.

JUNE 16. RECONSTRUCTION.

Insofar as our religion is the central element in our existence its reconstruction is of central importance as its fall has the most disastrous consequences. But the reconstruction of faith is not something confined to the worship, the numinous feelings, the relations to the unseen world. It is something that extends into the whole of life. And so we see how the community of faith not only comes into appearance in our religious life, where it modifies, transforms, corrects our constant tendencies to fear but in our domestic and our total cultural life.

Niebuhr, H.R., *Faith on Earth*, 118 note 14.

JUNE 17. LOYAL-DISLOYAL BEINGS?

"When the Son of Man comes, will he find faith on earth?" [My father] H. Richard Niebuhr spent years exploring substantive issues that this question attracts to itself, much as a magnet attracts susceptible particles into its field of energy. He explored not to locate the question's early significance in the Gospel according to Luke or to speculate on end-times but to inquire into the forms and structure of human faith as we experience faith in our times and thus into the nature of our social selfhood. While his other books give evidence of the breadth and of the many perspectives of his inquiry into faith, Faith on Earth is the most personal of all—it conducts us farther and deeper into the author's understanding of the fiducial constitution of our existence as loyal-disloyal beings who keep faith and break faith.

Niebuhr, R.R., "Preface," ix.

JUNE 18.   EDUCATING MINISTERS, ORDAINED OR LAY.

When teachers examine themselves and their [theological] schools for the sake of discovering how to overcome difficulties or how to improve their work they are quickly led to ask far-reaching questions about the nature and the purposes of education . . . they quickly discover that education is so closely connected with the life of a community that queries about the aims of reaching and learning cannot be answered unless ideas about the character and the purposes of society in which it is carried on are clarified first of all . . . [E]ducation, now as always, is concerned with the nurture of men and women whose business in life it will be to help humans to see their immediate perplexities, joys and sufferings in the light of an ultimate meaning, to live as citizens of the inclusive society of being, and to relate their present choices to first and last decisions made about them in the totality of human history by Sovereign Power.

Niebuhr, H.R., *Purpose of the Church*, 1, 2–3.

You can direct the thoughts and the hopes of persons to those facts and those truths which mitigate the cruelty of the natural world and give people the opportunity to assert the dignity of human life in the face of contempt of nature. You can help them to shape and to direct their hopes and aspirations until their lives are determined and molded by the ideal objects of their devotion . . . You may find real joy as a skilled [craftsperson] in separating hopes from illusions so that the one need not perish with the other.

Niebuhr, R., *Leaves from the Notebook*, 174.
cf. May 28 entry.

JUNE 19.   TEACHING OF GOD'S GRACE/ EMANCIPATION DAY (USA).

We bemoan the fact that our church members do not know the Bible, while at the same time we waste opportunities to make it available to them . . . It is the task of Christian Education to furnish imaginations with the story of salvation so that it may become a part of each individual's own history, absorbed in the context of his own particular life, be he young or older, rich or poor, from east or west . . . [The teacher as artist] acts to help the pupil make the gospel experience his own, its

JUNE   113

historical context invading the pupil's own, so that the gospel can live in that context, can snare it in imagination and discover for him or herself its meaning. As believer, the teacher is part of a community that lives in God's claim upon it, teaching of God's grace, probably unconscious of the fact that any teaching is going on.

Niebuhr, H., in Caldwell, *A Mysterious Mantle*, 118–19.

. . . I turn back to the prayer book [of my great grandmother, Lydia Niebuhr], which sits beside me as I write, itself a demonstration of my conviction that the sacred and secular are never easily separated. Thus, Lydia's book contains prayers from people who were not ordained or sanctioned to write them by any church. Here's how one begins, written by Robert Louis Stevenson: "We beseech Thee, Lord, to behold us with favor, folks of many families and nations gathered together in the peace of this roof, weak men and women subsisting under the covert of Thy patience. Be patient still; suffer us yet a while longer—with our broken purposes of good, with our idle endeavors against evil, suffer us a while longer to endure and (if it may be) help us to do better . . . Amen."

Niebuhr, G. [Jr.], *Beyond Tolerance*, xii–xiii.

JUNE 20.   PROVE OUR REPENTANCE.

We are not worthy of the rich inheritances of our common life. We confess that we have profaned the temple of this life by our selfishness and heedlessness. We have sought to gain advantages of our brothers and sisters who are bound to us by many different ties. Have mercy upon us, that we may express our gratitude for thy many mercies by contrition for our sins and that we may prove our repentance by lives dedicated more fully to thee and to the common good, through Jesus Christ our Lord.

Niebuhr, R., *Reinhold Niebuhr: Major Works*, 697.

JUNE 21.   NATIONAL [ABORIGINAL] INDIGENOUS PEOPLE'S DAY (CANADA).

The name did not register with me. "Benjamin Whipple was the Episcopal Bishop who went to see Lincoln to try to stop a mass hanging of the Sioux Indians." That sentence made me want to know more. I discovered that, yes, Whipple did go to see Lincoln about the Sioux, but the visit took place in a much larger, more impressive context: . . . In September 1862 the Dakota War spread death and terror across Minnesota, its principle victims white civilians; the state's leaders demanded Native Americans be exterminated. That did not stop Whipple. He recognized that moral authority, when kept sheathed like a sword in its scabbard eventually loses its purpose . . . Whipple sought a total reform of the Office of Indian Affairs. He knew what he wanted and he would have been succinct. He had seen up close the effects of alcohol sales, fraudulent dealing, and even violence by the men entrusted to keep the Indians' welfare in mind, rather than enrich themselves.

At one point, Lincoln needed to pause and absorb the urgency of the message and register his own grasp of Whipple's information . . . Later Lincoln would casually speak with a friend . . . 'When you see Lute [Lincoln's brother-in-law], ask him if knows Bishop Whipple. He recently came here the other day and talked with me about the rascality of the Indian business until I felt it down to my boots.'

Lincoln made a promise after that meeting—poignantly, when viewed in retrospect—to address America's other racial sin, after first dealing with slavery and secession. "If we get through this war," he said, "and I live, this Indian system shall be reformed!"

Niebuhr, G. [Jr.], *Lincoln's Bishop*, xi, xiv, 132.

O Lord, have pity upon this generation of your children . . . Assuage the passions of brutal persons and overcome the cowardice of those who are of faint heart. Grant us power and grace to resist evil, knowing that even though we ourselves are sinful [people] you have called us to be instruments of your justice.

Niebuhr, *Reinhold Niebuhr: Major Works*, 704.

JUNE 22. NOT DESPAIR.

Isaiah wrote a poem of gratitude to God. He thought that now the people would certainly repent. Surely now they would know God's care for them and would want to do what was right. Surely now they had seen the greatness of Holy One who could not excuse evil. "The whole earth is full of [God's] glory," he said. "How can [people] not be in awe of [God].?" But the people replied, "Let us eat, drink and be merry, for tomorrow we die!" Although Isaiah was greatly disappointed, he did not despair. The Lord would yet bring it about that they would know [the Holy One] and life after [the Sovereign's Ways].

Niebuhr, H., *One Story,* 65–66.

JUNE 23. NON-VIOLENT RESISTANCE.

There is no problem of political life to which the religious imagination can make a larger contribution that the problem of developing non-violent resistance. The discovery of elements of common human frailty in the foe and, concomitantly, the appreciation of all human life as possessing transcendent worth, creates attitudes which transcend social conflict and thus mitigate its cruelties. It binds human beings together by reminding them of the common roots and similar character of both their vices and their virtues. These attitudes of repentance which recognise that the evil is also in the self, and these impulses of love which claim kinship with all people in spite of social conflict are the peculiar gifts of religion to the human spirit. Secular imagination is not capable of producing them; for they require a sublime madness which disregards immediate appearances and emphasizes profound and ultimate unities . . .

For what the individual conscience feels when it lifts itself above the world of nature and the system of collective relationships in which the human spirit remains under the power of nature, is not a luxury but a necessity of the soul. Yet there is beauty in our tragedy. We are, at least, rid of some of our illusions. We can no longer buy the highest satisfactions of the individual life at the expense of social injustice. We cannot build our individual ladders to heaven and leave the total human enterprise unredeemed of its excesses and corruptions.

Niebuhr, R., *Moral Man and Immoral Society,* 254–55.

JUNE 24. CONSOLING GRACE.

All persons who live with any degree of serenity live by some assurance of grace. In every life there must at least be times and seasons when the good is felt as a present possession and not as a far-off goal. The sinner must feel oneself "justified," that is, he or she must feel that . . .

imperfections are understood and sympathetically appreciated as well as challenged. Whenever he or she finds themselves in a circle where they are "completely known and all forgiven" something of the mercy of God is revealed and one catches a glimpse of the very perfection which has eluded oneself. Perhaps the most sublime insight of Jewish prophets and the Christian gospel is the knowledge that since perfection is love, the apprehension of perfection is at once the means of seeing one's imperfections and the consoling grace which makes this realization bearable. This ultimate paradox of high religion is . . . constantly validated by the most searching experiences of life.

Niebuhr, R., *Reflections on the End of an Era*, 284–85.

JUNE 25.   ACROSS THE CHASM.

Historic events come to the believer as given. They can therefore not be anticipated by any philosophy of coherence. They presuppose an existential incoherence between human striving and the divine will. They can be appropriated only by faith, that is, existentially rather than speculatively, because the recognition of their truth requires a repentant attitude toward false completions of life from the human standpoint. Furthermore, they assert a relevance between a divine freedom and a human freedom across the chasm of the inflexibilities of nature which have no other message than death, to this curious animal, man and woman, who are more than an animal.

Niebuhr, R., *Christian Realism and Political Problems*, 201.

JUNE 26.   EITHER/OR.

Either we have a faith from the standpoint of which we are able to say, "I am persuaded, that either death, nor life . . . shall be able to separate us from the love of God which is in Christ Jesus our Lord" [Rom. 8:38–39], or we are overwhelmed by the incongruity of death and are forced to say with Ecclesiastes: "I said in mine heart concerning the estate of the sons of men . . . that they might see that themselves are beasts; . . . as the one dieth, so dieth the other; yea they all have one breath; so that a man hath no pre-eminence above a beast; for all is vanity" [Eccles. 3:18–19].

Niebuhr, R., *Discerning the Signs*, 128.

JUNE 27. JUSTICE TO THE WHOLE.

Only a combination of repose and anxiety, of serenity and preparedness, can do justice to the whole of our life and the whole of our world. For our life is a brief existence, moving within a great stream of finiteness. Yet the stream moves within its bed; and the flux of existence is held together by the eternal purposes of God. We ourselves stand beyond the flux in memory and hope. But we do not stand beyond it so completely that we can touch the eternal in the present moment by our own strength. We touch it by faith. That faith is the source of our serenity, even as alertness for the promises and perils of tomorrow is a reminder of our continued finiteness and sin. Both posterity and God are required to complete our life. [Both] tomorrow and today are in the hands of a God whose power is great enough to complete our incompleteness and whose mercy and forgiveness are adequate for the evils which we introduce into both the present and the future.

Niebuhr, R., *Discerning the Signs,* 109–10.

JUNE 28. SHOW US . . .

". . . And establish thou the work of our hands upon us; Yea, the work of our hands establish thou it" [Psalm 90:17].

The Ninetieth Psalm sings the melody and harmony of music. The thought of God's eternity and the idea of human transiency are interwoven in its verses like theme and counter-theme in a symphonic movement. As in so much music there is in it the sense of regret and melancholy for the impermanence of human things, of sorrow for the loveliness that was and is no longer. Yet . . . the Psalm does not end upon a note of melancholy resignation, but rather with a kind of trumpet call of passionate hope and assertion: Let the favor of the Lord our God be upon us, and establish thou the work of our hands; yea! The work of our hands, establish thou it!

Niebuhr, H.R., *Theology, History, and Culture,* 208.

. . . Show us, Almighty and Transcendent Being, what you are doing. And the Transcendent One made that very petition a part of the revelation of his work. For by this poem, too, in its setting, with its companion pieces, we are enabled to see, though dimly still, and more by faith than sight, that this whole story of our human life is the story of a supernal, everlasting creation and a cosmic redemption, of God's own artistry and God's own liberation from dullness and shame, from immorality and brutality, from destruction and decay . . .

Our own prayers will not be answered without our efforts. Our shabby work, our faithful cutting of corners, our efforts to get by, these will but furnish fuel for the world Gehennas where all the trash we people produce and accumulate must be destroyed if there is to be any glory. Yet even our best work cannot endure unless the transcendent power in being that presides over and works in all our working includes what we do in its deeds, a deed not of final destruction but of final recreation. Not of enslavement to futility but of liberation to action, not of death dealing but of life-giving.

Niebuhr, H.R., *Theology, History, and Culture,* 213–14.

JUNE 29.   SHUT UP/OPEN UP.

The distinction between coercive and persuasive power is not an ontological distinction. It is rather a phenomenal distinction . . . Coercion and persuasion are qualities of the worldly manifestation of power. Our human world shuts us up [coerces] and opens us toward [persuades] itself. Our lives in turn are a business of reacting—as any being reacts to the power of another being according to the laws of motion—and of responding, that is, animating our reactions with an increasing human intention. Jeremiah's angry protest, "thou hast deceived me, O Lord, and I was deceived"; [Roman Emperor and Stoic philosopher] Marcus Aurelius's cultivation of serenity and the death of passion; the existentialist's emancipation declaration that God has given him no script to follow— all of these are expressions of human intentions that have been infused into the perception and awareness that our lives are forever being closed up and set, by laws of motion and change not of our own making, on a course whose end we did not choose before it became our end.

Niebuhr, R.R., *Experiential Religion,* 29.

. . . This is the scene, the field, the world of power, in which our human nature appears. It calls for us to recognize ourselves as religious beings and as beings capable of faith.

Niebuhr, R.R., *Experiential Religion,* 32.

JUNE 30.   TO PRAY . . . ?

Many prayers in many faiths petition God to show the way to right action. But [the Serenity Prayer of my father] asks only for wisdom [and courage] to discern the right way on our own. It presumes that it's within our powers to accomplish this. Still, it is a prayer and I cannot imagine its message in a different mode . . . Whether Christian or not, why would anyone pray about this and not just think about it? What indeed does it mean to pray? I myself believe it's an inner activity natural to all humanity, and I'm certain that atheists and secular people pray, too, even when they scoff at the very idea. The reassuring truth is that the mode of hope in which prayer is cast is inevitable for all of us, and the habit of true prayer can develop easily. Yet, beyond the contemplative religious communities whose members devote themselves to this subject, not enough of us have thought about what prayer really is or might be.

Sifton, *Serenity Prayer,* **12–13.**

JULY
National Fragile X Awareness Month

God, grant us the grace to accept with serenity, the things we cannot change. Grant us the courage to change the things we ought to, and the wisdom to distinguish the one from the other.

Reinhold Niebuhr, in Elisabeth Sifton, *Serenity Prayer*, 7.
(see full discussion of prayer pp. 7–14, passim).

JULY 1. CANADA DAY.

O Lord, save your people. Save the nations from their arrogance and their folly, and grant them grace to walk peaceably with each other. Save the strong, the secure, the successful, and the wise, that they not glory in their might nor in their wisdom. Save the weak and the debased and all who are victims of heedless and cruel men, and reveal to them the final court and judgement where those of low degree are exalted and the disbalance of the world redressed. Save us, O Lord, from our sins and our anxieties, and grant us so sure a hold upon your grace that the peace which passeth understanding may keep our hearts, and we be enabled to walk serenely through the tumults and trials of these days, redeeming the time because the days are evil.

Niebuhr, R., *Reinhold Niebuhr: Major Works,* 703.

"I think the singular and plural versions of [Serenity Prayer] are related . . . because you can't engage in the social action that I think my father had in mind unless your heart changes in a deep, personal, and singular way. So the prayer is rightly thought of in both ways."

Sifton, in https://www.washingtonpost.com/local/obituaries/
elisabeth-sifton-revered-book-editor-and-publisher-dies-
at-80/2019/12/21/a482ded8–22d1–11ea-a153-dce4b94e4249_
story.html [accessed February 29, 2022].

JULY 2. THROUGH RISKS OF CONFIDENCE.

[As] thinking beings who are also moved by the ancient springs of religion, we respond by seeking an understanding of the world commensurate with our religious striving for alignment with true power . . . we awaken to our existence in the experience of taking responsibility for our lives, in acts of willing, of resolving, and of doubting. Here is another certitude: the agency that is me and us. And our whole world appears to us a world demanding of us enterprise and courage. As willing and doubting and asserting beings we respond in our religious striving through actions of willing, through decisions to discard old ways, and through risks of confidence beyond the range of visible evidences.

Niebuhr, R.R., *Experiential Religion,* 78.

JULY 3.   BASIS FOR TRUE CHARITY AND COMMON GOOD GOVERNMENT.

[The] combination of moral resoluteness about the immediate issues with a religious awareness of another dimension of meaning and judgment must be regarded as almost a perfect model of the difficult but not impossible task of remaining loyal and responsible toward the moral treasures of a free civilization on the one hand, while yet having some religious vantage point over the struggle. Surely it was this double attitude which made the spirit of Lincoln's, "with malice toward none; with charity for all" possible. There can be no other basis for true charity; for charity cannot be induced by lessons from copybook texts. It can proceed only from a "broken spirit and a contrite heart."

Niebuhr, R., *Irony of American History*, 172.

[John] Calvin believed that kings had a covenant with God to rule justly and the people had a covenant with God to obey. But he denied that this double covenant implied a contract between the ruler and the people. It was thus a simple matter for later Calvinists to insist that this covenant was triangular, between the ruler, the people, and God; that it was a covenant of justice; and that if the ruler broke it by injustice, the people were absolved of obedience. Thus justice, rather than mere order and peace, became the criterion for government; and democratic criticism became the instrument of justice.

Niebuhr, R., *Nature and Destiny of Man* (Vol. II), 282–83.

JULY 4.   INDEPENDENCE DAY (USA).

[American] idealism is too oblivious of the ironic perils to which human virtue, wisdom and power are subject. It is too certain that there is a straight path toward the goal of human happiness; too confident of the wisdom and idealism which prompt men and nations toward that goal; and too blind to the curious compounds of good and evil in which the actions of the best people and nations abound . . .

Niebuhr, R., *Irony of American History*,
in https://s-usih.org/2013/07/god-war-and-july-4–1976/
[accessed September 8, 2020].

JULY   123

We pray for all who have authority in the world, for the leaders of our
nation and for those who seek to bear office in all the nations, that they
may seek the peaceable fruits of justice; grant that they may know the
limits of human wisdom in the perplexities of the day, and calling upon
you in humility, and acknowledging your majesty, may learn the wisdom
of restraint the justice of charity.

Niebuhr, R., *Reinhold Niebuhr: Major Works*, 702.

JULY 5.   H. RICHARD NIEBUHR'S DEATH/ BROTHER'S TAMED CYNICISM/

National Injury Prevention Day (Canada).

Presented with thanks for what they have taught me . . . to the young men
and women who have studied with me.

Niebuhr, H.R., *Radical Monotheism*, 1960.

"Page by page the cynic—the same cynic that is in all of us—is tamed—
not broken, not forced into compromises, but tamed by the release of
impulse of sympathy, of maturer observation, of sincere analysis."

". . . The author's reluctance to have this book published is all the
more reason for the publisher's desire to have it see the light of day."

Publisher's notes in Fox, Reinhold Niebuhr: A Biography, 107.

"I don't know why I put the word 'tamed' in, but there was an undertone
of cynical reaction to all moral pretension right from the beginning of
my Detroit ministry, so that everything I have since elaborated was in
embryo in that early experience, both on the religious and on the political side . . . set me off on the path that I have since elaborated in various
ways."

Niebuhr, R., *Reminiscences of Reinhold Niebuhr*, 72-73.

[We pray] [f]or those who have been worsted in the struggle of life,
whether by the inhumanity of their fellows, their own limitations, or by
those hazards of life which beset all . . . that they may contend against injustice without bitterness, overcome their own weakness with diligence,
and learn to accept with patience that which cannot be altered.

Niebuhr, R., *Justice and Mercy*, 70.

JULY 6.   PRICE OF SWEAT AND DULL PAIN.

We went through one of the big automobile factories today. So artificial is life that these factories are like a strange world to me though I have lived close to them for many years. The foundry interested me particularly. The heat was terrific. The workers seemed weary. Here manual labor is drudgery and toil is slavery. The people cannot possibly find any satisfaction in their work. They simply work to make a living. Their sweat and their dull pain are part of the price paid for the fine cars we all run. And most of us run the cars without knowing what price is being paid for them.

Niebuhr, R., Leaves from the Notebook, 78.

JULY 7.   TRIBUTE TO THE CALLING.

If a minister wants to be a person among people, he or she needs only to stop creating devotion to abstract ideals which everyone accepts in theory and denies in practice, and to agonize about their validity and practicability in the social issues which he and others face in our present civilization. That immediately gives his ministry a touch of reality and potency and robs it of an artificial prestige which it can afford to dispense with, and is bound to be stripped of, the kind of prestige which is the prerogative of priests and professional holy men . . . Having both entered and left the parish ministry against my inclinations, I pay tribute to the calling, firm in the conviction that it offers greater opportunities for both moral adventure and social usefulness than any other calling if it is entered with open eyes and a consciousness of the hazards to virtue which lurk in it. I make no apology for being critical of what I love.

Niebuhr, R., Leaves from the Notebook, x, xii.

JULY 8.   BIND US TOGETHER.

In London on July 8 Dietrich [Bonhoeffer] preached a fiery sermon that was in sharp contrast to the enthusiastic reassurances most Germans were hearing from the pulpit about the bloodbath in the Reich. His text was the famous "repent or perish" passage in the Gospel of Luke, and while he made it very clear that he considered it inappropriate, even dangerous, to bring current events into the church service, his central pastoral point was that turning one's back on worldly crises, or trying to forget them, or dissociating oneself from them was as foolish as exulting in them . . . we must recognize the sins in our own hearts, repent, "and realize that no human being is ever right in the end." Accepting this spiritual truth is difficult, and the repentant sinner's situation is dangerous, for "we are no longer spectators, observers, judges . . . now, we ourselves are the ones addressed, we are the ones affected. God is speaking to us. It is meant for us . . . Lord, lead your people to repent and begin with us."

Sifton and Stern, *No Ordinary Men*, 49–50.

Almighty God, guide, we beseech you the nations of the world into the ways of justice and truth and establish among them the peace which is the fruit of righteousness. Temper the pride of victors by the knowledge that your judgment is meant for victors and vanquished. Transfigure the despair of the vanquished into hope, and let not the pride of the victors obscure the mercy of the judge before whom they will be judged. Bind us together, victors and vanquished, uneasy partners and former enemies, into a new community and thus make the wrath of all to praise you.

Niebuhr, R., *Justice and Mercy*, 98.

JULY 9. FAITH, HOPE. AND LOVE.

Faith is the capacity to transcend all the changes of history and to project an ultimate source and end of temporal and historical reality. Hope is the capacity to transcend all the confusions of history and project an ultimate end of all historical existence, that which does not annul history but fulfills it. Love is the capacity to recognize the social substance of human existence, and to realize that the unique self is intimately related to all human creatures.

Niebuhr, R., *Essential Reinhold Niebuhr*, 256.
[originally a 1967 *Christian Century* article]

The insistence of the Christian faith that the love of Christ is the final norm of human existence must express itself socially in unwillingness to stop short of the whole human community in expressing our sense of moral responsibility for the life and welfare others. The understanding of the Christian faith that the highest achievements of human life are infected with sinful corruption will help [persons] to be prepared for new corruptions on the level of world community which drive simpler idealists to despair. The hope of Christian faith that the divine power which bears history can complete what even the highest human striving must leave incomplete, and can purify the corruptions, is an indispensable prerequisite for diligent fulfillment of our historic tasks. Without it we are driven to alternate moods of sentimentality and despair, trusting human powers too much in one moment and losing all faith in the meaning of life when we discover the limits of human possibilities.

Niebuhr, R., *Children of Light*, 188–89.

JULY 10. DIMENSIONS OF TIME.

Time is a succession of events. Yet mere succession is not time. Time has reality only through a meaningful relationship of its successions. Therefore, time is real only as it gives successive expressions of principles and powers which lie outside of it. Yet every suggestion of the principle of a process must be expressed in terms of the temporal process, and every idea of the God who is the ground of the world must be expressed in some term taken from the world. The temporal process is like the painter's deception for the sake of truth.

Great art faces the problem of the two dimensions of time as well as the two dimensions of space. The portrait artist, for instance, is confronted with the necessity of picturing a character. Human personality is more than a succession of moods. The moods of a moment are held together in a unity of thought and feeling, which gives them, however seemingly capricious a considerable degree of consistency. The problem of the artist is to portray the inner consistency of a character which is never fully expressed in any one particular mood or facial expression. This can be done only by falsifying physiognomic details. Portraiture is an art which can never be sharply distinguished from caricature. A moment of time in a personality can be made to express what transcends the moment of time only if the moment is not recorded accurately. It must be made into a symbol of something beyond itself.

Niebuhr, R., *Beyond Tragedy*, 5–6.

JULY 11. DECEIVERS, YET TRUE.

We are deceivers, yet true, when we say that man and woman fell into evil. The story of the fall of humans in the Garden of Eden is a primitive myth which modern theology has been glad to disavow, for fear that modern culture might regard belief in it as a proof of the obscurantism of religion. In place of it we have substituted various accounts of the origin and the nature of evil in human life. Most of these accounts, reduced to their essentials, attribute sin to the inertia of nature, or the hypertrophy of impulses, or to the defect of reason [ignorance], and thereby either explicitly or implicitly place their trust in developed reason as the guarantor of goodness. In all of these accounts the essential point in the nature of human evil is missed, namely, that it arises from the very freedom of reason with which man is endowed. Sin is not so much a consequence of natural impulses, which in animal life do not lead to sin, as of the freedom by which a person is able to throw the harmonies of nature out of joint. One disturbs the harmony of nature when he or she centres their life about one particular impulse (sex or the possessive impulse, for instance) when one tries to make him or herself, rather than God, the centre of existence. This egoism is sin in its quintessential form. It is not a defect of creation but a defect which becomes possible because a person has been endowed with a freedom not known in the rest of creation.

Niebuhr, R., *Beyond Tragedy*, 10–11.

JULY 12. FULL DIMENSION OF HUMAN EXISTENCE.

The idea of the fall is subject to the error of regarding the primitive myth of the garden, the apple and the serpent, as historically true. But even if this error is not committed, Christian thought is still tempted to regard the fall as an historical occurrence. The fall is not historical. It does not take place in any concrete human act. It is the presupposition of such acts. It deals with an area of human freedom which, when once expressed in terms of an act, is always historically related to a previous act or predisposition. External descriptions of human behaviour are therefore always deterministic. That is the deception into which those are betrayed who seek to avoid the errors of introspection by purely external descriptions of human behaviour. What Christianity means by the idea of the fall can only be known in introspection. The consciousness of sin and the consciousness of God are inextricably involved with each other. Only as the full dimension of human existence is measured, which includes not only the dimension of historical breadth but the dimension of trans-historical freedom, does the fall of people achieve significance and relevance.

Niebuhr, R., *Beyond Tragedy*, 12.

JULY 13. SELF-SERVING BENEVOLENCE, PATERNALISM.

The fact that love was frequently used to cover up and to excuse social injustice has given the very word "charity" a bad connotation. It proves indeed that love in its purest form may not be as immediately relevant as either equality or liberty to the issue of establishing justice within the structures and traditions of community. But if love means wanting the welfare of the neighbor, it can never be irrelevant to any social situation. If love is defined exclusively in terms of attitudes which express themselves only in personal relations . . . it becomes irrelevant to any situation in which structures of justice must become instruments of love. Furthermore, love may easily be corrupted, so that a powerful person will use benevolence in personal relations as a substitute of granting justice in the basic organization of life. For in benevolence one displays his or her power with their goodness while justice challenges their power as incompatible with goodness. These facts are withheld from the wise but they are known by the "simple," particularly if they should be the victims of the "benevolence" of the powerful. Resentment against these hypocrisies are the root of the laboring person's objection to "paternalism." These corruptions can not however obscure the fact that it is always possible for the love or the self-love of individuals to perfect or to spoil even the most ideal structure of justice.

Niebuhr, R., *Self and the Dramas of History*, 185–86.

JULY 14. LOVE NEEDS . . . JUSTICE . . . NEEDS LOVE, WITH HOPE.

In so far as justice admits the claims of the self, it is something less than love. Yet it cannot exist without love and remain justice. For without the "grace" of love [the leavening ground and aim of justice], justice always degenerates into something less than justice . . . No possible historic justice is sufferable without the Christian hope.

Niebuhr, R., *Love and Justice*, 28.

But if justice requires that the interests of the self must be entertained, it also requires that they be resisted. Every realistic system of justice must assume the continued power of self-interest, particularly of collective self-interest . . . A simple Christian moralism counsels people to be unselfish. A profounder Christian faith must encourage people to creative systems of justice which will save society and themselves from their own selfishness.

Niebuhr, R., *Love and Justice*, 29.

That you might have to force a powerful factor in the community by a counter-weighing power did not occur to me. The element of power was not considered at all, because the persistence of individual and collective self-interest was simply not considered. As I saw this sprawling [1920s Detroit] industry, the moral pretensions in it, and the rather feeble little moralistic sermons that I preached, I was quite overwhelmed by the erroneousness of the whole show.

Niebuhr, R., *Reminiscences of Reinhold Niebuhr*, 27.

JULY 15. EXTENDING JUSTICE.

Mutual love informs and challenges the practice of justice to . . . extend the sense of obligation towards the other a) from an immediately felt obligation, prompted by an obvious need, to a continued obligation in fixed principles of mutual support; b) from a simple relation between a self and one "other" to the complex relations of the self and the "others"; and, c) finally from the obligations, discerned by the individual self, to the wider obligations which the community defines from its more impartial perspective.

Niebuhr, R., *Nature and Destiny of Man* (Vol. II), 248.

JULY 16.   DIMENSIONS OF DEPTH.

Justification by faith in the realm of justice means that we will not regard the pressures and counter pressures, the tensions, the overt and covert conflicts by which justice is achieved and maintained, as normative in the absolute sense; but neither will we ease our conscience by seeking to escape from involvement in them.

Niebuhr, R., *Nature and Destiny of Man* (Vol. II), 284.

If error and lie assail us we invoke the spirit and the power of truth on which we rely to maintain itself and its cause. If injustice prevails we pray not only for justice but to the spirit or power of justice to manifest itself again.

Niebuhr, H.R., *Radical Monotheism*, 54.

Prayer has to be engaged in habitually: One learns to pray by praying.

Sifton, *Serenity Prayer,* 187.

JULY 17.   POWER OF MEANINGFUL MYTH.

Every Christian myth, in one way or another, expresses both the meaningfulness and the incompleteness of the temporal world, both the majesty of God and his relation to the world. We are deceivers yet true, when we say that God created the world. Creation is a mythical idea which cannot be fully rationalised. It has therefore been an offense to the philosophers who, with the scientists, have substituted the idea of causality for it. They have sought to explain each subsequent event by a previous cause. Such an explanation of the world leads the more naïve thinkers to a naturalism which regards the world as self-explanatory because every event can be derived from a previous one. The more sophisticated philosophers will at least, with Aristotle, seek for a first cause which gives an original impetus to the whole chain of causation. But such a first cause does not have a living relationship with the events of nature and history. It does not therefore account for the emergence of novelty in each new event. No new fact or event in history is an arbitrary novelty. It is always related to a previous event. But it is a great error to imagine that this relationship completely accounts for the new emergence. In both nature and history each new thing is only one of an infinite number of possibilities which might have emerged at that particular juncture. It is for this reason that, though we can trace a series of causes in retrospect, we can never predict the future with accuracy. There is a profound arbitrariness in every given fact, which rational theories of causation seek to obscure. Thus they regard a given form of animal life as rational because they can trace it historically to another form or relate it in terms of genus and species to other types of life. Yet none of these relationships, whether historical or schematic, can eliminate the profound arbitrariness of the givenness of things.

Niebuhr, R., *Beyond Tragedy*, 7–8.

JULY 18.   TEMPTATIONS AND ROLE OF ART.

The idea of creation relates the ground of existence to existence and is therefore mythical rather than rational[.] The fact that it is not a rational idea does not make it untrue or deceptive. But since it is not rational it is a temptation to deceptions. Every mythical idea contains a primitive deception and a more ultimate one. The primitive error is to regard the early form in which the myth is stated as authoritative. Thus the Christian religion is always tempted to insist that belief in creation also involves belief in an actual forming of man and woman out of a lump of clay, or in an actual creative activity of six days. It is to this temptation that biblical literalism succumbs. But there is also a more ultimate source of error in the mythical statement of religious belief. That is to regard the relation of each fact and event in history to a Divine Creator as obviating the possibility of an organic relation to other facts and events according to a natural order. By this error, which Etienne Gilson (Footnoted with: In his *Unity of Philosophical Experience)* calls "theologism," Christian theology is constantly tempted to deny the significance of the natural order, and to confuse the scientific analysis of its relationships. At the rise of modern thought, the seventeenth-century French philosopher, Malebranche, developed a doctrine of "occasionalism" which expressed this error of Christian theology in its most consistent form. But it has been a persistent error in Christian thought and one which arises naturally out the mythical statement of the idea of creation. The error is analogous to that of certain types of art which completely falsify the natural relations of objects in order to express their ultimate significance.

Niebuhr, R., *Beyond Tragedy*, 9–10.

JULY 19.   TWO FORMS OF PEACE.

There are two forms of peace within the limits of understanding. The one is the peace of nature which leaves human freedom out of consideration; the other is the peace of human reason which is achieved by denying or obscuring the hopes, fears and ambitions, transcending reason and the impulses and desires, lying below it. Both are simple forms of peace. Both are too simple. The peace of God, on the other hand, is not simple. There is pain and sorrow in it. That at least is the peace of God which has been revealed in the cross of Christ. It passeth understanding to such a degree that the very revelation of it has been an offense to the wise . . . The God who is revealed in Christ is not so easily understood. There is indeed peace in the Holy One and with God's self. God is the calm source from which all life springs and the serene end in which all life finds its fulfillment. But strangely and paradoxically there is also sorrow and suffering in the Holy One's heart; and it is that sorrow and suffering that God finally overcomes the world's disquiet.

Niebuhr, R., *Discerning the Signs,* 176–77.

JULY 20.   MEASURING FULL DIMENSIONS.

The idea of the fall is subject to the error of regarding the primitive myth of the garden, the apple and the serpent, as historically true. But even if this error is not committed, Christian thought is still tempted to regard the fall as an historical occurrence. The fall is not historical. It does not take place in any concrete human act. It is the presupposition of such acts. It deals with an area of human freedom which, when once expressed in terms of an act, is always historically related to a previous act or predisposition. External descriptions of human behaviour are therefore always deterministic. That is the deception into which those are betrayed who seek to avoid the errors of introspection by purely external descriptions of human behaviour. What Christianity means by the idea of the fall can only be known in introspection. The consciousness of sin and the consciousness of God are inextricably involved with each other. Only as the full dimension of human existence is measured, which includes not only the dimension of historical breadth but the dimension of trans-historical freedom, does the idea of the fall of [humanity] achieve significance and relevance.

JULY   133

It is interesting to note that Christian theology has usually regarded
the fall as an historical occurrence, even when it did not accept the primitive myth of the Garden of Eden. It therefore spoke of a perfection before
the fall as if that too were an historical era. Even the sophisticated dia-
lectical theology of Barth and his school speaks of the perfection before
the fall as historical, and consequently elaborates a doctrine of human
sinfulness which approaches, and sometimes surpasses, the extremism
of the historic doctrine of total depravity. The perfection before the fall
is an ideal possibility which men can comprehend but not realise. The
perfection before the fall is, in a sense, the perfection before the act. Thus
we are able to conceive of a perfectly disinterested justice; but when we
act our own achievements will fall short of this standard.

Niebuhr, R., *Beyond Tragedy*, 11–13.

JULY 21.   OUTRAGE OF TRUTH.

We are deceivers, yet true, when we affirm that God became human to redeem the world from sin. The idea of eternity entering time is intellectually
absurd. This absurdity is proved to the hilt by all the theological dogmas
which seek to make it rational. The dogmas which seek to describe the
relation of God the Father (the God who does not enter history) and God
the son (the God of history) all insist that the Son is equal to the Father
and is yet not equal to Him. In the same way all the doctrines of the two
natures of Christ assert that he is not less divine for being human and
temporal and not less human and temporal for being fully divine. Quite
obviously it is impossible to assert that the eternal ground of existence
has entered existence and not sacrificed its eternal and unconditioned
quality, without outraging every canon of reason. Reason may deal with
the conditioned realities of existence in their relationships and it may
even point to the fathomless depth of creativity out of which existential
forms are born. But it cannot assert that the Divine Creator has come into
creation without losing God's unconditioned character. The truth that the
Word was made flesh outrages all the canons by which truth is usually
judged. Yet it is the truth. The whole character of the Christian religion
is involved in that affirmation. It asserts that God's word is relevant to
human life. It declares that an event in history can be of such a character
as to reveal the character of history itself; that without such a revelation
the character of history cannot be known. It is not possible to arrive at

an understanding of the meaning of life and history without such a revelation. No induction from empirical facts can yield a conclusion about ultimate meaning because every process of induction presupposes some canon and criterion of meaning. That is why metaphysical systems which pretend to arrive at ultimate conclusions about the meaning of life are either covert theologies which unconsciously rationalise some revelation, accepted by faith; or they merely identify rationality with meaning, a procedure which forces them into either pantheism or acosmism. They must either identify the world with God on the supposition that temporal events, fully understood in all their relationships, are transmuted from finiteness and contingency into an unconditioned totality; or they must find the existential world evil in its finiteness because it does not conform in its contingent, existential relationships to a rational idea of unity.

For Christian faith the world is neither perfect nor meaningless.

Niebuhr, R., *Beyond Tragedy*, 14–15.

JULY 22.   POINTING BEYOND HISTORY.

In Christian thought Christ is both the perfect human, "the second Adam" who had restored the perfection of what man or woman was and ought to be; and the Son of God, who transcends all possibilities of human life. It is this idea which theology sought to rationalise in the doctrines of the two natures of Christ. It cannot be rationalised and yet it is a true idea. Human life stands in infinity. Everything it touches turns into infinity. Every moral standard, rigorously analysed, proves to be no permanently valid standard at all short of perfect and infinite love. The only adequate norm of human conduct is love of God and of man and woman, through which all persons are perfectly related to each other, because they are all related in terms of perfect obedience and love to the centre and source of their existence. In the same way all evil in human life is derived from an effort to transmute finite values into infinities, to seek infinite power, and infinite wealth and infinite gratification of desire. There is no sharp line between the infinity in humans and the infinity beyond man and woman and yet there is a very sharp line. One always remains a creature and his or her sin arises from the fact that one is not satisfied to remain so. He or she seeks to turn creatureliness into infinity; whereas their salvation depends upon subjecting their creaturely weakness to the infinite good of God. Christ, who expresses both the infinite possibilities of love in human life and the infinite possibilities beyond human life, is thus a true revelation of the total situation in which human life stands. There is every possibility of illusion and deception in this statement of the Christian faith. People may be deceived by the primitive myth of the Virgin Birth and seek to comprehend as a pure historical fact, what is significant precisely because it points beyond history. Or they may seek to explain the dogma of the Incarnation in terms which will make it an article in a philosophical creed. Such efforts will lead to varied deceptions; but the deceptions cannot destroy the truth of the Incarnation.

Niebuhr, R., *Beyond Tragedy,* 16–17.

JULY 23.   SELF-SERVING GAMES.

The great political game of 'Power, power, who gets the power? is attracting Christians now as it has done before. Capitalists, fascists, proletarians, agriculturalists, industrialists, intelligentsia all have their ambitions and delusions. The Christian revolutionary intelligentsia are among the worst. They are persuaded of their own disinterestedness and how they would love to wield power for the sake of their brothers and sisters. But how can they believe that they will be uncontaminated by the exercise of power when they look at the past?

Niebuhr, R.R., "Foreword," in *H. Richard Niebuhr, Theology, History and Culture,* ix.

JULY 24.   AS THE DIALOGUE PROCEEDS.

An apparently tough-minded common sense has insisted in all ages that "Seeing is believing" and "What I can't see, I never will believe in!" But it is soon reminded that it disbelieves many things it sees, such as the smallness of the stars compared with the earth, while it believes many statements about the existence and nature of things it does not and cannot see, such as certain historical events to which it constantly refers, or principles like those of human equality and justice, or constructs like those of the atom and the unconscious . . . seeing and believing seem to be exclusive of each other; seeing is accompanied by assurance, believing by uncertainty. But as the dialogue proceeds it becomes apparent there is more than one kind of seeing, more than one sort of believing; that the relations between them are intricate; and that assurance is attached in various measures to each.

Niebuhr, H.R., *Faith on Earth*, 12–13.

JULY 25. FAITH AND SIGHT.

Problems of faith and sight have, of course, occupied members of the community of Christian believers ever since the earliest hearers of the gospel asked its preachers to produce some sign from heaven validating its truth, or to show them the Father or the resurrected Christ . . . faith was defined as essentially a relation to the unseen. Though the emphasis in the Letter to the Hebrews is on the unseen future on which the believer relies, yet what is unseen in present and past is also the object of faith, for, it affirms, "by faith we understand the world was created by the word of God, so that what is seen was made out of things which do not appear [Heb.11:1] . . . Similarly, in the Fourth Gospel, Jesus Christ is represented as pronouncing his blessing on "those who have not seen and yet believe" (20:29), and in the First Letter of Peter it is the unseen Jesus Christ who is the object of that genuine faith—more precious than gold—by which salvation is obtained. "Without having seen him you love him; though you do not see him you believe in him" (I:8).

Niebuhr, H.R., *Faith on Earth*, 14.

JULY 26. 26TH OF JULY MOVEMENT (PRECURSOR TO THE 1959 CUBAN REVOLUTION).

Besides the sense of the holy and the need for superhuman aid we encounter in religion the desire for ecstasy, for transport out of the ordinary round of routine existence into the realms of wonder, of increased sensitivity, of enlarged views, of freedom from constraint, of "surprises of joy."

Niebuhr, H.R., *Radical Monotheism*, 55.

The definition of faith as conviction of the reality of the unseen is accompanied in the pages of the New Testament by another one according to which believing is conviction of the reality of what others have seen. So the author of the Gospel of Luke and of Acts begins the account "of things that have been accomplished among us" by reference to the eyewitnesses while, more explicitly, the Gospel of John concludes with the statement, "Now Jesus did many other signs in the presence of the disciples, which are not written in this book; but are ~~not~~ written that you may believe that Jesus is the Christ, the Son of God, and that believing you may have life in his name" (20:30–31) . . . The contrast is not between faith and sight but, in part at least, between unbelief and belief in the testimony of those who have seen or claim to have done so.

Niebuhr, H.R., *Faith on Earth*, 14–15.

JULY 27.   WORLD DAY FOR GRANDPARENTS AND THE ELDERLY.

It is evidently possible for persons to believe—not only to profess belief—in one thing and yet to act in opposition to that belief. In a sociological study of "The Negro Problem" in America the "American Creed"—significantly so called—was contrasted with American practice; and the dilemma of the nation was discovered in the conflict between its faith and its action. "The American Dilemma," writes the author, Gunnar Myrdal, "is the ever-raging conflict between, on the one hand, the valuations persevered on the general plane which we shall call the "American Creed," where the American thinks, talks, and acts under the influence of high national and Christian precepts, and, on the other, the valuations on specific planes of individual and group living where personal and local interests; economic, social and sexual jealousies; considerations of community prestige and community; group prejudice against particular persons or types of people; and all sorts of miscellaneous wants, impulses, and habits dominate his outlook." . . . Similar problems have arisen everywhere when nations or other groups have espoused principles and not been content with the simple aims of surviving and being powerful.

Niebuhr, H.R., *Faith on Earth*, 5.

JULY 28.   OVERTONES OF TRUST AND DISTRUST.

In the midst of all questionings and arguments about faith; in the controversies of the religious sects and philosophical schools; among the contentions as defenders of this and that faith attack others with different beliefs, we become aware of a strange fact. Belief and disbelief, trust and distrust, fidelity and infidelity toward each other is present in all those who contend or agree with each other as they argue about faith . . . Belief and trust and fidelity and their opposites are forever present as active attitudes in the very subjects who make them the objects of their inquiry or disputation . . . Complete disinterestedness may be possible in our encounter with things or even thoughts. But as we deal with thinking people we raise questions: Can they be trusted? Where are they trying to lead me? What are they defending? This page is being read with some trust or distrust of the writer as a person or as representing a class; it is being written also with overtones of trust and distrust of various classes, of fidelity and infidelity to a cause.

Niebuhr, H.R., *Faith on Earth*, 20.

JULY 29.   BELIEF AND AFFIRMING.

Questions *about* faith, about its relations to action, to sight and under-standing, about its objects and circular movements are important to us only because we have previously been required to answer the questions *of* faith. These have been put to us in direct encounter with all the objects of our trust and distrust, belief and disbelief, loyalty and infidelity. The primary situation in which faith appears as a problem is of the sort in which Descartes found himself as he looked upon the "very proud and magnificent palaces" erected by ancient moralists and discovered that he distrusted them as being "built nothing but sand and mud." Or, on the positive side, it is the situation in which one answers the question about what he or she can believe by affirming their own existence on the basis of confrontation with themselves as thinking beings.

Niebuhr, H.R., *Faith on Earth*, 20–21.

JULY 30.   INTERNATIONAL DAY OF FRIENDSHIP.

We hear [the direct question of faith] raised in encounters . . . when fa-miliar disbelief is challenged. Then it may be the sort of question Jesus raised for his disciples: "Why are you so fearful, O you of little faith?" or put to Mary: "I am the resurrection and the life . . . Do you believe this?" (Matt. 8.26, John 11:25, 26].

We become aware of these primary questions of faith usually in those times when our confidence in the hitherto trusted is shaken or when we are moved to rely on the previously untried; but they are being constantly addressed to us in all our daily encounters with our companions and our world. They accompany like an undertone all the transactions and communications between people and all their dialogues of perception and conception with common objects. We are forever being asked and asking: Do you believe me? Do you trust me? Are you trustworthy and believable? Are you faithful to me and to our common cause?

Niebuhr, H.R., *Faith on Earth*, 22.

JULY 31.   FAITH AND UNDERSTANDING.

Faith seeks understanding in a double way. It seeks to understand what it believes but also how it believes. As man and woman, the knower seeks clarity about this knowing activities as well as known realities, as one the valuer finds him or herself impelled to inquire in their choosing no less than into the nature of chosen and rejected values, so the believing human wants to know how he or she believes as what they believe. Why one is obliged or compelled to pursue such insights may not know this side of its achievement.

Niebuhr, H.R., *Faith on Earth*, 23.

AUGUST

National Immunization Awareness Month
(Canada and USA)

Is fearing a pathological condition, temporary and negative in its import
for our understanding of "true" human nature? Or is it normal and normative, disclosing a universal feature of human existence? And if it is
the latter, how can it have any special meaning for Christians . . . or for
would-be Christians or post-Christians? Could we, for example, borrow
the language of Calvin and Jonathan Edwards to say of this sense of being
shipwrecked that it is the work of the Holy Spirit?

Niebuhr, R.R., "The Widened Heart," 141.

It may well be true that we must distinguish between pathological and
nonpathological fearing, although our conception of human health is
forever changing . . . Fearing is the perception of the immensity of power
and of the weakness of any claims of ours. While we are instinctively
inclined . . . to see dread and fearing as a reflection of our poverty, if we
fully attend to what it opens to view we perceive not merely emptiness
but contrast; contrast between self and field of power, between small and
great.

Niebuhr, R.R., *Experiential Religion*, 93-94.

AUGUST   141

AUGUST 1.   WHATEVER THY HEART CLINGS TO?/ CANADIAN EMANCIPATION DAY.

At the beginning of the modern era, Luther vigorously and repeatedly affirmed that God and faith belonged together so that all statements about God which are from some other point of view than that of faith in God are not really statements about God at all. "What does it mean to have a god . . . or what is God?" And the answer was that "trust and faith of the heart alone makes both God and idol . . . For the two, faith and God, hold close together. Whatever then thy heart clings to . . . and relies upon, that is properly thy god."

Niebuhr, H.R., *Meaning of Revelation*, 17.

AUGUST 2.   GOD: SPEAKING AND BEYOND.

When a Christian says "God" he does not mean that a being exists who is also the beginning of a solar system or of the cosmos, or the great mathematician who figures out a world in which mathematicians can take delight. What one means, what he or she points to with the word "God," is a being infinitely attractive which by its very nature calls forth devotion, joy, and trust. This God is always "my God," "our Good," "our beginning" and "our end." To speak about God otherwise, in the first place at least, would be like speaking about beauty in a picture to which one did not respond with delight, as though color and texture and balance, just as they are in themselves or impersonally considered, were beauty.

Niebuhr, H.R., *Meaning of Revelation*, 18–19.

AUGUST 3.   FAITH IS ACTIVE.

The faith we speak of . . . in the classic book of Christianity, the Bible, speaks, is not intellectual assent to the truth of certain propositions, but a personal, practical trusting in, reliance on, counting upon something. So we have faith in democracy not insofar as we belief that democracy exists, but insofar as we rely upon the democratic idea or spirit to maintain itself and to influence the lives of people continuously. We have faith in the people not insofar as we believe in the existence of such a reality "the people" but insofar as we count upon the character of what we call the people to manifest itself steadfastly in the maintenance of certain values. Faith, in other words, always refers primarily to character and power rather than to existence. Existence is . . . necessarily implied; but there is no direct road from assent to the intellectual proposition that something exists to the act of confidence and reliance upon it. Faith is an active thing, a committing of self to something that is also active, that has power or is power.

Niebuhr, H.R., *Radical Monotheism*, 116–17.

AUGUST 4.   FINAL AND SPECIAL STRIVINGS.

[T]he healthy functioning of the whole body is in a sense a goal that a physician will have in view as he or she pursues the proximate end of improving circulation. The question of the ultimate objective of the whole Church and of the seminaries in the Church does not reduce questions about proximate ends to questions about means, but it poses the problem of the final unifying consideration that modifies all the special strivings.

Niebuhr, H.R., *Purpose of the Church*, 28–29.

As people grow accustomed to the concrete and specific objects which distract them on first sight, they will learn again to regard all things in their relationships.

It is in relationships and in totalities that life's meaning is revealed.

Niebuhr, R., *Leaves from the Notebook*, 59.

The profession that God governs the course of human affairs for good is a judgement which puts together the hazards and fortuitous moments *of life* in the streets . . . and affirms that this whole of experience—incomplete, asymmetrical, and often dissonant—is good.

Niebuhr, R.R., in Primeaux, *Richard R. Niebuhr on Christ*, 197.

AUGUST 5.   GOAL OF CHURCH.

Devotion directed toward Jesus Christ is at least partly directed by him to the One he loves and who loves him, and to the world created and redeemed by the love of God. Nothing less than God—albeit God in the mystery of his being as Father, Son and Holy Spirit—is the object toward

AUGUST 143

which Scripture, Church, and Jesus Christ himself direct those who begin by loving them.

. . . No substitute can be found for the definition of the goal of the church as the increase among people of the love of God and neighbor . . . Any adequate discussion of theme of love of God and neighbor and of its relevance to the Church and school requires all the resources of the theological curriculum from the study of the Scriptures though systematic theology, the philosophy, psychology and history of religions, Christian and social ethics to pastoral theology, Christian education and homiletics.

Niebuhr, H.R., *Purpose of the Church,* **31.**

AUGUST 6.   HIROSHIMA DAY . . . MAN'S TRAGEDY.

In the language of Christianity love of God and neighbor is both "law" and "gospel"; it is both the requirement laid on man and woman by the Determiner of all things and the gift given, albeit in incompleteness, by the self-giving of the Beloved. It is the demand inscribed into infinitely inspiring human nature by the Creator; its perversion in idolatry, hostility and self-centeredness is the heart of [human] tragedy; its reconstruction, redirection and empowerment is redemption from evil. Love of God and neighbour is the gift given through Jesus Christ by the demonstration in incarnation, words, deeds, death and resurrection that God is love— a demonstration we but poorly apprehend yet sufficiently discern to be moved to a faltering response of reciprocal love.

Niebuhr, H.R., *Purpose of the Church,* **32.**

AUGUST 7.   INCOMPLETE POSSIBILITIES.

The purpose of the gospel is not simply that we should believe in the love of God; it is that we should love God and neighbor. We love in incompleteness, not as redeemed but in the time of redemption, not in attainment but in hope. Through Jesus Christ we receive enough faith in God's love toward us to see at least the need for and the possibility of a responsive love on our part. We know enough of the possibility of love to God on our part to long for its perfection; we see enough of the reality of God's love toward us and neighbour to hope for its full revelation and so for our full response . . . What then is love and what do we mean by God and by neighbor when we speak of the ultimate purpose of Church, and so of theological education, as the increase of love of God and neighbor among men and women?

Niebuhr, H.R., *Purpose of the Church*, 33, 34–35.

AUGUST 8.   WHAT THEN IS LOVE?

By love we mean at least these attitudes and actions: rejoicing in the presence of the beloved, gratitude, reverence and loyalty toward him and her. Love is rejoicing over the existence of the beloved one; it is the desire that he or she be rather than not be; it is longing for one's presence when he or she is absent; it is happiness in the thought of him or her; it is profound satisfaction over everything that makes one great and glorious. Love is gratitude: it is thankfulness for the existence of the beloved; it is the happy acceptance over everything that one gives without the jealous feeling that the self ought to be able to do as much; it is gratitude that does not seek equality; it is wonder over the other's gift of him and herself in companionship. Love is reverence: it keeps its distance even as it draws near; it does not seek to absorb the other in the self or want to be absorbed by it; it rejoices in the otherness of the other; it desires the beloved to be what one is and not seek to refashion another into a replica of the self or to make him or her a means to the self's advancement. As reverence love is and seeks knowledge of the other, not by way of curiosity nor for the sake of gaining power but in rejoicing and wonder. In all such love there is an element of that "holy fear" which is not a form of flight but rather deep respect for the otherness of the beloved and the profound unwillingness to violate his or her integrity.

Niebuhr, H.R., *Purpose of the Church*, 35.

AUGUST 9.   LOVE AS LOYALTY.

Love is loyalty; it is the willingness to let the self be destroyed rather than that the other cease to be; it is the commitment of the self by self-binding will to make the other great. It is loyalty, too, to the other's cause—that for the sake of which the nation exists—that there is no love of God where

God's cause is not loved, that which God loves and to which the Holy One has bound . . . in sovereign freedom.

Niebuhr, H.R., *Purpose of the Church*, 35–36.

[Abraham] Heschel was the great interpreter of the Hebrew Prophets, and Pa always emphasized that it was the Prophet's vision of God's transcendent righteousness that gives us a standard and the dynamic for ethical action. So it was no surprise that he and Heschel hit it off from the start: there was so much for them to share and explore together. "Prophecy is a sham unless it is experienced as a word of God swooping down on man and converting him into a prophet," Heschel had once written, and my mother observed, "I think others would agree with me that the word of God indeed swooped down on these two friends." . . . They needed each other.

Sifton, *Serenity Prayer*, 335, 334.

AUGUST 10. GOD.

What, further, do we mean by the word God when we speak of the love of God? Not less than this surely—the Source and Center of all being, the Determiner of destiny, the Universal One—God the Father Almighty, Maker of Heaven and Earth. By God we cannot mean first of all love itself as the relation that binds all things together; the proposition that God is love cannot be converted without loss and error in the statement that love is God. Neither do we mean by God any lovely being easily made the object of our affection. We encounter no demand in ourselves or in our world to love that to which we are naturally attracted. Neither is there any promise and hope in the idea that we shall come to love with rejoicing, gratitude, reverence and loyalty, all that now easily arouses in us the movements of our desire. The movement of our love toward all these things though they go by the name of God or gods, is the way of our idolatry; it is the movement toward the many away from the One, toward the partial instead of the universal, toward the work of our hands rather than toward our Maker. The demand and the promise refer to the One beyond all these.

Niebuhr, H.R., *Purpose of the Church*, 36.

AUGUST 11.   GNAWING PROBLEMS.

The problem of humans is how to love the One on whom he or she is completely, absolutely dependent; who is the Mystery behind the mystery of human existence in the fatefulness of its selfhood of being this person among these people, in this time and all time, in the thus and so-ness of the strange actual world. It is the problem of reconciliation to the One from whom death proceeds as well as life, who makes demands too hard to bear, who sets us in the world where our beloved neighbors are objects of seeming animosity, who appear as God of wrath as well as God of love. It is the problem that arises in its acutest from when life itself becomes a problem, when the goodness of existence is questionable, as it has been for most humans at most times; when the ancient and universal suspicion arises that one is happiest who was never born and the next fortunate who died young.

Niebuhr, H.R., *Purpose of the Church*, 36–37.

AUGUST 12.   RECONCILING LOVE.

Reconciliation to God is reconciliation to life itself; love to the Creator is love of being, rejoicing in existence, in its source, totality and particularity. Love to God is more than that, however, great as this demand and promise are. It is loyalty to the idea of God when the actuality of God is mystery; it is the affirmation of a universe and the devoted will to maintain a universal community at whatever cost to the self. It is the patriotism of the universal community, the kingdom of God, as a commonwealth of justice and love, the reality of which is sure to become evident. There is in such love of God a will-to-believe as the will-to-be-loyal to everything God and his kingdom stand for. Love to God is the conviction that there is faithfulness at the heart of things: unity, reason, form and meaning in the plurality of being. It is the accompanying will to maintain or assert that unity, form and reason despite all appearances. The dark shadow of this love is our combative human loyalty which in its love of gods—principles of religion, empires and civilizations, and all partial things—denies while it seeks to affirm the ultimate loyalty and so involves us in apparently never-ending religious animosities which at the same time unite and divide neighbors, as they forge close bonds of loyalty to each other in a common cause among closed societies disloyal to each other.

Niebuhr, H.R., *Purpose of the Church*, 37.

AUGUST 13. MY NEIGHBOUR/NEIGHBOUR?

Who, finally, is my neighbor, the companion whom I am commanded to love as myself or as I have been loved by my most loyal neighbor, the companion whose love is also promised me as mine is promised him or her? He and she is the near one and the far one; the one beside the road I travel here and now; the one removed from me by distances in time and space; in convictions and loyalties. She is my friend, the one who has shown compassion toward me; and my enemy, who fights against me. He is the one in need, whose hunger, nakedness, imprisonment and illness I see or ought to see the universal suffering servant. She is the oppressed one who has not risen in rebellion against my oppression nor rewarded me according to my deserts as individual or member of a heedlessly exploiting group. He is the compassionate one who ministers to my needs: the stranger who takes me in; the father and mother, sister and brother. In her the image of the universal redeemer is seen as in a glass darkly.

Niebuhr, H.R., *Purpose of the Church*, 38.

AUGUST 14. CHRIST IN MY NEIGHBOR.

Christ is my neighbor, but the Christ in my neighbor is not Jesus; it is rather the eternal son of God incarnate in Jesus, revealed in Jesus Christ. The neighbor is in past and present and future, yet he or she is not simply humankind in its totality but rather in its articulation, the community of individuals and individuals in community. He is Augustine in the Roman Catholic Church and Socrates in Athens, and the Russian people, and the unborn generations who will bear the consequences of our failures, future persons for whom we are administering the entrusted wealth of nature and other greater common gifts. She is a human and he is angel and she is animal and inorganic being, all that participates in being. That we ought to love these neighbours with rejoicing and with reverence, with gratitude and with loyalty is the demand we dimly recognize in our purer moments in science and religion, in art and politics. That we shall love them as we do not now, that is the hope which is too good to be true. That we are loved by them and by God, that is the small faith, less than the mustard seed in size, which since the time of Abraham and of Jesus Christ remains alive, makes hope possible, encourages new desires and arouses people to anticipated attainments of future and possibility.

Niebuhr, H.R., *Purpose of the Church*, 38–39.

AUGUST 15.   WHEN ALL IS SAID AND DONE.

When all is said and done the increase of this love of God and neighbor remains the purpose and the hope of our preaching of the gospel, of all of our church organization and activity, of all our ministry, of all our efforts to train men for the ministry, of Christianity itself.

Niebuhr, H.R., *Purpose of the Church*, 39.

Involvement with photography has led me to realize how effective preaching must have form and drama, as well as highly visual quality . . . We all need education in the arts to help us see and feel the basic forces that shape us and our environment.

Niebuhr, R.R., in Primeaux, *Richard R. Niebuhr on Christ*, 218.

AUGUST 16.   WILL AS TOTAL ORGANIZED SELF.

The ideal of love is first of all a commandment which appeals to the will. What is the human will? It is neither the total personality nor yet the rational element in personality. It is the total organized personality moving against the recalcitrant elements in the self. The will implies a cleavage in the self but not a cleavage, primarily between reason and impulse. The will is a rational organization of impulse. Consequently, the Christian ideal of a living will does not exclude the impulses and emotion in nature through which the self is organically related to other life. Jesus therefore relates the love of God to the natural love of parents for their children: "If ye then, being evil, know how to give good gifts unto your children, how much will your Father which is in heaven give good things to them that ask him?" . . . The moral will is not a force imposed upon the emotions. It utilizes whatever forces of nature carry life beyond itself. But since the forces of nature carry life beyond itself only to enslave it again to the larger self of family, race, and community, Christian ethics never has . . . an uncritical attitude toward impulses of sociality. They all stand under the perspective of the "how much more" and under the criticism, "If yet love those who love you what thanks have ye."

Niebuhr, R., *Interpretation of Christian Ethics*, 210–11.

AUGUST 17.   EQUALITY.

Equality is always the regulative principle of justice; and in the ideal of equality there is an echo of the law of love, "Thou shalt love thy neighbour *as thyself*."

If the question is raised to what degree the neighbor has a right to support his life through privileges and opportunities of the common life, no satisfactory, rational answer can be given to it, short of implying equalitarian principles: He or she has much right as you yourself.

Niebuhr, R., *Interpretation of Christian Ethics,* 108.

AUGUST 18.   QUALIFYING EQUALITY.

This does not mean that any society will ever achieve perfect equality. Equality, being a rational, political version of the law of love, shares with it the quality of transcendence. It ought to be, but never will be fully realized. Social prudence will qualify it. The most equalitarian society will probably not be able to dispense with special rewards as inducements to diligence. Some differentials in privilege will be necessary to make the performance of certain social functions possible. While a rigorous equalitarian society can prevent such privileges from being perpetuated from one generation to another without regard to social function, it cannot eliminate privileges completely. Nor is there any political technique which would be a perfect guarantee against abuses of socially sanctioned privileges. Those who possess power, however social restrained, always have the opportunity of deciding that the function which they perform is entitled to more privilege than any ideal scheme of justice would allow . . . [Equality] remains, nevertheless, a principle of criticism under which every scheme of justice stands and a symbol of the principle of love involved in all moral judgements.

Niebuhr, R., *Interpretation of Christian Ethics,* 108–109.

AUGUST 19.   EXPERIENCES OF FAITH.

The Captain and perfecter of Christian faith remains aloof from the demands of historical science for simple, sharp evidence, hemmed in by the disagreeing crowd of our predecessors and contemporaries, remote and vague in the resulting social and historical confusion. Clarity does not reach us from a source that is itself not clear to perception that has been shaped by a human world of conflict. All the dogmatic labors of a theologian may devote to the definition of Christ, all of the research that a historian may expend in the search for the historical Jesus, by whatever one may devise, will fail to bestow light of the figure of Jesus, until [all] understand what it is our world/age that endows our own experience with resonance to the world of Jesus and that enables us to recognize his conduct and his method of taking hold of the known and paying deference to the unknown as authoritative, augmenting and attractive to us in our enigmatic world.

Therefore, we do not ask: What gives Jesus clarity? We ask: What gives him importance in a radial world? What kind of experience is greater than and surrounds the conflicts of testimonies and interests? What makes believing nevertheless a "natural" relation to this person about whose definition all contend in vain? . . . Where do [people] make a beginning in their own experience of faith in this power-world that they may recognize the new beginning that Christ himself represents and embodies? For the biblical figure of Jesus is insignificant to those who are not subjects of a double perception: a perception of him in this world and of ourselves in our own world of coalescing in some fashion.

Niebuhr, R.R., "The Widened Heart," 132.

AUGUST 20. BUILDING LOVE VIA JUSTICE.

[I]t is true that beyond and above every human relation as ordered by a fixed structure of justice, by custom, tradition and legal enactment, there remain indeterminate possibilities of love in the individual and personal encounters of those who are in the structure. Whether persons meet their brothers and sisters with generosity or with envy, with imagination or with ambitions of dominion, is a question which cannot be fully solved by the structure of justice which binds them to their companions. Human actions can, to a degree, corrupt even the highest structure and they can also partially redeem the worst structure. The fact that slavery was essentially wrong proves the invalidity of regarding structures of justice as irrelevant to love. Yet it did make a difference to a slave whether he or she was subject to a kind or to a cruel master. The institution was wrong because the disproportions of power in the institution of slavery were such that they could predispose even decent people to unconscious cruelties. But the most adequate institution is still only a bare base upon which the higher experiences of love must be built.

Niebuhr, R., Reinhold Niebuhr: Major Works, 842–43.

AUGUST 21. LOVE COMMAND NECESSARY, BUT INSUFFICIENT?

The commandment to love the neighbor as the self must finally culminate in the individual experience in which one self seeks to penetrate deeply into the mystery of the other self and yet stand in reverence before a mystery which he has no right to penetrate. This kind of love is a matter of law in the sense that the essential nature of persons, with his and her indeterminate freedom, requires that human relations should finally achieve such an intimacy. But it is also a matter of grace because no sense of obligation can provide the imagination and forbearance by which this is accomplished. Such intimacy is of course related to sacrificial love, for the intermingling of life with life predisposes to sacrificial abandonment of the claims of the self for the needs of the other.

Niebuhr, R., Reinhold Niebuhr: Major Works, 843.

AUGUST 22. INSEPARABLE LOVES.

In both law and gospel the love of God and the love of neighbor are inseparably related. Historically they are associated in Judaism and Christianity in the two tables of the Ten Commandments, in the double summary of the law offered by Jesus, in apostolic preaching, in the theology and ethic of Catholic and Protestant churches . . . God does not exist as God-for-us or become known or loved as God except in his and our relation to the neighbor . . . The interrelation of self, companion and God are so intricate that no member of this triad exists in his or her true nature without the others, or can be known or loved without the others.

Niebuhr, H.R., Responsibility of the Church, 94.

AUGUST 23. AFFECTIVE FAITH.

However else we interpret faith, we must make room in our minds for its affectionate character. Affective faith is an awakening, a suffering of a whole frame of mind that endows the individual with a resonance that lies at the foundation of his existence. It qualifies all his interactions with other men, with himself, and with his near and ultimate environment.

Niebuhr, R.R., *Experiential Religion,* 46–47.

AUGUST 24.   OUR FINAL SECURITY.

O God, who has taught us to pray for the coming of your kingdom on this earth, give us grace to build our communities after the fashion of your kingdom, to set no boundaries around them which you would not set, to quiet the tumult within them by brotherly and sisterly love and to work the more diligently for the better concord in them, because our final security lies in the city which has foundations, whose builder and maker is God.

Niebuhr, R., *Justice and Mercy,* 49.

AUGUST 25.   PAINFUL TENSION.

The individual is not discrete. He or she cannot find their fulfillment outside of the community; but they cannot also find fulfillment completely within society. In so far as he finds fulfillment within society she must abate . . . individual ambitions. One must "die to self" if he and she would truly live. In so far as one finds fulfillment beyond every historic community he or she lives in painful tension with even the best community, sometimes achieving standards of conduct which defy the standards of the community with a resolute "we must obey God rather than mortals." Sometimes one is involved vicariously in the guilt of the community when he or she would fain live a life of innocency . . . There are no simple congruities in life or history. The cult of happiness erroneously assumes them.

Niebuhr, R., *Irony of American History,* 62.

AUGUST 26.   WISDOM AND SERENITY.

. . . It is possible to soften the incongruities of life endlessly by the scientific conquest of nature's caprices, and the social and political triumph over historic injustice. But all such strategies cannot finally overcome the fragmentary character of human existence. The final wisdom of life

AUGUST

requires, not the annulment of incongruity, but the achievement of serenity within and above it.

Niebuhr, R., Irony of American History, 62–63.

AUGUST 27.   GRACE OF RESPONSIBILITY.

Grant us, Our Father, the grace of honest and true self-knowledge that we may not think of ourselves as more highly than we ought and the grace of responsibility for our neighbor wherever he may be this wide world.

Now may grace, mercy and peace of Our Father/Abba and our Lord be with us now and forever more.

Niebuhr, R., "Chapel Talk on Romans 13:8," Audio Tape 26.

AUGUST 28.   ANTIPHONAL MOVEMENT.

The human situation makes it natural for us to go out from ourselves: "For whosoever seeketh to gain his or her life will lose it, but whoso loseth their life will find it." That is the basic law of human existence, and the one impulse in life. The other impulse is always to draw all life into ourselves. While there are relativities of good and evil, we all have a sense of universal law, and we know that a consistent self-regard is evil and that a consistent self-forgetfulness is good. For life is not made up of consistent self-regard and consistent self-forgetfulness. Rather, there is the antiphonal movement, the dialectic between going out from oneself and returning to oneself. When we examine our lives, on any level, we find our consciences accusing or else excusing us.

Niebuhr, R., Justice and Mercy, 40.

AUGUST 29.   ACCUSING/EXCUSING OURSELVES.

There is an interesting ambiguity in the words ambition and ambitious. Sometimes when we praise a being we say he or she is very ambitious. Sometimes when we condemn them we say they are very ambitious. Is being ambitious a virtue or a vice? Probably it is both, because ambition contains the urge to be excellent in your field or discipline. It also contains the urge to get head of other people! Academics, and probably also clergy, are apt to be critical of politicians who are obviously ambitious.

We are all ambitious, and we are all jealous of somebody else who has a greater eminence. The politician happens to display his or her ambition more publicly than anybody else. Always, it comes back to accusing or excusing ourselves.

Niebuhr, R., *Justice and Mercy*, 41.

AUGUST 30.   BY GRACE.

There is a healthy, but not cynical, realism about our selfishness. Martin Luther said—and this is frequently misunderstood—"Sin bravely, if also you have great faith." This means, don't be so morbid about the fact that you're selfish; don't deny that you are self-regarding, but work in life and hope that by grace—this perhaps is the door to the real answer—you will be redeemed. By grace.

Niebuhr, R., *Justice and Mercy*, 43.

AUGUST 31.   INTERNATIONAL OVERDOSE AWARENESS DAY.

Today even Christians do not emphasize common grace enough. We do not become unselfish by saying so. But, thank God, there are forces in life and in history that draw us out of ourselves and make us truly ourselves. This is grace: common grace, prevenient grace. Grace is every impulse or power which operates against the pull of my self-regard, and makes me truly a self by helping me to forget myself. This is the basic answer of the Christian faith.

Niebuhr, R., *Justice and Mercy*, 43.

Eternal God, creator and redeemer of men and women . . . Have mercy upon distressed persons, upon those who are imprisoned or afflicted in mind, body, or estate. Have compassion upon the dying and upon those who stand in the fear of death, that they may know, whether they live or die, they are with you.

Niebuhr, R., *Justice and Mercy*, 118.
cf. Lydia Niebuhr (front matter quotation).

SEPTEMBER
Gospel Music Heritage Month

A poem in [Wystan Auden's book] Nones, "Music is International," delivered as the Phi Beta Kappa poem at the Columbia University commencement in 1947, contains the passage; "Deserving nothing, the sensible soul/ Will rejoice at the sudden mansion/ Of any joy: besides there is a chance/ We may some day need very much to/ Remember when we were happy."

Sifton, *Serenity Prayer,* 319.

The only Kingdom which can defy and conquer the world is one which is not of this world . . . In every moment of existence those "who are of the truth" hear the Christ's voice, warning, admonishing and guiding them in their actions.

Niebuhr, R., *Beyond Tragedy,* 284.

SEPTEMBER 1.   HALLOWING ALL RELATIONS.

Grant us, our Father, grace to work while it is day, for the night comes when no one can work. Let our work be done this day with sense of our responsibility in our several callings. Save us from sloth and waywardness. Keep us humble in your sight and before our brothers and sisters, so that neither pride nor indifference may destroy the bond which we have with our co-workers. May our love of you hallow all our relations, and our service to our brothers and sisters complete our reverent obedience.

Niebuhr, R., Reinhold Niebuhr: Major Works, 698.

SEPTEMBER 2.   MAKING TOLERABLE.

Perhaps we should draw the conclusion that our common life, particularly among the nations is made tolerable by the knowledge of all this. We are sufferable only when somebody has the power and the courage to stand against us. The history of Western democracy and the pageant of its development rest upon this insight about common grace. An English historian once said: "Modern democracy rests upon the insight that what I think to be just is tainted by my own self-interest. I have just enough residual virtue to know that it is tainted, and that someone has to stand again me, and declare his different conviction."

Niebuhr, R., Justice and Mercy, 44.

SEPTEMBER 3.   DYNAMICALLY BALANCING.

All our justice rests upon, on the one hand, a political elaboration of our mutualities, and on the other hand, upon elaboration of delicate balances of power that represent us from being as self-regarding as we might be.

Niebuhr, R., Justice and Mercy, 44.

SEPTEMBER 4.   *AS* WE FORGIVE.

We should try to be as rigorous in judging ourselves as we are in the judging of others, which we never are, of course . . . St. Paul puts the whole of human life in the context of a great drama of divine forgiveness. "And be kind to one another, forgiving one another as God in Christ forgave you." We must move from the nicely calculated less or more of how good or how selfish we are, to the recognition instead that we all stand in the need of forgiveness. "Forgive us our sins our trespasses or debts, sins of commission or omission; as we forgive those who sin against us." The important word is *as*—we forgive.

Niebuhr, R., *Justice and Mercy*, 44.

SEPTEMBER 5. CONSTANT ULTIMATE RECONCILIATION.

Forgiving one another does not mean a condescending forgiveness of the virtuous person for the unvirtuous person. It means that no one can forgive who does not know that he or she is tainted with the same self-regard as the person he is forgiving. How could our family life exist without this? Family life begins with the impulse of nature, two people meeting each other, falling in love with each other. But as they live together, something more grows up which is a of matter of the spirit, ultimately what the New Testament calls reconciliation, mutual forgiveness, mutual forbearance. Sometimes this can be done with a little sense of humor rather than some obvious form of reconciliation. But constant reconciliation goes on in the sense that we know we hurt each other even when we try not to, or that we hurt our children or that they hurt us, and yet we continue bearing and forbearing with each other with, we hope, more understanding. Thank God for the ultimate redemption where there is forgiveness of sin.

Niebuhr, R., *Justice and Mercy*, 45.

SEPTEMBER 6. MERCIES/FORGIVENESS.

[Eternal God] of all mercies, teach us to be merciful, as you are merciful. [Abba] of all forgiveness, help us to forgive others as you have forgiven us.

Grant, O Lord, to the living, grace; to the church and to all [humankind], peace and concord; to us and all your servants, life everlasting.

Niebuhr, R., *Justice and Mercy*, 45.

SEPTEMBER 7.   LABOUR DAY (IF 1ST MONDAY OF MONTH).

Mother and I visited at the home of ____today where the husband is sick and was out of employment before he became sick. The folks have few connections in the city. They belong to no church. What a miserable existence it is to be friendless in a large city. And to be dependent upon a heartless industry. The man is about 55 or 57 I should judge, and he is going to have a desperate time securing employment after he gets well. These modern factories are not meant for old people. They want young men or women, and they use them up pretty quickly. Your modern worker, with no skill but what is in the machine, is a sorry individual. After he or she loses the stamina of youth, they have nothing to sell. I promised 1 would try to find him a job. I did it to relieve the despair of that family, but I will have a hard time making good on my promise. According to the ethics of our modern industrialism persons over fifty, without special training, are so much junk. It is a pleasure to see how such an ethic is qualified as soon as the industrial unit is smaller and the owner has a personal interest in his or her people. I could mention quite a few such instances. But unfortunately the units are getting larger and larger and more inhuman. I think I had better get in contact with more of these victims of our modern industrialism and not leave that end of our work to mother [Lydia] alone. A little such personal experience will help much to save you from sentimentality.

Niebuhr, R. *Leaves from the Notebook*, 149.

The domination of one life by another is avoided most successfully by equilibrium of powers and vitalities so that weakness does not invite enslavement by the strong . . . But an equilibrium of power is not brotherhood, or sisterhood. The restraint of the will-to-power of one member of the community by the counter-pressure of power by another member results in a condition of tension. All tension is covert or potential conflict. The principle of equilibrium of power is thus a principle of justice in so far as it prevents domination and enslavement.

Niebuhr, R., *Nature and Destiny of Man* (Vol. II), 266.

SEPTEMBER 8.   PARDON DAY.

"O God, you have bound us together in this life. Give us grace to understand how our lives depend on the courage, the industry, the honesty, and the integrity of all who labor.

May we be mindful of their needs, grateful for their faithfulness, and faithful in our responsibilities to them; through Jesus Christ our Lord. Amen."

May we remember too, Lord, that all our work and labor is in vain if we do not do it for your glory.

Niebuhr, R., in https://www.facebook.com/PotwinChurch/
posts/a-prayer-from-reinhold-niebuhr-on-this-labor-dayo-god-
you-have-bound-us-together/439638499408109/
[accessed September 7, 2020 (Labour Day)].

SEPTEMBER 9.   FAITH, JUDGMENT, GRACE'S MERCY.

Grant us grace to apprehend by faith the power and wisdom which lie beyond our understanding; and in worship to feel that which we do not know, and to praise even what we do not understand; so that in the presence of your glory we may be humble, and the knowledge of your judgment we may repent; and so in the assurance of your mercy, we may rejoice and be glad.

Niebuhr, R., *Justice and Mercy*, 37.

SEPTEMBER 10.   A CURIOUS PARADOX.

[Albert Camus] just lost his life in an automobile accident . . . [He was] described in many of the obituary notices as a leading French existentialist. But he himself denied he was an existentialist . . . he was partly a Christian believer and partly an agnostic. He was an agnostic because he said, "I think death is absurd." There is irony in the fact that he died in the most absurd way in an automobile accident driven by his friend at ninety miles an hour. But why should anybody, an intelligent man, or anyone, say that death is so absurd? For it is one of the things that belongs to our existence. "As dying, and behold, we live," says St. Paul. There must be a quality of life that takes in the curious paradox of life that man has such dignity and is yet so miserable in his anxiety about death and, further-more, knows that he ought not to be. Christian faith is no sentimental thing. It is a faith that takes all the dimensions of life into consideration, including in Pascal's phrase, "not only the dignity of man and woman, but the misery of [all]." Such a faith affirms that despite all these paradoxes, paths of meaninglessness, and tragedies, a person can, in the words of John Adam, "rejoice in God and in his creation."

Niebuhr, R., *Justice and Mercy*, 34.

SEPTEMBER 11. 9/11 ATTACKS/TRAGEDY (USA, 2001)/ASSASSINATION OF S. ALLENDE (CHILE, 1973).

The 9/11 attacks had created an appalling symbol over New York that served to keep the shock of the atrocity alive and vivid. Its twin towers fallen, the World Trade Centre burned for days on end, throwing a pil-lar of smoke high above Manhattan into the radiant, late summer sky. If you commuted into the city you saw it every morning. For any Jew or Christian with a biblical imagination, the sight might make a demonic inversion of the story in Exodus, in which God appears by day as a pillar of smoke, leading the Israelites into freedom. But the smoke hanging over New York Harbor rose from the fires of cremation. People built shrines to the dead in the train stations, an inherently religious act whether or not they recognized it as such. Flyers with photographs of missing family members were taped to the walls . . . Many of the pictures showed happy moments, a man or woman enrobed at graduation, dancing at a wedding, or holding a toddler aloft. Commuters would break stride and stop. Some left bouquets. Others scrawled messages, promising never to forget . . . another force was at work amid the horror—a constructive force, alive in the grass roots, defined by neighborliness and an active commitment to the preservation of peace and the safety and rights of vulnerable people.

Niebuhr, G. [Jr.], *Beyond Tolerance*, 4–5.

SEPTEMBER 12. BEYOND TRAGEDY.

The Christian view of history passes through the sense of the tragic to a hope and an assurance which is "beyond tragedy." The cross, which stands at the centre of the Christian world-view, reveals both the seriousness of human sin and the purpose and power of God to overcome it. It reveals man or woman violating the will of God in their highest moral and spiritual achievements [in Roman law and Jewish religion] and God absorbing this evil into God's self in the very moment of its most vivid expression. Christianity's view of history is tragic insofar as it recognizes evil as an inevitable concomitant of even the highest spiritual enterprises. It is beyond tragedy insofar as it does not regard evil as inherent in existence itself but as finally under the dominion of a good God.

Niebuhr, R., *Beyond Tragedy*, x–xi.

SEPTEMBER 13. GRANDPARENTS DAY.

I come from a family that has, among its traditions, a tendency to take religion seriously, by which I mean it has been a part of our daily lives—not as a narrow, personal piety [that is not a part of our tradition], but instead as a way of understanding society and our relationship and responsibilities to it. I trace the family tradition back four generations, to my great grandfather after whom I'm named. An immigrant, he ran away from his German home as a teenager and made his way to the American Midwest, where he quickly found work as a farmhand. I have always admired his daring in making that move, but I have since found far more in him to appreciate than that. Gustav underwent a conversion experience not long after he arrived in the United States, went to seminary and eventually emerged as a leading figure in the old German Evangelical Synod of North America. He worked for reconciliation and cooperation between Reformed Protestants [his branch] and Lutherans. To outsiders, the differences between such groups may seem obscure, even baffling. But they were real and remain so. The question is, how far apart should they keep people? My great grandfather passed on his perspective to two of his sons. My grandfather, H. Richard Niebuhr, a theologian at Yale, worked successfully to unite denominations. His older brother, my great-uncle, Reinhold Niebuhr, taught at Union Theological Seminary in New York and took the bold step in the 1930s in demanding that Christians cease targeting Jews for conversion. Both men were committed Christians. But they had no use for legalistic literalism, for aggressive fundamentalism or its treacherous near-cousin, political militancy. As Reinhold Niebuhr would write, "Absolutism, in both religious and political idealism, is a splendid incentive to heroic action, but a dangerous guide in immediate and concrete situations . . . The fanaticism which in the individual may appear in the guise of a harmless or pathetic vagary, when expressed in political policy, shuts the gates of mercy on humankind."

Niebuhr, G. [Jr.], *Beyond Tolerance,* x–xi.

SEPTEMBER 14. NEEDING EACH OTHER.

While the vertical dimension of human striving, classically expressed in the religious yearning for perfection, adds depth and richness to communal life, a consistent vertical impulse must destroy community. For persons make life tolerable for each other in community only as they recognize the persistence and inevitability of the fragmentary character of their life. They need each other precisely because they are not whole without the other. Thus men and women need each other and can only be fulfilled in each other.

Niebuhr, R., *Pious and Secular America,* 114.

SEPTEMBER 15. INTERNATIONAL DAY OF DEMOCRACY.

. . . [C]apricious disproportions of power generate various forms of domination and enslavement. Human society requires a conscious control and manipulation of the various equilibria which exist within it. There must be an organizing center within a given field of social vitalities. This center must arbitrate conflicts from a more partial perspective than is available from any party to a given conflict; it must manage and manipulate the processes of mutual support so that the tensions inherent in them will not erupt into conflict; it must coerce submission to the social process by superior power whenever the instruments of arbitrating and composing conflict do not suffice, and finally it must seek to redress the disproportions of power by conscious shifts of the balances whenever they make for injustice.

Niebuhr, R., *Nature and Destiny of Man* (Vol. II), 266.

SEPTEMBER 16.   CHECK-AND-BALANCE NECESSITY.
CHILDREN OF DARKNESS

Humans' capacity for justice makes democracy possible; but our inclination to injustice makes democracy necessary . . . The preservation of a democratic civilization requires the wisdom of the serpent and the harmlessness of the dove. The children of light must be armed with the wisdom of the children of darkness but remain free from their malice. They must know the power of self-interest in human society without giving it moral justification. They must have this wisdom in order that they may beguile, deflect, harness and restrain self-interest, individual and collective, for the sake of the community.

Niebuhr, R., *Children of Light,* xiii, 40–41.

SEPTEMBER 17.   INTENSIVE AND EXTENSIVE CONFESSIONS.

We confess that we are not worthy of the riches of life for which generations of men have labored that we might enter into this heritage. We confess the sorry confusion of our common life, the greed which disfigures our collective life and sets a person against his or her brothers and sisters. We confess the indifference and callousness with which we treat the sufferings and the insecurity of the poor, and the pettiness which mars the relations between us. May we with contrite hearts seek once more to purify our spirits, and to clarify our reason so that a fairer temple for the human spirit may be built in human society.

Niebuhr, R., *Reinhold Niebuhr: Major Works,* 701.

SEPTEMBER 18.   HEALING OF DIVISIONS.

We pray O Lord for your church, that it may be healed of its divisions by your grace; that it may teach your word with courage to a sinful world, and may mediate with true charity your love and mercy to all people. Strengthen every ministry of reconciliation therein with your spirit. Grant that it may be a true community of grace in which the pride of race or nation is humbled, where the strong and the mighty are brought to judgement, and the meek and lowly are lifted up. Make it more faithful to its Lord, and more instant to meet the needs of people.

Niebuhr, R., *Reinhold Niebuhr: Major Works,* 701.

SEPTEMBER 19.   INCLUSIVITY OF LOVE.

It was the demand to holiness which Jesus translated and interpreted . . . by interpreting the perfection in which one is called upon to imitate God as inclusive love . . . The words Jesus probably used, were: "Let your love therefore be inclusive as God's love includes all." While this reconstruction is speculative it is not idle speculation because the words fit into the context of the Sermon on the Mount, particularly those passages in which parochial loyalties are criticized from the standpoint of more universal loyalty, as for instance in the admonition "love your enemies" and in the question: "If ye [merely] love those which love you what thanks have you?"

Niebuhr, R., *Pious and Secular America*, 117–18.

SEPTEMBER 20.   THROUGH MY DEPRESSIONS.

I must confess my ironic embarrassment as I lived through my depressions, which had the uniform characteristic of an anxious preoccupation with real or imagined future perils. The embarrassment particularly was occasioned by the incessant correspondence about a prayer I had composed years before, which the old Federal Council of Churches had used and was later printed on small cards to give to soldiers. The prayer read: "God grant us the grace to accept with serenity the things we cannot change; the courage to change the things that should be changed; and the wisdom to distinguish the one from the other."

Niebuhr, R., "View from the Sidelines," 251.

SEPTEMBER 21.   CONTENT WITH . . . MINIMAL CONSOLATION/INTERNATIONAL DAY OF PEACE.

Many friendly and inquiring correspondents asked for the original inspiration of the [serenity] prayer, whether I was really its author, or whether it had been St. Francis of Assisi or even an admiral who had used it in shipboard services. I received about two such letters a week and every answer to an inquiring correspondent embarrassed me because I knew that my present state of anxiety defied the petitions of this payer. I confessed my embarrassment to our family physician who had a sense of humor touched with gentle cynicism. "Don't worry," he said, "Doctors and preachers are not expected to practice what they preach." I had to be content with this minimal consolation.

Niebuhr, R., "View from the Sidelines," 251–52.

SEPTEMBER 22. BEYOND CLEVERNESS IN PRAYER.

[P]rincipled, rock-solid understanding of faith, hope, and charity, even in the darkest night of despair is not, I fear, what a simple enjoyment of the Serenity Prayer's superficial charm can aspire to. All too often, the Serenity Prayer has been construed as a way to say something clever about a life's difficulties, rather than a true petition for grace and wisdom in an impossible world, though I think most AA members understand it rightly. Perhaps it's that for many people praying is a kind of reassuring, pleasant activity which in itself they find soothing. The contrition and renunciation that one must experience to arrive at real hope or reassurance aren't part of the scheme.

Sifton, *Serenity Prayer,* 342.

SEPTEMBER 23. PERSEVERANCE.

We must persevere under all trials. We shall probably never have enough courage to change what must be changed. The grace to accept with serenity that which cannot be changed will not easily come to us. And the wisdom to discern the one from the other takes more than our lifetime to acquire.

Sifton, *Serenity Prayer,* 349.

SEPTEMBER 24. FOR WHOM THE SERENITY PRAYER?

In an inanely amoral, frivolous, and profit-driven world, we are urged to fill ourselves with pride and self-esteem and to armor ourselves with pretensions. We may lose the ability to hear such a [serenity] prayer. Solemn rebuke from self-important priests would have them fall appropriately on deaf ears. But the prayer is not grim, and it came from a free heart, from someone who trusted that the joyful life of attentive, listening, awe-filled, loving people must go on. The Serenity Prayer was meant for them.

Sifton, *Serenity Prayer*, 347–48.

SEPTEMBER 25. HEART-SPRUNG GAIETY/TO THE END OF LIFE.

Buoyant, even hilarious high spirits marked the public and private behavior of my father's friends and associates, and you knew their gaiety sprang from serious, dedicated hearts. They worked so hard. They were so very loving. And their labors were informed, in the end, by the humble recognition that it is not within our human powers to understand their final tally.

Sifton, *Serenity Prayer*, 348.

When my father died, he was buried in Stockbridge, which is famous in American history as the town where the great Jonathan Edwards . . . preached to a tiny congregation of frontier people and Indians. Edwards took the themes of the moral world as his central subject. The stringent clarity, the passionate ascetic power of America's first and in many ways greatest theologian shines as clearly today as it did when he wrote about this eternal work of the present tense: "Gracious and holy affections have their exercise and fruit in Christian practice. I mean, they have that influence and power upon him who is the subject of 'em that they cause that [it] should be the practice and business of his life. This implies . . . that he persists in it to the end of life, so that it may be said not only to be his business at certain seasons, the business of Sabbath days, or certain extraordinary times, or the business of a month, or a year, or of even seven years, or . . . under certain circumstances, but the business of his life . . . which he perseveres in through all changes, and under all trials, as long as he lives. The necessity [of this] in all true Christians is most clearly and fully taught in the Word of God."

Sifton, *Serenity Prayer*, 348–49.

SEPTEMBER 26. AMERICAN FAMILY DAY.

Eternal God, who has set the solitary in families and ordained that a man shall leave his father and his mother and cleave unto his wife, and they shall be one flesh; under your providence these your children have found, and learned to love and cherish each other. Grant your children grace, that the solemn vows said this day may surely be performed by everything that knits their lives together, by shared tasks and common interests, by sharing each other's joys and sorrows and by bearing common responsibilities and cares.

May their emotions of love, springing from their hearts, nourish the will to integrity, which is more constant than any emotion and is both the crown and servant of love. O God, who has made us coworkers with you and introduced us to the awesome mystery of creation, bless this union with children; and grant their parents wisdom, imagination, and patience to nurture new life in all goodness and godliness and every grace of life.

Our Father, who knows the weakness of our nature, give these your children, the spirit of gratitude for each other's virtues and good intentions, and forbearance of each other's frailties and foibles, that the years may continue to strengthen their union, and time may add to its glory and its grace.

Niebuhr, R., *Justice and Mercy*, 127.

Vom Vater hab ich Statur,
des Lebens ernste Fuebrung;
Von Mutter hab ich die Frob-Natur
die Lust zum Fabulieren
My father gave my stature tall,
And rule of life decorous;
My mother my nature genial
And joy in making stories;
"This fits RN to a T."

Samuel Press citing Goethe and applying to Reinhold Niebuhr, in Chrystal, "Man of the Hour and the Time," 416 note 3. (For actual poem and its translation, see Chrystal, *Young Reinhold Niebuhr*, 23 and note 12 for further source.)

SEPTEMBER 27. THE PATRIARCH WEIGHS IN.

True faith . . . rests not alone in the revealed Word . . . But also upon the most intimate self-revelation which one can only describe with the all-inclusive word, grace . . . Faith is in the last analysis a personal certainty which not only says, "The Lord has said," but which prides itself on personal fellowship with the Lord and joyfully cries out to the doubter: "We see his glory—we speak of that which we know and bear witness to that which we have seen.

Niebuhr, G. [Sr.], in Chrystal, *A Father's Mantle*, 115.

Word and deed—that is what finally counts. Where a joyous and definite confession of faith in the Savior and works of self-sacrificing love as a follower of Jesus are lacking there no longer exists any right to church consciousness. We are truly evangelical so long as we hear the voice of the Good Shepherd and walk in his footsteps.

Niebuhr, G. [Sr.], in Chrystal, *A Father's Mantle*, 118.

SEPTEMBER 28. A CENTER TO HOLD?

[A human being] is indeed like a cork that is drawn down the river of time, carried away as with a flood. But one could not be altogether that, because he or she knows about it; [we] speculate about it as the Psalmist (90) does, and about the significance of it. [We] stand outside of the river of time, so that [we] can anticipate our depth either with hope or with melancholy. Also, [we] can create. [We are] not the only creatures because [we are] not quite in the river of time, although [we] might forget how much of a creature [we are] when we begin to create . . . This drama of human history is indeed partly our construct, but it stands under a sovereignty much greater than ours. "A thousand years are in thy sight but as yesterday when it is past, and as a watch in the night" [citing Ps. 90:2].

Niebuhr, R., *Justice and Mercy*, 52–53.

SEPTEMBER 29. DELIBERATIONS ON JUSTICE-MAKING AND -KEEPING.

Humans transcend the social and historical process sufficiently to make it possible and necessary to deliberately to contrive common ends of life, particularly the end of justice. We cannot count on inadvertence and the coincidence of private desires alone to achieve common ends. On the other hand, [man or woman] is too immersed in the welter of interest and passion in history and their survey over the total process is too short-range and limited to justify the endowment of any group or institution of "planners" with compete power. The "purity" of their idealism and the pretensions of their science must always be suspect. One simply does not have a "pure" reason in human affairs; and if such reason as [he or she] has is given complete power to attain its ends, the taint will become the more noxious. The controversy between those who would "plan" justice and order and those who trust in freedom to establish both is, therefore, an irresolvable one. Every healthy society will live in the tension of that controversy until the end of history; and will prove its health by preventing either side from gaining complete victory.

Niebuhr, R., *Irony of American History*, 107–08.

The inclination "to give each [person] his [and her] due " is one of the ends of discipling the exercise of power. But a sense of humility which recognizes that nations are even more incapable than individuals of fully understanding the rights and claims of others may be an even more important element in such a discipline. A too confident sense of justice always leads to injustice. In so far as people and nations are "judges in their case" they are bound to betray the human weakness of having a livelier sense of their own interest than of the competing interest. That is why "just" persons and nations may easily become involved in ironic refutations of their moral pretensions . . . Genuine community is established only when the knowledge that we need one another is supplemented by the recognition that "the other," that other form of life, or that other unique community is the limit beyond which our ambitions must not run and the boundary beyond which our life must not expand.

Niebuhr, R., *Irony of American History*, 138–39.

SEPTEMBER 30. DIMENSION OF DEPTH/ORANGE SHIRT DAY (CANADA).

[Orange Shirt Day is to honour and remember Indigenous children who attended residential schools [in Canada].

While common sense maintains the idea of moral responsibility for human actions and attaches moral guilt to anti-social actions, a high religion goes beyond common sense in that it excludes no action, not even the best, from the feeling of guilt. This result is due to the fact that religion sees all reality including human personality, in such a dimension of depth, that some transcendent possibility always stands above every actuality, as a vantage-point from which actual achievements are found wanting. Thus the ideal of perfect love gives a perspective upon every action which prompts the confession, "Are we not all unprofitable servants?"

Niebuhr, R., *Interpretation of Christian Ethics*, 79.

OCTOBER

National Bullying Prevention Month,
and Action

No democratic society can afford to capitulate to the pride of dominant groups. The final end of such appeasement is the primitivistic homogeneity of Nazism. On the other hand it is foolish to disregard race pride as a mere vestige of barbarism when it is in fact a perpetual source of conflict in human life.

A democratic society must use every stratagem of education and every resource of religion to generate appreciation of the virtues and good intentions of minority groups, which diverge from the type of the majority, and to prompt humility and charity in the life of the majority. It must seek to establish contacts between the groups and prevent the aggravation of prejudice through segregation. It must uncover the peculiar hazards to right judgment which reveal themselves in inter-group relations . . .

. . . It would be more helpful if we began with the truer assumption that there is no unprejudiced mind and no judgment which is not, at least partially, corrupted by pride . . .

. . . Our knowledge that there is no complete solution for the problem would save us from resting in some proximate solution under the illusion that it is an ultimate one.

Niebuhr, R., *Children of Light*, 143–45.

OCTOBER 1. NO COMPLACENT REST.

A business person is forced to earn his or her livelihood within terms of an economic system in which perfect honesty would probably lead to self-destruction. According to the sensitivity of his [or her] spirit one will find some compromise between his or her immoral actions to which one is tempted by the necessities of the social system in which he or she operates and the ideal possibilities which one's conscience projects. But there is no compromise at which one can rest complacently. Even though the highest moral possibility transcends the limits of one's imperfect freedom, there is always an immediately higher possibility which he or she might take. A general sense of religious guilt is therefore a fruitful source of a sense of moral responsibility immediate situations . . . The human, as the creature of both necessity and freedom, must, like Moses, always perish outside the promised land. One can see what he or she cannot reach.

Niebuhr, R., *Interpretation of Christian Ethics* **(1956), 76.**

OCTOBER 2. INTERNATIONAL DAY OF NON-VIOLENCE.

The most basic and fruitful conception flowing from the ancient myth [of the Fall] is the idea that evil lies at the juncture of nature and spirit. Evil is conceived as not simply the consequence of temporality or the fruit of nature's necessities. Sin can be understood neither in terms of human reason alone, nor yet in terms of the circumscribed harmonies in which the human body is bound. Sin lies at the junction of spirit and nature, in the sense that the peculiar and the unique characteristics of human personality, in both its good and evil tendencies, can be understood only by analyzing the paradoxical relation of freedom and necessity, of finiteness and the yearning for the eternal in human life.

Niebuhr, R., *Interpretation of Christian Ethics* **(1956), 74–75.**

There is no problem of political life to which religious imagination can make a larger contribution than [the] problem of developing non-violent resistance. The discovery of elements of common frailty in the foes and, concomitantly, the appreciation of all human life as possessing transcendent worth, creates attitudes which transcend social conflict and thus mitigate its cruelties.

Niebuhr, R., *Moral Man and Immoral Society,* **254–55.**

OCTOBER 3.   PESSIMISTIC CONCLUSIONS?

The Christian analysis of life leads to conclusions which will seem morbidly pessimistic to moderns, still steeped as they are in their evolutionary optimism. The conclusion most abhorrent to the modern mood is that the possibilities of evil grow with the possibilities of good, and that human history is therefore not so much a chronicle of the progressive victory of the good over evil, of cosmos over chaos, as the story of an ever increasing cosmos, creating ever increasing possibilities of chaos.

Niebuhr, R., *Interpretation of Christian Ethics (1956)*, 92.

OCTOBER 4.   NECESSITY OF PROPHETIC CHRISTIANITY.

Since the vertical dimension in human life, revealing the ultimate possibilities of good and the depth of evil in it, is a reality which naïve philosophies may obscure but cannot destroy, it will be necessary for our generation to return to the faith of prophetic Christianity to solve its problems. At the same time, it will be necessary for prophetic Christianity, with a stronger emphasis upon its prophetic and a lesser emphasis upon its nationalistic inheritance, to develop a more adequate social ethic within terms of its understanding of the total human situation. The approach of the historic Christian Church to the moral issues of life has been less helpful than it might have been, partly because a literal interpretation of its mythical basis destroyed the genius of prophetic religion, and partly because Christianity, in the effort to rationalize its myths ran upon the rocks either of the Scylla of a too optimistic pantheism or the Charybdis of a too pessimistic and otherworldly dualism.

Niebuhr, R., *Interpretation of Christian Ethics (1956)*, 93.

OCTOBER 5.   LAW OF OUR EXISTENCE.

The structure of human nature is such that one can not complete him or herself within oneself. Love and brotherhood or sisterhood are the law of their existence. Furthermore, there are no natural limits of brotherhood and sisterhood. The law of love is universal. There are indeterminate possibilities of realizing a wider brotherhood and sisterhood in history. But the natural limits are never completely transcended. One is never quite universal man or woman in history; but black human and white human,

European and Asiatic, American and Russian. Furthermore each kind of person introduces the corruption of sin into this finiteness by claiming for his [or her] partial and peculiar [human]hood more ultimate significance than it possesses. If the transcendent reality of brotherhood [and sisterhood] is not emphasized the partial and corrupted definitions of selfhood, as we have them in history, can become perversely normative as they did in Nazism. The liberal democratic world saved itself from this perversity by the hope of a complete historical realization of universal being. Future ages are bound to invalidate this hope.

Niebuhr, R., *Discerning the Signs*, 90–91.

OCTOBER 6. IMPARTING AND RECEIVING.

Look with mercy upon this company of your people, the church. You have called us out of many lands and places to serve you in the ministry of your word. Teach us rightly to divide the word of truth. Grant that our love may grow in all knowledge and discernment. Help us each to walk worthily in the vocation in wherewith we are called, forbearing one another in love and endeavoring to keep the unity of the spirit in the bond of peace. Teach us that we impart and receive from each other whatever gift of the spirit you have given to each.

Niebuhr, R., *Reinhold Niebuhr: Major Works*, 700–701.

OCTOBER 7. IS POWER GOOD?

The Lord of heaven and earth is indeed the faithful, loyal Father, and Jesus Christ is indeed of one nature, one faithfulness, with that [*Abba*]. We may describe what happens to faith by saying that the two great problems of existence are solved at least in principle. The first of these is the problem of the goodness of Power. The great anxiety of life, the great distrust, appears in the doubt that the Power whence all things come, the Power which has thrown the self and its companions into existence, is not good. The question is always before us, Is Power good? Is it good to and for what it has brought into being? Is it good with the goodness of integrity? Is it good as adorable and delightful? On the other hand we know something of what true goodness is. We recognize goodness in every form of loyalty and love.

Niebuhr, H.R., *Faith on Earth*, 100.

OCTOBER 175

OCTOBER 8.   IS GOOD POWERFUL?

Our second great problem is whether goodness is powerful, whether it is not forever defeated in actual existence by loveless, thoughtless power. The resurrection of Jesus Christ from the dead, the establishment of Jesus Christ in power, is at one and the same time the demonstration of the power of goodness and the goodness of power.

Niebuhr, H.R., *Faith on Earth*, 100.

OCTOBER 9.   MINISTRY OF RECONCILIATION.

We pray, O Lord, for your church, that it may be healed of its divisions by your grace; that it may teach your word with courage to a sinful world; and may mediate with true charity your love and mercy to all [people]. Strengthen every ministry of reconciliation therein with your spirit. Grant that it be a great community of grace in which the pride of race or nation is humbled, where the strong and the mighty are brought to judgment, the meek and lowly are lifted up. Make it more fruitful to its Lord, and more instant to meet the needs of [all].

Niebuhr, R., *Reinhold Niebuhr: Major Works*, 701.

OCTOBER 10.   WORLD MENTAL HEALTH DAY.

To the extent that a considerable portion of preaching today fastens upon the phenomenon of anxiety (which has been carefully studied and described by existentialism), a similar view of isolated man [or woman] dominates our perspective on the communion of saints. For anxiety as a basic mood and affection qualifying every interest in the world-self relation arising out of that mood is an impetus toward self-seclusion; it dramatizes the isolation of the self . . . A minister who pictures him [or herself] only as the counselor of the psychically disturbed will easily find their institutional relations and duties a source of embarrassment. This is not to say that the ministry should not embody these functions in preaching and the pastorate, but it is also necessary to find other real relations to the humanity dwelling in the congregation and parish.

Niebuhr, R.R., "Problem of Preaching at Easter," 412.

OCTOBER 11.   OUR INDIVIDUALITY . . . OUR HUMANITY.

Unless the gospel is uttered in such a say that it evokes in us not only a sense of our individuality but also of our humanity, there is little point in dwelling on the Christ who is for us . . . [I]t requires a fresh appropriation of the image of Jesus Christ as the head of the race, the last Adam, the recapitulator, the [person] in whose own humanity our own image is reflected and simultaneously freed of its distortions.

Niebuhr, R.R., "Problem of Preaching at Easter," 412.

OCTOBER 12.   THANKSGIVING DAY (CANADA, IF 2ND MONDAY).

Eternal God, creator and redeemer of all, we thank you for this new day and for all your mercies which reveal the constancy of your love toward your children. Grant us grace to begin this day in your fear and with your favor; to perform our tasks as unto you; to live with all who share our work and our common life in the spirit of charity and goodwill. Banish all fears from our hearts that we may know that peace which the world cannot give or take away. Awaken us from the sloth and sleep of sin and grant us the power to obey your will with steadfast purpose and resolute hearts.

Niebuhr, R., *Justice and Mercy*, 118.

OCTOBER 13.   SELF'S CAPACITY TO TRANSCEND.

The self's capacity to view every situation in which it is involved, and to view itself from a standpoint beyond the situation makes for the indeterminate character of all human desires and the corresponding indeterminateness of the qualms of conscience about the legitimacy of those desires and lusts. [B]oth desires and qualms of conscience about the desires are indeterminate; and both are fruits of the self's capacity to transcend every situation, historical or natural, which offers either preliminary restraints upon its ambitions, limits for its desires or justifications of its undue selfishness.

Niebuhr, R., *Self and the Dramas of History*, 20.

OCTOBER 14. LIMITLESSNESS OF AMBITIONS/ SECURITIES.

There are no limits to human ambitions or securities. Whether people have one house or three or five, and whether the house boasts of two or twenty rooms, is not determined by some logical principle or some primary need because human desires always transcend elementary needs. The scope beyond the primary need invariably includes cultural as well as purely physical values.

Niebuhr, R., *Self and the Dramas of History*, 21.

OCTOBER 15. LADDERS OF AMBITION/LADDERS OF ANXIETY.

The ladder of ambition and achievement is inevitably accompanied by a ladder of anxiety. The poor person is anxious lest he [or she] lack sufficient income to satisfy the basic needs of one's family. The rich person is anxious that he [or she] may not be able to conform to the living standards of one's neighbors. [One] is also anxious lest envy of his [or her] wealth destroy, rather than enhance, respect for one's personhood. Human anxieties grow with achievement and the anxieties contain both concern of the social or artistic achievement and for the social prestige, which may follow upon the achievement either contemporaneously or ultimately.

Niebuhr, R., *Self and the Dramas of History*, 21–22.

OCTOBER 16. QUALMS OF CONSCIENCE.

The qualms of conscience are just as indeterminate as the lust and ambitions of persons, ranging from the one of easy conscience because he [or she] has desisted from a previous crime, to the one who has an uneasy conscience because his [or her] privileges are inconsistent with a standard of justice which one has set for [oneself], or because one is involved in a social evil from which he [or she] sees no escape, or from which a little more courageous action on one's part might offer the way of escape.

Niebuhr, R., *Self and the Dramas of History*, 22.

OCTOBER 17. INTERNATIONAL DAY FOR ERADICATION OF POVERTY.

We are universal as creatures who have need of food and shelter, perhaps locomotion and communications in modern existence, and we are dependent upon each other for these goods . . . we are free spirits with a certain dignity and we must carry each other's burdens, the strong, particularly, must carry the burdens of the weak in order to protect the dignity of our humanity. This is the point of "Bear one another's burdens" [Galatians 6:2].

Niebuhr, R., *Justice and Mercy*, 107.

Grant us grace, our Father, to measure the height of our dignity as free spirits, and the depth of our misery and the breadth of our responsibility. Judge us in our vanities and our pretensions. Have pity on us, for only your infinite pity is adequate to the infinite pathos of our human existence.

Niebuhr, R., *Justice and Mercy*, 111.

OCTOBER 18. CHARITY, PITY, POWER, AND INJUSTICE.

Those who benefit from social injustice are naturally less capable of understanding its real character than those who suffer from it. They will attribute ethical qualities to social life, if only the slightest gesture of philanthropy hides social injustice. If the disinherited treat these gestures with cynicism and interpret unconscious sentimentality as conscious hypocrisy, the privileged will be properly outraged and offended by the moral perversity of the recipients of their beneficiaries. Since liberal Protestantism is, on the whole, the religion of the privileged classes of Western civilization, it is not surprising that its espousal of the ideal of love, in a civilization reeking with social injustice, should be cynically judged and convinced of hypocrisy by those in whom bitter social experiences destroy the sentimentalities and illusions of the comfortable . . . philanthropy combines genuine pity with the display of power and that the latter element explains why the powerful are more inclined to be generous than to grant social justice.

Niebuhr, R., *Moral Man and Immoral Society*, 80, 127.

OCTOBER 19. JUDGMENT IN HISTORY AND AT THE END OF HISTORY.

The judgment of God is executed not only at the end of history. It is executed periodically in history. The mighty persons sin against people as well as God. The expanding self of mighty persons grows too tall and affronts God. But wherever life exceeds its just bounds it also grows too broad and destroys other life near it. The mighty persons are like tall trees whose branches rob neighbouring trees of the sunshine they require for their life. In other words, the social sin of the mighty is that they demand too high a price from society for the services they render. They not only demand it but get it. They get it because they control the organs by which society comes to self-consciousness and thinks and acts. Whether the mighty persons are priestly rulers, military chieftains or economic overlords they always become involved in the same self-destructive process. At first they create social peace and a modicum of justice by their power. Then they disturb social peace and destroy justice by the exactions of their power. They involve society in internal strife by demanding exorbitant rewards for the service they render; also they involve it in external strife by using their control of their fellow [humans] for the satisfaction of their imperial ambitions beyond the borders of their own social system. Thus injustice is the social consequence of pride; and the inevitable fruit of injustice is self-destruction.

Niebuhr, R., *Beyond Tragedy*, 202–203.

OCTOBER 20. LEAVING . . . WITH MIXED FEELINGS.

I always thought I was a fairly brutal realist, but I am beginning to suspect that the whole thing is a pose to hide the sentimental preacher. At any rate now that the time has come to sever my connections with the church I find it almost impossible to take the step. There is nothing quite like the pastoral relationship. I would almost be willing to sacrifice the future for the sake of staying here and watching the lovely little kiddies grow up, and see the young boys and girls that I have confirmed blossoming into manhood and womanhood. There must be something bogus about me. Here I have been preaching the gospel for thirteen years and crying, "Woe unto you if all men speak well of you," and yet I leave without a serious controversy in the whole thirteen years. It is almost impossible to be sane and Christian at the same time, and on the whole I have been more sane than Christian. I have said what I believe, but in my creed the divine madness of a gospel of love is qualified by considerations of moderation which I have called Aristotelian, but which an unfriendly critic might call opportunistic. I have made these qualifications because it seems to me that without them the Christian ethic degenerates into asceticism and becomes useless for any direction of the affairs of a larger society. I do not say that someone ought not to undertake an ascetic revolt against civilization. Certainly there would be a peace in it which no one can find who tries to adapt the principles of love to a civilization built upon the drive of power and greed.

Niebuhr, R., Leaves from the Notebook, 195–96.

OCTOBER 21. FITTING ADJUSTMENTS?

Those of us who make adjustments between the absolute ideal of our devotion and the necessities of the immediate situation lack peace, because we can never be sure that we have our adjustment at the right place. Every moral position which has left the absolute basis is in danger of becoming a rationalization of some selfish purpose. I am not unconscious of the fact that my tendency to criticize others so severely for their alleged rationalizations and hypocrisies springs from my own sense of insecurity. I persevere in the effort to combine the ethic of Jesus with what might be called Greek caution because I see no great gain in ascetic experiments. I might claim for such a strategy the full authority of the gospel except that it seems to me more likely to avoid dishonesty if one admits that the principle of love is not qualified in the gospel and that it must be qualified in other than the most intimate human associations. When one deals with the affairs of a civilization one is trying to make the principle of love effective as far as possible, but one cannot escape the conclusion that society as such is brutal, and that the Christian principle may never be more than a leaven in it. There has never been a time when I have not been really happy in the relationships of the parish ministry. The church can really be a community of love and can give one new confidence in the efficacy of the principles of brotherhood [and sisterhood] outside of the family relation. The questions and qualms of conscience arise when one measures the church in its relationships to society, particularly to the

OCTOBER 181

facts of modern industry. It is at this point where it seems to me that we had better admit failure than to claim any victory.

Niebuhr, R., Leaves from the Notebook, 197–98.

OCTOBER 22. RECALCITRANCE TO HUMILITY.

The admission of failure may yet lead to some kind of triumph, while any premature confidence in the victory of a Christian ethic will merely obfuscate the conscience. Modern industry, particularly American industry, is not Christian. The economic forces which move it are hardly qualified at a single point by really ethical considerations. If, while it is in the flush of its early triumphs, it may seem impossible to bring it under the restraint of moral law, it may strengthen faith to know that life without law destroys itself. If the church can do nothing else, it can bear witness to the truth until such a day as bitter experience will force a recalcitrant civilization to a humility which it does not now possess.

Niebuhr, R., Leaves from the Notebook, 197–98.

OCTOBER 23. OUR DIGNITY AS CO-WORKERS.

O God, the sovereign of nations, teach us how we may build a common life in which the nations of the world may find peace and justice. Show us what we ought to do. Show us also what are the limits of our power and what we cannot do. Recall us to our dignity as co-workers with You now and evermore.

Niebuhr, R., "Teach Us" in "Reinhold Niebuhr: Prayers,"
https://www.harvardsquarelibrary.org/poetry-prayers-visual-arts/
reinhold-niebuhr-prayers/ [accessed October 22, 2020.]

OCTOBER 24. INTERCESSIONS.

O God, we pray for all sorts and conditions of people:

For all who toil in the burden and heat of the day, that they may enjoy the rewards of their industry, that they may not be defrauded of their due, and that we may never cease to be mindful of our debt to them for making our life tolerable;

For those in authority, who have power over others, that they may not use it for selfish advantage but be guided to do justice and to love mercy.

For those who have been worsted in the battles of life, whether by the inhumanity of others, their own limitations, or the fickleness of fortune, that they may contend against injustice without bitterness, and learn how to accept what cannot be altered, with patience;

For the rulers of nations that they may promote peace among the peoples and establish justice in our common life.

For the teachers and ministers of Your power, for artists, scientists and interpreters of the spiritual life, that they may not corrupt the truth to which they are committed;

For prophets and seers who awaken us from our sloth, that they may hold their torches high in a world darkened by prejudice.

O God, who has bound us together in this bundle of life, give us the grace to understand how our lives depend upon one another and our responsibilities to You.

Niebuhr, R., "For All People" in "Reinhold Niebuhr: Prayers," https://www.harvardsquarelibrary.org/poetry-prayers-visual-arts/ reinhold-niebuhr-prayers/ [accessed October 22, 2020.]

OCTOBER 25. CONSPICUOUS UNRECONCILEDNESS.

The ecumenical world of those who are unreconciled to each other is the world of those unreconciled to God. This strange human race has never been reconciled to God—but now its unreconciledness is more conspicuous than ever. On the one hand, it manifests itself in the despair that does not know it is despair—the despair of those who try to forget by seeking the enjoyment of the immediate moment or of that near moment to come, the despair that seeks the fulfillment of life's purpose in the satisfaction of the lust for a momentary prestige, for a momentary possession, or for an additional few years of personal or national life. On the other hand, there is the despair that the most sensitive of minds of our ecumenical world voice and communicate—the explicit despair that recognizes no meaning, purpose, or hope in this human existence. Individuals and nations live in an ecumenical world—a great household—but the larger it grows the deeper the suspicion and distrust of the source whence mankind came and of the end toward which it moves. Whether that in which we live, move and have our being, is nothingness, or a great game of chance—it is the enemy, against which man [or woman] maintains themselves for a while, unreconciled; in the natural mind which is enmity to God or fear of the Holy One as enemy.

Niebuhr, H.R., *Responsibility of the Church,* 136.

OCTOBER 26. PAINFUL MENTAL AND SPIRITUAL STRUGGLE.

The duty of the church in this ecumenical age cannot, I am sure, be fulfilled if it is not more fully reconciled within itself and all its parts, to the one God, the God and [Abba] of its Lord Jesus Christ. And it may be that if we become more fully reconciled to God, and to one another in God, we shall then know how to carry on our ministry of reconciliation to those who are near and to those who are far. But even this knowledge will not come automatically, not without painful mental and spiritual struggle.

Niebuhr, H.R., *Responsibility of the Church,* 136–37.

OCTOBER 27. RECONCILIATION: CALLED TO SERVE.

The commission to go into the world with the ministry of reconciliation may come to persons on a hill-top in the hinterlands rather than in a chamber in the capital city. Yet knowing that a sovereign rules over our intentions, the good as well as the evil, the little as well as the great, we dare not carry on our work in the seminaries in this ecumenical age, without the painful and awful awareness that this Church we serve has been called to serve in the ministry of reconciliation to all the world. We cannot meet the call to this ministry by introducing special courses, by adding to an overloaded curriculum further special inquiries. The question is one about the spirit and the context in which we do all that we do.

Niebuhr, H.R., *Responsibility of the Church,* 137.

OCTOBER 28.   PETITIONS.

Teach us each day what you have us do, and help us to perform our tasks with diligence and humility. Give us grace in this fellowship to be helpful to each other in our several responsibilities. Save us from seeking to impress our sisters and brothers, or from being afraid of their judgements when we are sure of your commandment for us. Look with favor upon this company of your people, bound together in the common tasks and disciplines of your church. Help us to search for your word of truth diligently and not be content with the letter of your words, since it is her spirit which gives life. Help us to profit from the prophets and ages of every age, the people of faith who out of weakness were made strong, and the people of learning who have sought rightly to divide the truth. Give us above all the spirit of love, seeing that if we have all knowledge and understand all mysteries and have not love, it profits us nothing. Grant us to be members one of another in the body of which Christ our Lord is the head.

Niebuhr, R., *Justice and Mercy*, 117–18.

OCTOBER 29.   RELEVANCE OF JUDGMENT AND MERCY.

The task of any movement devoted to "social Christianity" must be not so much to advocate a particular nostrum for the solution of various economic and social evils, but to bring a full testimony of a gospel of judgment and grace to bear upon all of human life, upon the individual in the final heights of individual self-consciousness, where it transcends all social institutions and historical situations, and upon human communities which do, on their own level, make contact with the kingdom of God, whenever individuals recognise that a judgment and mercy of God are relevant to their collective as well as to their individual actions, and to the actions by which they order their common life as well as to actions in which they express themselves above and beyond every particular order or system.

Niebuhr, R., "Christian Faith and Social Action," 137.

OCTOBER   185

OCTOBER 30.   PURPOSES AND IMPEDIMENTS.

For on the one hand Christians must seek to serve God, that is, consider
the ultimate purpose of their toil, no matter how inadequate may be
the structure of justice in which they are forced to toil. But on the other
hand they must always reconsider the organizations and arrangements
through which the toil of people is organized so that impediments to life's
more ultimate purposes may be removed.

Niebuhr, R., *Christian Realism and Political Problems*, 136.

OCTOBER 31.   REFORMATION DAY (IF LAST
SUNDAY).

When may we expect that more radical renaissance which our religious
need and the religious need of our fellow and sister people appear to require? Fundamentally I believe that we can expect it from no other kind
of source than from the kind represented in Luther's experience. He made
all things new in his day. He could translate the Gospel into the vulgar
tongue of his day. He found freshly minted parables. He brought forth
new symbols because he wrestled with, he encountered, he experienced,
he heard, he searched out himself-before-God and God-before-himself.
What he communicated was not the word of God in the Scriptures but
the word that he had heard of God speaking to him, Martin Luther, in the
Scriptures. It was not the word that anyone could hear but which came
to the ears of an agonized listener, of one who was fighting for his life,
who was crying for help and heard the distant answer of the helper . . . Of
this, I think we can be certain, that a new religious language and a new
symbolism do not in the first place grow out of our need to communicate
to our sisters and brothers something we already know but out of our
encounter and communication with the actuality of our own existence
in, with, before God—in all of our searching out of what we do not yet
know but experience in twilight, sense as present, recognize as inescap-
ably there and still have no word for it.

Niebuhr, H.R., *Theology, History, and Culture*, 32–33.

The new ecumenical spirit between Protestants and Catholics will profit
by a new appreciation of the values both branches of Christendom have in
common—though one branch may emphasize unity and order while the

other emphasizes liberty. But the Jesuit spirit of liberty and "new World Council" spirit of unity reveal that these contrasting and supplementary values are not the exclusive possession of either side.

Niebuhr, R., "Toward New Intra-Christian Endeavors," 116.

NOVEMBER

National Family Caregivers Month (USA)

I do not believe that we can meet in our day the need which the church was founded to meet by becoming more orthodox or more liberal, more biblical or more liturgical. I look for a resymbolization of the message and the life of faith in the One God. Our old phrases are worn out; they have become clichés by means of which we can neither grasp nor communicate the reality of our existence before God. Retranslation is not enough; more precisely, retranslation of traditional terms—"Word of God," "redemption," incarnation," "justification," "grace," "eternal life"—is not possible unless one has direct relations in the immediacy of personal life to the actualities to which people in another time referred with the aid of such symbols. I do not know how this resymbolization in pregnant words and in symbolic deeds (like the new words of the Reformation and the Puritan movement and the Great Awakening, like the symbolic deeds of the Franciscans and the social gospel era) will come about. I do count on the Holy Spirit and believe that the words and deeds will come to us. I also believe, with both the prophets and, of all people, Karl Marx, that the reformation of religion is the fundamental reformation of society. And I believe that nothing very important for humankind will happen as a result of our "conquest" of space or as a result of the cessation of the cold war unless the human spirit is revived within itself.

Niebuhr, H.R., *Responsibility of the Church*, 144.

NOVEMBER 1.   ALL SAINTS DAY.

Around the corner from the Cathedral of the Assumption in downtown Louisville, Kentucky, a bolt of what must have seemed to be pure spiritual lightning erupted out of the blue one spring day in 1958. No one actually saw it, but the incident is known among many thousands because the person to whom it occurred would write so eloquently of it later. His experience—some admirers would call it an "epiphany," an elastic word that can mean a sudden insight or a real manifestation of the divine— was about being swept by a feeling of transcendent joy in humanity, as if the barriers between people had been abruptly uprooted, leaving an overpowering sense of oneness. "In Louisville, at the corner of Fourth and Walnut, in the middle of the shopping district, I was suddenly overwhelmed with the realization that I loved all these people, that they were mine and I theirs, that we could not be alien to each other even though we were total strangers." The words are Thomas Merton's, one of the most famous Catholic writers on spirituality in American history, recorded in his journal, *Conjectures of a Guilty Bystander.*

Niebuhr, G. [Jr.], *Beyond Tolerance*, 160.

NOVEMBER 2.   ALL SOULS DAY.

Bishop Williams is dead. I sit and stare at the floor while I say that to myself and try to believe it. How strangely a vital personality defies the facts of death. Nowhere have I seen a personality more luminous with the Christ spirit than in this bishop who was also a prophet . . . His fearless protagonism of the cause of democracy in industry won him the respect and love of the workers of the city as no other churchperson possessed it . . . But society resists every effort to bring its processes under ethical restraint so stubbornly that one must finally be satisfied with preserving one's moral integrity in a necessary and yet futile struggle . . . The bishop did not change Detroit industry, but if the church ever becomes a real agency of the kingdom of God in an industrial civilization, his voice, though he is dead, will be in its counsels.

Niebuhr, R., *Leaves from the Notebook*, 72-73.

NOVEMBER 3.   ATTACHING EMOTIONS TO TASKS.

It is very difficult to persuade people who are committed to a general ideal to consider the meaning of that ideal in specific situations. It is even more difficult to prompt them to consider specific ends of social and individual conduct and to evaluate them in light of experience . . . very little is done to attach emotion to the specific tasks and projects. Is the industrial life of our day unethical? Are nations imperialistic? Is the family disintegrating? Are young people losing their sense of values?

Niebuhr, R., *Leaves from the Notebook,* 74.

NOVEMBER 4.   REALISM!

In political and moral theory "realism" denotes the disposition to take all factors in a social and political situation, which offer resistance to established norms, into account, particularly the factors of self-interest and power . . . This definition of realism implies that idealists are sub-ject to illusions about social realities, which indeed they are. "Idealism" is, in short, in the esteem of its proponents, characterized by loyalty to moral norms and ideals, rather than to self-interest, whether individual or collective. It is . . . characterized by a disposition to ignore or be indif-ferent to the forces in human life which offer resistance to universally valid ideals and norms. This disposition . . . is general whenever persons are inclined to take the moral pretensions of themselves or their brothers and sisters at face value; for the disposition to hide self-interest behind the façade of pretended devotion to values, transcending self-interest, is well nigh universal . . . One is a curious creature with so strong a sense of obligation to his and her people that one cannot pursue his and her own interests without pretending to serve their wider community.

Niebuhr, R., *Christian Realism and Political Problems,* 119–120.

NOVEMBER 5   ELABORATIONS.

General programs tend to be a screen for particular interests in society and as their weapons in social controversy. Thus medieval conceptions of natural law were used by aristocratic classes to put the rising middle class at a moral disadvantage; and modern "natural rights" concepts were used with similar purpose by the bourgeois classes to prove that a system of "natural liberty," which would be to their advantage, was in accord with the "laws of nature" and of "nature's God"; and the modern industrial classes are naturally inclined to view processes, defined as "historical dialectic," as giving a kind of cosmic support to their particular struggle in society.

Niebuhr, R., *Christian Faith and Social Action,*" 125.

NOVEMBER 6. NEGATIVE AND POSITIVE FORCES.

The relevance of a genuine and vital Christian faith is that it unmasks the errors of a false and abstract idealism by two forces, one negative and one positive. The negative force is the contrite recognition in the Christian faith, as expounded in the New Testament, that the law is not redemptive but may be the servant of sin . . . The laws and ideals which we regard as guarantors of justice and bearers of our goodness can be personally used as instruments of the ego.

Niebuhr, R., *"Christian Faith and Social Action,"* 129.

The real problem of a Christian social ethic is to derive from the Gospel a clear view of the realities with which we must deal in our common or social life, and also to pressure a sense of responsibility for achieving the highest measure of order, freedom, and justice despite the hazards of [our] collective life.

Niebuhr, R., *"Christian Faith and Social Action,"* 131.

NOVEMBER 7. LOVE'S RELEVANCE.

The relevance of the law of love to the field of social institutions and collective relations is established whenever the religious awareness of the individual, in conscious relation to the divine, is related to the intricacies and complexities of social relations. In that sense, a Christian social ethic requires competent technical judgments. But the relevance of the law of love rests upon a more basic religious consideration. It is established whenever religious experience bears testimony both to the law of love and to that of self-love. For to understand the law of love as a final imperative, but not to know about the persistence of the power of self-love in all of life but particularly in the collective relations of humankind, results in an idealistic ethic with no relevance to hard realities of life. To know about the power of self-love, but not to know that its power does not make it normative, is to dispense with ethical standards and fall into cynicism. But to know both the law of love as the final standard and the law of self-love as a persistent force is to enable Christians to have a foundation for a pragmatic ethic in which power and self-interest are used, beguiled, harnessed, and deflected for the ultimate end of establishing the highest and most inclusive possible community of justice and order.

Niebuhr, R., "Christian Faith and Social Action," 135–36.

NOVEMBER 8.   NATIONAL ABORIGINAL VETERANS DAY (CANADA).

O God, whom the heavens cannot contain, yet who visits the humble with your presence, and loves a contrite heart, give us eyes to see our share in the common sins of humankind, so that we will not walk in pride and deceive ourselves. In all our doings, reveal yourself to us, a God both of wrath and mercy, who visits the sins of the fathers and mothers upon the children to the third and fourth generations and who shows mercy to them that love you. We are consumed by your anger and sustained by your mercy. Such knowledge is too wonderful for us. We cannot attain to it. Yet we know that in an evil world we are sustained by your grace coming to us in the goodness of generous souls, in forgiving hearts, in the beneficence of nature, of the glory of the day, the rhythm of the seasons, and in the whole solemn mystery of life. Make us more worthy of the swift and solemn trust of life.

Niebuhr, R., *Justice and Mercy*, 75.

NOVEMBER 9.   KRISTALLNACHT . . . NIGHT OF THE BROKEN GLASS.

I should like, as a Christian speaking to Jews, to express my genuine admiration for the Jewish spirit and my sense of shame that an allegedly Christian civilization can sink to such depths of cruelty.

Niebuhr, R., in Littell, "Reinhold Niebuhr and the Jewish People," 15.

Hear us, our Father, we pray for all who are in special need of your grace; for the sick and the anxious, for the dying and for those who stand in the fear of death. Teach them that neither life nor death can separate them from the love of God.

We pray for those who have great authority that they may know the limits of human wisdom, and may seek your counsels to supply their need. We pray for doctors and nurses and all who are ministers of your mercy, that they may be fit vehicles of your grace, and for all teachers and guides of youth that they rightly divide the word of truth and lead people to wisdom and to the fear of the Lord which is the beginning of wisdom.

Niebuhr, R., *Justice and Mercy*, 73–74.

The pastoral responsibility of the Church for society is . . . direct as well as indirect. Compassion and concern for the Jewish people as a whole, pastoral interest in the defeated nations and in the victors who stand in great moral danger characterizes the Church which responds to the God who not only creates [humans] but also their societies. As the interdependence of people increases in industrial and technical civilization the responsibility for dealing with the great networks of interrelationship increases. If the individual sheep is to be protected the flock must be guarded.

Niebuhr, H.R., *Responsibility of the Church*, 73.

NOVEMBER 10.   INTERCESSIONS.

We pray, O Lord, for the millions of distressed people throughout the earth. May our hearts go out to them, more especially since they bear in their bodies the costly price of our freedom and security.

O Lord, show yourself to all who seek you, give peace to all who are anxious and afraid, and challenge all the strong and the secure that they may know their strength is not their own, and that they are not as secure as they think they are.

Niebuhr, R., *Justice and Mercy*, 75.

NOVEMBER 11. REMEMBRANCE DAY (CANADA)/ VETERANS DAY (USA).

I can see one element in this strange fascination of war which persons have not adequately noted. It reduces life to simple terms. The modern person lives in such a complex world that one wonders how his or her sanity is maintained as well as it is. Every moral venture, every social situation and every practical problem involves a whole series of conflicting loyalties, and one may never be quite sure that he or she is right in giving himself or herself to the one as against the other. Shall one be just and sacrifice love? Shall he strive for beauty and do it by gaining the social privileges which destroy his sense of fellowship with the under- privileged? Shall she serve his family and neglect the state? Or be patriotic to the detriment of the great family of humankind? Shall he be diligent at the expense of his health? Or keep healthy at the expense of the great cause in which she is interested? Shall he be truthful and therefore cruel? Or shall she be kind and therefore a little soft? Shall he strive for the amenities of life and make life less robust in the process? Or shall she make courage the ulti-mate virtue and brush aside the virtues which a stable and therefore soft society has cultivated? Out of this mesh of conflicting claims, interests, loyalties, ideals, values and community one is rescued by the psychology of war which serves the state at least a momentary priority over all other communities and which makes courage the supreme virtue.

Niebuhr, R., *Leaves from the Notebook*, 17–18.

NOVEMBER 12. ONCE MORE REVEALED.

I talked to a young captain at camp last week who told me how happy he was in the army because he had "found himself" in military service. Our further conversation led me to suspect that it was this simplifica-tion of life which had really brought him happiness; that and his love of authority.

Unfortunately, all these momentary simplifications of the complexi-ties of life cannot be finally satisfying, because they do violence to life. The imperiled community may for a moment claim a kind of unqualified loyalty which no community or cause has the right or ability to secure in normal times. But judgment returns to sobriety as events become less disjointed and the world is once more revealed in all its confusion of good in evil and evil in good. The imperiled community was threatened because of its vice as much as because of its virtue, and the diabolical foe reassumes the lineaments of our common humanity. Physical courage is proved unequal to the task of ennobling man or woman without the aid of other virtues, and the same people who have been raised to great heights by the self-forgetfulness of war have been sunk into new depths of hatred. There is only momentary peace in all-consuming passion, except it be a passion for what is indubitably the best. And what is the best?

Niebuhr, R., *Leaves from the Notebook*, 18–19.

NOVEMBER 13.   AWARENESS AND PRAGMATICS.

. . . [D]ialogue and service together, can be found in teachings of Gandhi, King, Pope John Paul II and others who have waged campaigns for peace in recent decades. They have left deep imprints on millions of people. King drew Protestants, Catholic, Jews, Unitarians, Buddhists, agnostics, and atheists to the cause of civil rights. In 1965, a religiously mixed group marched together in Selma, Alabama, right into the truncheons of Alabama law enforcement authorities. Bloody Sunday, as the event came to be called, proved crucial to bringing about the political momentum to pass the federal Voting Rights Act. Within two years, King had taken on broader work, becoming an outspoken critic of American involvement in the Vietnam War . . . He also wrote an essay called "The World House" in which he identified the "great new problem of mankind," the divisions that separated people from recognizing that they lived together and had a responsibility to one another. "We have inherited a large house, a great 'world house' . . . a family unduly separated in ideas, culture, and interest, who, because we can never again live apart, must learn somehow to live with each other in peace."

Niebuhr, G. [Jr.], *Beyond Tolerance*, 65–66.

NOVEMBER 14.   BASIS OF ALL MORAL LIFE.

The law of love is indeed the basis of all moral life; it cannot be obeyed by a simple act of the will because the power of self-concern is too great, and that the forces which draw the self from its undue self-concern are usually forces of "common grace" in the sense that they represent all forms of

NOVEMBER 195

social security or to bethink itself of its social essence and to realize itself by not trying too desperately for self-realization.

Niebuhr, R., *On Man's Nature and His Communities,* 125.

NOVEMBER 15. BANEFUL EFFECT OF GENERAL AND ABSTRACT PROGRAMS.

It is important to understand [the] baneful effect of general and abstract programs upon the social life of [humans]. Two reasons may be given why evil flows from these too inclusive and abstract programs: (1) These generalizations fail to take the endless contingencies of history into account; (2) General programs and panaceas are stubbornly held and not easily amended by empirical data. General programs tend to be a screen for particular interests in society and their weapons in social controversy.

Niebuhr, R., "Christian Faith and Social Action," 125.

NOVEMBER 16. PANACEAS' TEMPORARY PROTECTION.

Panaceas do not ... merely hide special economic or social interest. They may have another purpose which is of particular concern for students of morals and religion. They tend to obscure the tension between individual and social morality. This tension is a serious problem for all religiously sensitive individuals. The social order is involved in collective forms of egotism, its injustices, in conflicts of self-interest, and in subordinations of life to life which are an affront to the sensitive conscience. There is, therefore, a strong tendency to develop "ideologies of conscience" as well as ideologies of interest. The middle classes ease their conscience by the conviction that the "natural systems of liberty" would make for justice in the long run even if in the short run it manifested obvious injustices. When this failed to materialize it was a natural inclination of the religious conscience to invest a collectivist alternative with more moral capital that it did not deserve. This was done primarily by contrasting the "motives of service" which were supposed to rule the collectivist order as against the "motives of profit: in the old order.

Niebuhr, R., "Christian Faith and Social Action," 125.

NOVEMBER 17.   SERENITY PRAYER'S ORIGINS.

The circumstances under which the Serenity Prayer was composed and the reasons that it took on such a life of its own are themselves inspiring and knowing them might help us to appreciate its consoling, challenging power.

Sifton, *Serenity Prayer,* 11.

At some point during the late 1943 or early 1944, [Dean Robbins] suggested to Pa that the little prayer about grace, courage and wisdom, which he remembered from a summer church service, might be appropriate for inclusion in material that he was helping the Federal Council of Churches prepare for army chaplains in the field. Ministering to soldiers was an essential task . . . it was indeed included in the Book of Prayer and Services for the Armed Forces, prepared by the Commission on Worship for the FCCC and the Christian Commission for Camp and Defense Communities. This was its first publication in any form and in any language, and it's because of this little booklet that eventually it became famous. I have been told that booklet was translated into German, presumably for use in an occupied Germany . . . A short while later Alcoholics Anonymous, then a fledgling small organization scarcely a decade old, with my father's permission, also started to use the prayer in their regular meetings.

Sifton, *Serenity Prayer,* 292.

NOVEMBER 18.   SUBTLE PRAYER CHANGES.

The Serenity Prayer is not just a familiar, agreeable cliché. After all, its instructions are tremendously difficult and puzzling to follow.

I don't know when or how AA simplified the text—perhaps from the very beginning. Their version frames the prayer the first-person singular and simplifies the opening. It omits the spiritually correct but difficult idea of praying for grace to accept with serenity that which we cannot change, and focuses instead on the simpler notion of obtaining serenity to accept what cannot be changed. My father let this happen and didn't fuss when the wordings were altered though he minded. There are, after all, several large difference between the two formulations.

Another change is more serious. In the second clause, courage to change which should be changed becomes, in the AA rendering, simply courage to change what can be changed. Goodness me, just because something can be changed doesn't mean that it must be! More important, this way of putting it reduces the scope of the imperative. It speaks merely of what we might manage to alter at a given moment, to *change what we can change*. But there are circumstances that *should be changed* yet may seem beyond our powers to alter, and these are the circumstances under which prayer is most needed.

Sifton, *Serenity Prayer*, 11, 292–93 (italics in original).

NOVEMBER 19. ACCEPTING AND CHANGING INCAPACITIES.

After half a century, there are plenty of riffs done on the prayer, and some of them are ghastly, others quite cheery. I like a goofy one that turned up in the Calvin and Hobbes comic strip. Calvin says to Hobbes, "Know what I pray for?" Hobbes: "What?" Calvin: "The strength to change what I can, the inability to accept what I can't, and the incapacity to tell the difference." Hobbes: "You should lead an interesting life." Calvin: "Oh, I already do!"

It is easy enough to see that the Serenity Prayer came out of, and was affected by, the challenges and dangers of a very difficult, fractured time. Now sixty years later, our lives are darkened again by grim foreboding about new threats, and civil society even more fractured and frantic. Trust, hope and courtesy in the public sphere have radically diminished, and this naturally affects our inner lives, too: how can it not?

Sifton, *Serenity Prayer*, 295, 14.

NOVEMBER 20. PERTINENCE OF GRACE IN PRAYER.

Yet, we are not facing a new spiritual crisis: this is the same old crisis in a new form. Living in history, living in full, always offers as much despair as hope, as much danger as possibility. So it is no wonder that so many millions find daily strength and resolve in praying for grace to accept with serenity that which we cannot change, courage to change what we should change, and the wisdom to discern the one from the other.

Sifton, *Serenity Prayer*, 14.

NOVEMBER 21. NEVER-ENDING PILGRIM'S PROGRESS.

We climb the mountain of revelation that we may gain a view of the shadowed valley in which we dwell and from the valley we look up again to the mountain. Each arduous journey brings new understanding, but also new wonder and surprise. This mountain is not one we climbed once upon a time; it is a well-known peak we never wholly knew, which must be climbed again in every generation, on every new day. There is no time in human history, there is no moment in the church's past, nor is there any set of doctrines, any philosophy and theology of which we might say, "Here the knowledge possible through revelation and the knowledge of revelation is fully set forth." Revelation is not only progressive but it requires of those to whom it has come that they begin the never-ending pilgrim's progress of the reasoning Christian heart.

Niebuhr, H.R., *Meaning of Revelation*, 100.

NOVEMBER 22. NATIONAL HOUSING DAY/CLASS CONFLICTS.

The class conflicts of human history are, on the whole, contests between those who have, and those who lack, economic power, the latter of whom are driven by want, hunger, and resentment to challenge the power of the economic overlords. These conflicts may not be overt; but they have not been absent in any society. They have become, however, increasingly overt and acrimonious in modern industrial society . . . The issue between the classes has become more than the question of an equitable distribution of property. It is the issue about the very legitimacy of the right of property. The Christian idea that we are God's stewards of all we possess remained a force in Calvinistic as in Catholic thought. But the idea of stewardship easily degenerated into the idea of philanthropy as a justification for property distinctions. Thus Calvinism laid the foundation for the hypocrisies of bourgeois and plutocratic idealism in which charity became a screen for injustice.

Niebuhr, R., *Children of Light*, 87, 95.

NOVEMBER 199

NOVEMBER 23. "MORE THAN SIMPLY TOLERATE PEOPLE."

Commitment to individual rights and commitment to the idea of a common life are not mutually exclusive. It has been enunciated in American past, perhaps most memorably in January of 1941, as the United States prepared to enter a global war. President Roosevelt briefly described four principles that utterly distinguish democracy from tyranny. They are freedom of speech, freedom of worship, freedom from want (especially hunger), and freedom from fear, which he said could be achieved by an eventual reduction in world armaments. What makes the list so compelling still is the way that he linked two ideas that we typically understand as individual rights (free speech and worship) with two others that are societal goods, vast projects intended for the betterment of humanity. The four principles served as the basis for "a moral order" and a "good society," he said. "Freedom means the supremacy of human rights everywhere . . . each individual has an inherent worth and dignity. And to assume that is to do more than simply tolerate people. It is to extend to them a recognition of their uniqueness—articulated with particular eloquence by the twentieth-century Jewish philosopher Martin Buber.

Niebuhr, G. [Jr.], *Beyond Tolerance,* 52–53.

NOVEMBER 24. EASIER TO GIVE TO CAESAR.

Christendom has often achieved apparent success by ignoring the precepts of its founder. The church, as an organization interested in self-preservation and in the gain of power, has sometimes found the counsel of the Cross quite inexpedient as have national and economic groups. In dealing with such social evils as war, slavery, and social inequality, it has discovered convenient ambiguities in the letter of the Gospels which enabled it to violate their spirit and to ally itself with the prestige and power those evils had gained in their corporate organization. In adapting itself to the conditions of civilization which its founder had bidden it to permeate with the spirit of divine love, it found that it was easier to give to Caesar . . . if the examination of what might belong to God were not too closely pressed.

Niebuhr, H.R., *Responsibility of the Church,* 3.

NOVEMBER 25. "GRACE WHICH COMPLETES AND CORRECTS."

"Time is too short for me to tell the stories of Gideon, Barak . . . of David and Samuel and the prophetic. Through faith, they overthrew kingdoms, established justice . . . Their weakness was turned to strength' [Hebrews 11:32].

Our Father, look with pity upon us too weak for the tasks which are set before us, unable fully to obey your commands or to discern your will. Grant us, by faith, a wisdom beyond our wisdom, that in your light, we may see light and also a measure of your strength, which is made perfect in our weakness. So, amidst all that is fragmentary and contrary to our existence here, we may lay hold upon your grace, which completes, and corrects what is amiss.

Niebuhr, R., *Justice and Mercy,* 124.

NOVEMBER 26. THANKSGIVING DAY (USA, 4TH THURSDAY OF NOVEMBER).

The grace which determines the lives of [humans] and nations is manifest in all the special circumstances, favours, and fortunes of geography and climate, of history and fate, which lead to eminence despite the weakness and sinfulness of the beneficiary of such eminence.

If we know that we have been chosen beyond our deserts, we must also begin to realise that we have not been chosen for our particular task in order that our life may be aggrandized . . . It can be justified only if it results in good for whole community of mankind . . . If ever a nation required the spirit of genuine contrition and humility, it is ours.

Niebuhr, R., in Davis and Good, *Reinhold Niebuhr on Politics,*
269–70.

Conversion is the very heart of the Christian faith, for it is the change of mind which the reception of the gospel of the Kingdom brings with it. Such conversion is antithetical to substitution. In the Christian life human eros is not supplanted by divine agape but the divine agape converts the human eros by directing it in gratitude toward God and toward the neighbor in God.

Niebuhr, H.R., *Responsibility of the Church,* 60.

Obviously one could not, in these times celebrate Thanksgiving by sing-
ing "For Peace and Plenty" . . . Fruits and grain enough there were, to be
sure, but not peace exactly, and surely not plenty. What might be an honest Thanksgiving celebration for a group of junior and intermediate girls
and boys many of whom lacked so greatly of the things they reasonably
desire? . . . This Thanksgiving celebration therefore, might be the occasion to come to grips with the age-old "problem of evil." At least it might
be possible to work out an approach to it.

Niebuhr, H., in Caldwell, *A Mysterious Mantle*, 119.

NOVEMBER 27.   PRAYING FOR . . .

We thank thee for the glimpses of nobility in human life which redeem
it from sordidness and reassure us that thy image is in the heart of man
[and woman]. We are grateful for ties which bind us to our [sisters and
brothers]; for our common toil in industry and marts of trade; for our
joint inheritance as citizens of this nation; for traditions and customs
hallowed by age through which our passions are ordered and channeled;
for the love of beauty and truth and goodness by which we transcend the
chasms of race and nation; for the faith of our fathers and mothers by
which we claim kinship with the past and gain strength for the present;
for the love of dear ones in our homes and for the enlarging responsibilities and sobering duties of family life; for the security of older people
who redeem us from fretfulness; and for the faith and courage of youth
through which we are saved from sloth.

Niebuhr, R., *Reinhold Niebuhr: Major Works*, 697.

NOVEMBER 28.   LIFE AND DEATH OF CHRIST AS A PARABLE.

In interpreting the present, we use the life and death of Christ as a parable and an analogy. The scribes and the Pharisees now sit in Peter's seat,
and in the churches of St. Paul priests plot defense against the disturber
of the people; disciples are corrupted by thirty pieces of silver; money-
changers and those who sell human victims for vain sacrifices conspire
with Pilates who wash their bloody hands in public; poor unreasoning
soldiers commit sins which are not their own; betrayals and denials take

place in every capital; and so, out of cumulative self-deceit and treachery, out of great ignorance, out of false fears and all the evil imaginations of the heart, crosses are constructed not only for thieves but for the sons of God. We see through the use of the great parable how bodies are now being broken for our sake and how for the remission of sins the blood of the innocents is being shed. Not with complete clarity, to be sure, yet in a glass darkly, we can discern in the contemporary confusion of our lives the evidence of a pattern in which, by great travail of humans and God, a work of redemption goes on which is like the work of Christ.

Niebuhr, H.R., *Meaning of Revelation*, 91.

NOVEMBER 29. DOING AND SUFFERING IS LIKE THIS.

We learn to know that what we are doing and what is being done to us—how by an infinite suffering of the eternal victim we are condemned and are forgiven at the same time; how an infinite loyalty refuses to abandon us either to evil or nothingness, but works out our salvation with a tenacity we are tempted to deplore. The story of Jesus, and particularly of his passion, is the great illustration that enables us to say, "What we are now doing and suffering is like this."

Niebuhr, H.R., *Meaning of Revelation*, 91.

[Suffering] is a subject to which academic ethical theory, even theological ethics, usually pays little attention. Yet everyone with any experience of life is aware to the extent to which the characters of people he [or she] has known have been given their particular forms by the sufferings through which they have passed. But it is not simply what has happened to them that has defined them; their responses to what has happened to them have been of even greater importance, and these responses have been shaped by their interpretations of what they suffered.

Niebuhr, H.R., *Responsible Self*, 59.

NOVEMBER 30. THE HEROIC SOUL.

A sense of ultimate security and ultimate fulfillment may beguile a few from their immediate tasks. But the heroic soul will be the freer to seek for possible securities in history if he possesses a resource against immediate insecurities. The city of God is no enemy of the land of promise. The hope of it makes the inevitable disappointments in every land of promise tolerable.

Niebuhr, R., *Discerning the Signs*, 93.

DECEMBER
Month of the Advent Season

Nothing that is worth doing can be achieved in our lifetime; therefore we must be saved by *hope*. Nothing which is true or beautiful or good makes complete sense in any immediate context of history; therefore we must be saved by *faith*. Nothing we do, however virtuous, can be accomplished alone; therefore we must be saved by *love*. No virtuous act is quite as virtuous from the standpoint of our friend or foe as it is from our own standpoint. Therefore we must be saved by the final form of love which is *forgiveness*. [emphasis added]

Niebuhr, R., *Irony of American History*, 63.

DECEMBER 205

DECEMBER 1. ADVENT SEASON/WORLD AIDS DAY/NATIONAL DAY OF GIVING.

The final question about our existence is whether it makes sense. An obvious answer to that question is that it does not make sense as simply as either the pietists or the rationalists assume. Life is full of contradictions and incongruities, not to speak of its tragic dissonances. Our meanings are surrounded by a penumbra of mystery . . .

Niebuhr, R., *Pious and Secular America,* 123.

DECEMBER 2. ON HOPE.

Hope is a particular form of faith; hope is faith related to the future. Hope can be as egoistic as faith in that we face the same problems of immaturity and maturity. Thus, we might hope that our nation will always be great as it is now, or we might hope that an umbrella of security will be established over our family against all other families; or we might hope that Western civilization will survive untouched . . . Those forms of hope are not really mature hope. To have mature hope is to rejoice in the whole drama of human history, including the terrible anxieties of a nuclear age. We do not know if we will survive or whether the great powers will destroy each other in their fateful struggle on the abyss of nuclear annihilation. But we hope that we have the wisdom and responsibility to escape this fate, in which case we could have a more universal community. In a sense we are saved by hope, in that we believe not only in the goodness of life but we believe in the meaningfulness of the great drama of life . . . We do not have to flee from history into eternity, but eternity is a quality which is gained by faith and love in history.

Niebuhr, R., *Justice and Mercy,* 34–35.

DECEMBER 3. JUDGMENT AS RIGHT-WISING.

Eternal God, Father Almighty, maker of heaven and earth, we worship you. Your wisdom is beyond our understanding, your power is greater than we can imagine, your thoughts are above our thoughts; as high as the heaven is above earth, your majesty judges all human majesties. Your judgment brings princes to naught, and makes the judges of the earth as vanity; for before the mountains were brought forth or over the earth and the worlds were made, even from everlasting to everlasting you are God.

Niebuhr, R., *Justice and Mercy,* 37.

DECEMBER 4.   MATURE OR SENTIMENTAL?

When we talk about love, we have to become mature or we will become sentimental. Let us not say that we as Christians are potential martyrs, or that we are more unselfish than other people. That is not what love means if we take it modestly. Basically, love means that life has no meaning except in terms of responsibility; responsibility toward our family, toward our nation, toward our civilization and, now, by the pressures of history, toward the universe of [humankind] which includes our enemies. "The greatest of these is love"—"Thou shall love thy neighbour as thyself"— that is the basic meaning of love, as the permanent abiding value of life.

Niebuhr, R., Justice and Mercy, 35.

DECEMBER 5.   POWER AND WISDOM VIA FAITH.

Give us grace to apprehend by faith the power and wisdom which lie beyond our understanding; and in worship to feel that which we do not know, and to praise even what we do not understand; so that in the presence of your glory we may be humble, and in the knowledge of your judgement we may repent; and so in the assurance of your mercy, we may rejoice and be glad.

Niebuhr, R., Justice and Mercy, 37.

DECEMBER 6.   NATIONAL DAY OF REMEMBRANCE AND ACTION ON VIOLENCE AGAINST WOMEN/ ACROSS CHASMS AND COMMUNITIES.

There must be some way of bridging across chasms and communities because we face a world that has no institutions. We still stand on the edge of war with the possibilities of misadventure and miscalculation; one has the uneasy feeling about that as we sit to the Lord's words about the last judgment. We may be doing all ordinary things and then . . . in one moment interruption comes . . . Even if the nuclear dilemma crisis is not the ultimate judgment it is certainly pen-ultimate, and as pen-ultimate strikes us with humility. The Christian gospel breeds a clarity without which we can never live and certainly cannot live in a nuclear age.

Let us pray:

God give us the grace of firmness in the light as thou givest us to see the light. The grace also of recognizing that in thy sight no man or woman living is justified, that we relate to our sisters and brothers and pay heed to our foes with malice to none and charity to all, through Christ our Lord.

Niebuhr, R., "Advent Sermon in an Atomic Age," Audio Tape 8.

DECEMBER 7. COMING TO TERMS WITH SIDELINES.

Sidelines are on the one hand filled with athletes who have been injured in the battles of the arena, and on the other hand with spectators. My view of life since my stroke had to be informed by both perspectives. I was dismissed from the battle, but I was also a spectator to engagements that had hitherto occupied me. Emancipation from the endless discussion of committee meetings, trying to solve problems in political and religious communities, that had hitherto occupied so much of my time, was a desirable freedom from the chores of a democratic society; but it also meant an emancipation from responsibility—a doubtful boon, because responsibility engages us in the causes of moral, political, and religious movements.

Niebuhr, R., "View from the Sidelines," 252.

DECEMBER 8. SIDELINE'S ADVANTAGE.

There is some advantage in the spectator's view as opposed to the advocate's. One can see all the strange forms of spirit and culture that a common faith may take, without disloyalty to one's inherited beliefs. It can be exciting when one ceases to be a consistent advocate and polemical agent of a belief system. If I feel at times, that an attitude from the sidelines may betray the irresponsibility of a pure spectator, I console myself with the fact that my current loyalty to causes, while less copious, is also more selective. And on the two main collective moral issues of our day—the civil rights movement which seeks democratic improvements for our black minority, and opposition to the terrible and mistaken war in Vietnam—the thoroughly ecumenical cooperation among the biblical faiths gives one a reassuring confidence that unpolemical attitudes are not in contrast to moral commitments. My semi-retirement has brought me nearer to other common moral commitments of the three [Abrahamic] faiths.

Niebuhr, R., "View from the Sidelines," 252–53.

DECEMBER 9.   DOUBLENESS OF THE MIND.

Rejoicing and dreading do not exclude each other. As Schleiermacher wrote: "Joy does not displace sorrow rather both overspread one's entire being." This quality deserves stressing.

Despair and dreading do not banish rejoicing, nor does gladness extinguish fearing. They are not contradictories; they are opposites and hence do not root each other out. So it is possible to be conscious at one and the same time of being "shipwrecked" and of "being under way." In his Confessions Augustine puzzled over this doubleness of the mind, "that when in a joyful mind I remember an earlier sadness, my mind hath joy, and my memory sadness" (X, xiv). It shows how life can be appropriately portrayed as an oscillation between these two encompassing affections. Indeed, it seems to be almost a law of human existence that these two affections and their corresponding images are superimposed, and neither is likely to disappear completely. [We are], however, more aware of dread in joy than of joy in dreading. And therefore all of a [person]'s experiences are similarly deeply conditioned by these two tonalities of being-in-the-world.

Niebuhr, R.R., *Experiential Religion*, 104.

DECEMBER 10.   HUMAN RIGHTS DAY / THOMAS MERTON'S AND KARL BARTH'S DEATHS (1968).

We should have come at last to the conclusion that the paradox of humanity's tribal and universal nature must exhibit, and be solved by, the most diverse resources in his nature.

The harnessing of the national interest to the project of guarding these human rights and liberties will not assure necessarily a quick triumph ... The historical tribal roots of prejudice have too long accumulated, and the marks of racial distinction are too obvious to guaranteed the triumph over them, even by a united and powerful national consensus. All that may be said is that the problem will probably concern the

DECEMBER 209

nation for at least a century even as the tolerable solution of the problem of economic justice required the resources of democracy throughout the nineteenth century.

Niebuhr, R., *On Man's Nature and His Communities,* 105.

We thank thee, our Father, for life and love, for the mystery and majesty of human existence, for the world of beauty which surrounds us and the miracle of our conscious life by which we behold the wonders of the universe . . . We confess that we have profaned the temple of this life by our selfishness and heedlessness . . . Have mercy on us, that we may express our contrition for our sins and that we may prove our repentance by lives dedicated more fully to thee and to the common good, through Jesus Christ our Lord.

Niebuhr, R., *Reinhold Niebuhr: Major Works,* 697.

DECEMBER 11. SOLUTION BEYOND ALL OUR SOLUTIONS.

Spiritually an organization such as UNESCO [United Nations Educational, Scientific and Cultural Organization], as well as the whole modern generation, needs a faith which recognizes the completion of life within and above its fragmentariness, the final solution beyond all our solutions . . . The spiritual problem of UNESCO is exactly the spiritual problem of modern people, who must find a way of engaging in impossible tasks and not be discouraged when he [or she] fails to complete any of them . . . It needs, in short, an apprehension of the grace which makes it possible for [persons] to say "We are perplexed but not unto despair" [II Cor. 4:8.].

Niebuhr, R., in Davis and Good, *Reinhold Niebuhr on Politics,* 260.

Man or woman is not a measure of all things but must be measured by things greater than him or herself. Unless we get out of our planetary provincialism, our narrow selfish way of thinking and looking at things, and cultivate a cosmic faith, we can never understand the many problems we are facing, nor realize the brotherhood and sisterhood of humans.

Niebuhr, H.R., in J. Diefenthaler, "H. Richard Niebuhr," 184.

DECEMBER 12. AS SUFFERING LOVE.

To believe that the suffering Messiah will return at the end of history as a triumphant judge and redeemer is to express the faith that existence cannot ultimately defy its own norm. Love may have to live in history as suffering love because the power of sin makes a simple triumph of love impossible. But if this were the ultimate situation it could be necessary either to worship the power of sin as the final power in the world or to regard it as a second God, not able to triumph, but strong enough to avoid defeat. The vindication of Christ and his triumphant return is therefore an expression of faith in the sufficiency of God's sovereignty over the world and history, and in the final supremacy of love over all the forces of self-love which defy, for the moment, the inclusive harmony of all things under the will of God.

Niebuhr, R., *Nature and Destiny of Man* (Vol. II), 290.

DECEMBER 13. LAST JUDGMENT'S IMPORT/ DEATH OF ELISABETH NIEBUHR-SIFTON.

The symbol of the last judgement in New Testament eschatology contains three important facets of the Christian conception of life and history. The first is expressed in the idea that it is Christ who will be the judge of history. Christ as judge means that when the historical confronts the eternal it is judged by its own ideal possibility, and not by the contrast between the finite and the eternal character of God. The judgement is upon sin and not finiteness. This idea is in logical accord with the whole Biblical conception of life and history, according to which it is not the partial and particular character of human existence which is evil, but rather the self-love by which [persons] disturb the harmony of creation as it would exist if all creatures obeyed the divine will.

Niebuhr, R., *Nature and Destiny of Man* (Vol. II), 291–92.

DECEMBER 14. DIVINE MERCY AND FORGIVENESS.

The second facet in the symbol of the last judgement is its emphasis upon the distinction between good and evil in history. When history confronts God the differences between good and evil are not swallowed up in a directionless eternity. All historical realities are indeed ambiguous.

DECEMBER   211

Therefore no absolute distinction between good and evil is possible. But this does not obviate the necessity and possibility of a final judgement upon good and evil. To be sure the righteous, standing before the last judgement, do not believe themselves to be righteous, and their uneasy conscience proves the final problem of history to be that, before God, "no [person] living is justified." There is no solution to this final problem short of the divine mercy and the "forgiveness of sins."

Niebuhr, R., *Nature and Destiny of Man* (Vol. II), 292.

DECEMBER 15. FEARS OF DEATH AND JUDGMENT.

The third facet in the symbol of the last judgment is to be found in its locus at the "end" of history. There is no achievement or partial realization in history, no fulfillment of meaning or achievement of virtue by which man can escape the final judgement. The idea of a "last" judgement expresses Christianity's refutation of all conceptions of history, according to which it is its own development, to emancipate man and woman from the guilt and sin of their existence, and to free them from judgment.

Many a court of opinion may dismiss us with a: "Well done, thou good and faithful servant"; but we will deceive ourselves if we believe such a judgement to be final. If men and women are fully aware, they will discern an accent of the fear of judgment in the fear of death. The fear of death arises from merely the ambiguity of finiteness and freedom which underlies all historical existence; but the fear of judgment is prompted by awareness of the mixture of sin and creativity which is the very substance of history.

Niebuhr, R., *Nature and Destiny of Man* (Vol. II), 293–94.

DECEMBER 16. THE DISQUIETING CONCLUSION.

If we analyze the different dimensions of human existence, the social and the vertical, we come to the disquieting conclusion that the roots of religious imagination are much more in the intensities of consciousness and conscience and sense of guilt than they are in all our social experience. Most of our social experiences, practically speaking, tend to idolatry, whether the idolatry of nation or denomination. As we pray together, we pray together idolatrously asking God to bless us: "Me and my wife, John and his wife, us four, no more."

Give us grace, our Father, to measure the heights of our dignity as free spirits, and the depths of our misery and the breadth of our responsibility. Judge us in our vanities and pretensions. Have pity on us, for only your infinite pity is adequate to the infinite pathos of human existence.

Niebuhr, R., *Justice and Mercy*, 110–11.

DECEMBER 17.   DANGEREOUS "WITHOUT'S."

A God *without* wrath brought men and women *without* sin into a kingdom *without* judgment through the ministrations of a Christ *without* a Cross.

Niebuhr, H.R., and Marty, *Kingdom of God in America*, 193 italics added.

My intention has not been to dismiss older ways of thinking but to begin to take our older ways and still older issues of religion and faith and God and place them in the light that is thrown in our own perceptions of the new man [and woman] today who has their being in a world of power that is forever disquieting him and reshaping her. Is it not possible that this person, whom we all know well, is experiencing the terrible joy of being made and made again by a ruling power that he [or she] knows but does not know that they know? Is it not possible that in his and his daily despair and occasional gladness they can accept these moments of awakening, in a world where Jesus of Nazareth has gone before, as telling them what God is? God is our determination and our freedom, our living and our dying.

Niebuhr, R.R., *Experiential Religion*, 140.

DECEMBER 18.   CHRIST . . . EXPECTED/NOT EXPECTED.

The basic distinction between historical and non-historical religions and cultures may be succinctly defined as the difference between those which expect and those which do not expect a Christ. A Christ is expected wherever history is regarded as potentially meaningful but as still awaiting the full disclosure and fulfillment of is meaning. A Christ is not expected wherever the meaning of life is explained from the standpoint of either nature or supernature in such a way that a transcendent revelation of history's meaning is not regarded as either possible or necessary. It is not regarded as necessary when one's capacity for freedom and self-transcendence is believed to be infinitely extensible until the ambiguities of history are left behind and pure eternity is achieved. The significance of a Christ is that this [One] is a disclosure of the divine purpose, governing history within history.

Niebuhr, R., Nature and Destiny of Man (Vol. II), 4–5.

DECEMBER 19.   DISCLOSURE.

A Christ is expected wherever history is thought of as a realm of fragmentary revelation of a purpose and power transcending history, pointing to a fuller disclosure of that purpose and power. [The Human One] is expected because this disclosure is regarded as both possible and necessary. It is regarded as possible because history is known to be something more than the nature-necessity in which it has its roots. It is regarded as necessary because the potential meaningfulness of history is recognized as fragmentary and corrupted. It must be completed and clarified.

Niebuhr, R., Nature and Destiny of Man (Vol. II), 5.

DECEMBER 20.   GENUINE STUMBLING BLOCK.

No Christ could validate himself as the disclosure of a hidden divine sovereignty over history or as a vindication of the meaningfulness of history, if a Christ were not expected . . .

If history is not regarded as potentially meaningful, the claim that potential meaning has been realized and that obscurities and ambiguities in history have been clarified would not be credible.

The true Christ must be a stumbling block in the sense that he must disappoint, as well as fulfill, expectations. He must disappoint some expectations because Messianic expectations invariably contain egoistic elements, which could not be fulfilled without falsifying the meaning of history. Every Messianic expectation contains an explicit or implicit assumption that history will be fulfilled from the particular locus of the civilization and culture which has the expectation.

Niebuhr, R., *Nature and Destiny of Man* (Vol. II), 15–16.

DECEMBER 21   MESSIANIC HOPES.

On the egoistic-nationalist level Messianism looks forward to the triumph of the nation, empire or culture in which the Messianic hope is expressed. This means that history is regarded as obscure and that life is threatened with meaninglessness primarily because the collective life of nation or empire, which is the primary source of meaning, is known to be more finite than it pretends to be. The symbol of its insecurity is the power of its foes. The fulfillment of life's meaning is thus contained in the triumph of our nation or civilization over its foes . . . It must be added that it is not only impossible for the highest forms of Christian prophetism to remain free of egoistic corruptions; it is also impossible for the most advanced civilization to be safe against reversions to the very primitive egoistic-nationalistic interpretations of history, as for instance in Nazism.

Niebuhr, R., *Nature and Destiny of Man* (Vol. II), 18.

DECEMBER 22.   SIGNIFICANCE OF IMPORTANT SYMBOL.

On the second level of Messianism [the ethical-universalistic level of Messianism], the problem of history is not the impotence of our race, empire or nation, and the answer to the problem of history, therefore, cannot be the triumph of our people over our foes. The problem of history is the impotence of the good against the evil forces in history. The momentary triumph of evil in history is seen as a threat to the meaningfulness of history and this threat is overcome by the hope of the coming of a Messianic king who will combine power and goodness. This is the significance of the figure of the Messianic "shepherd king," an important symbol not only in Hebraic but in Babylonian and Egyptian Messianism. The shepherd king is gentle despite his power. As a judge he rises to the heights of imaginative justice in which justice and mercy become one, for he "shall not judge after the sight of his eyes, neither reprove after the

DECEMBER 215

hearing of his ears; but with righteousness shall he judge the poor, and reprove with equity for the meek of the earth" (Isaiah 11: 3–4).

Niebuhr, R., *Nature and Destiny of Man* (Vol. II), 19.

DECEMBER 23. SHEPHERD KING?

The hope of a shepherd king is a very profound expression of the ethos of historical cultures. Its weakness lies in the fact that it hopes for an impossible combination of the divine and the historical. The God who is both powerful and good by reason of being the source of all power, and not some particular power in history, cannot remain good if the Holy One becomes a particular power in human society. Perfect goodness in history can be symbolized only by the disavowal of power. But this did not become clear until the One appeared who rejected all concepts of Messianic dominions and became a "suffering servant." The great contribution of prophetic Messianism consists in the fact that it interpreted history too profoundly to allow the solution of the Messianic king to remain tenable. It saw history involved in the inevitable tragedy of tempting the rulers and the nations, who performed a special mission in history, to the sins of pride and injustice.

Niebuhr, R., *Nature and Destiny of Man* (Vol. II), 22–23.

DECEMBER 24. EVE OF ITS APPEARANCE.

The truth which is revealed in Christ must be apprehended by faith. Faith, as far as it uses our natural endowments, draws on poetic and imaginative capacities rather than rational ones. The point of the Christian story is that we see a clue to the character of God in the character and drama of Christ; and we have some understanding of the fact that the similarity of love between God and Christ is partly revealed by the dissimilarity of power in the historical and trans-historical. The divine goodness is a part of the divine majesty and power; but it can appear in history only in powerless, rather than powerful, terms.

Niebuhr, R., *Discerning the Signs*, 143–44.

By such acceptance the believer is lifted in principle above the egoistic corruptions of the truth in history: "as many as received him, to them gave he the right to become the children of God" (John 1:12).]

Niebuhr, R., *Nature and Destiny of Man* (Vol. II), 215.

DECEMBER 25.   I BELIEVE . . .

I believe the Christmas story. It expresses the idea that the great God of the universe has purposes which are relevant to humanity's purposes. This is very difficult to believe. Human values must achieve cosmic validity if any religion is to live. Yet there must be to this belief some suggestion of the mystery of life and of the majesty of the divine which transcends human life. True religion therefore must be conscious of the difficulty and the absurdity of the human claiming kinship with the divine, of the temporal trafficking with the eternal. If the divine is made relevant to the human, it must transvalue our values and enter the human at the point where one is lowly rather than proud and where one is weak rather than strong. Therefore believe that God came in the form of a little child born to humble parents in a manger "because there was no room for them in the inn" (Luke 2:8).

But if I put all this in rational terms I lose something of the rich variety of the Christmas story. I prefer, therefore, to do what I did on Christmas day: I like to sing "Hark the herald angels sing" and "O come, all ye faithful." I like to hear the soprano of boy's voices rejoicing, "Glory to God in the highest." (Why should these urchins who have such a difficult challenge keeping quiet in their choir stalls suggest the song of angels to me?).

Niebuhr, R., *Essays in Applied Christianity*, 29–30.

DECEMBER 26.   DRAMAS OF HISTORY.

The dramas of history contain many facts and sequences which must be rationally correlated. But the frame of meaning in which these acts and sequences are discerned must be apprehended by faith because it touches the realm of mystery beyond rational comprehension. The ultimate question always remains whether the mystery is so absolute as to annul the meaning of the historical drama or whether there is a key of meaning in

DECEMBER 217

the mystery, a light "that shines in the darkness [John 1]," which clarifies, rather than annuls, all the strange and variegated dramas of history.

Niebuhr, R., *Self and the Dramas of History*, 242.

Grant us grace, O Lord, that the praise we give you as we begin the day may diffuse the thoughts and actions of this day. Be with us as we do our work and meet our friends and co-workers, and study the Scriptures and search out the riches of your wisdom.

Niebuhr, R., *Justice and Mercy*, 113.

DECEMBER 27. POSSIBILITY WITHIN IMPOSSIBLE.

The world community, toward which all historical forces seem to be driving us, is [humankind]'s final possibility and impossibility. The task of achieving it must be interpreted from the standpoint of a faith which understands the fragmentary and broken character of all historic achievements and yet has confidence in their meaning because it knows their completion to be in the hands of a Divine Power, whose resources are greater than those of men and women, and whose suffering love can overcome the corruptions of one's achievement, without negating the significance of our striving.

Niebuhr, R., *Children of Light*, 189–90.

DECEMBER 28. WIFE'S PREACHER-HUSBAND.

The task of the preacher as Reinhold Niebuhr saw it was to show Christian faith as relevant to life, in both its individual and social dimensions. For him, the Christian faith was "a present fact, and a present truth about life that illumines our existence and gives meaning, relieves us of some of the miseries of guilt in which all persons are involved, explains the curious paradox of human freedom and human necessity of human freedom in spite of the fact that we are living in the necessities of nature." The "effort to establish relevance and the effort to establish applicability," these followed from his basic assumption; so he suggested to his theological students that a good part of their education should be "concerned with validating the foolishness of God as wisdom, but also in relating this wisdom to the wisdom of the world . . . For forty years I preached almost every Sunday in various parts of the country. This experience taught me much. 'Making sense' out of the symbols and professions of faith has always been the responsibility of preacher and teacher."

Niebuhr, U., "Introduction," in Niebuhr, R., *Justice and Mercy*, 5.

DECEMBER 29.   IN FAITH.

In faith we seek to make decisions in our existential present, knowing that the measure of faith is so meager that we are always combining denials with our affirmations of it. Yet in faith in the faithfulness of God, we count on being corrected, forgiven, complemented, by the company of the faithful and by many others to whom God is faithful though they reject the Holy One. To make our decisions in faith is to make them in view of the fact that the world of culture—man's achievement—exists within the world of grace—God's Kingdom.

Niebuhr, H.R., *Christ and Culture*, 255–56.

The burden of Jesus' conduct is to disclose the worlds opposing and informing him as a theater of action. The motive of that action is the divine good-pleasure. The quality of that action is generosity. The mass of that action is power. The appearance of that action is Jesus' own persona. The goal of that action is human faithfulness wrought out of the experience of diminishment and enlargement in which that great action may appear again in glory. God-ruling is a powerful, generous, and swift good-pleasure intersecting the human world at every point, now making [people] small, now making them great, but never letting them be.

Niebuhr, R.R., *Experiential Religion*, 137.

DECEMBER 30.   VIA INTERCESSIONS . . .
AN ULTIMATE MEANING.

Prayer is meditation and reflection and suggestion and also communion with God. In that communion the heart of man and woman may be changed; may not the heart of God also be affected? In such a social community as the Kingdom of God, as it exists at any time, the relationship of all members may and must be changed through the activity of the one.

Niebuhr, H.R., in Fowler, *To See the Kingdom*, 48 note 109.

DECEMBER

Finally, all concern for immediate correlations and coherences and meanings falls away. The Christian faith stands in the sense of an ultimate meaning. We may be persuaded that God is on our side—not against somebody else—but on our side in this ultimate sense. We are "sure that neither death nor life, nor angels, nor principalities, nor things present, nor things to come, . . . will be able to separate us from the love of God in Christ Jesus our Lord" [Romans 8].

It is on that level of meaning that the Christian faith makes sense. The lower levels are a threat, not only to the sense of the meaning of life, but finally to the morals of life. We must not deny that there is a kind of religion that enhances the ego and gives it an undue place in the world. But from the standpoint of our faith we should take our humble and contrite place in God's plan of the whole, and leave it to the Consummator to complete the fragmentation of our life.

Niebuhr, R., *Justice and Mercy*, 22.

DECEMBER 31: ENDINGS: UNTIL SUCH A DAY . . . A NEW BEGINNING.

When we believe we are perishing we see ourselves in a world surrounded by foes. We interpret the presence of the foes with the suspicious attitude of those who see death, in the whole environment. When the cross comes into view the scene is changed. It does not make our enemies into friends, to be sure, but does bring us at least daily to the realization that foes and friends in our environment are all under the control of the final prevailing love of God. We learn somehow to say, "I am persuaded that neither life nor death, nor the heedlessness of nature, nor the blind operation of natural laws, nor the fateful forces of history, nor the cruelty of men or women, nor the strange forces within me nor any other awful thing can separate us from the love of God which is in Christ Jesus our Lord." Here is a new beginning for a wisdom which is not the strategy of survival but the strategy of salvation, reconciliation, resurrection. It is the kind of wisdom which we see exemplified in the struggles of sick people who believe they are getting well and in the bravery under opposition which folk in occupied countries manifest when they are assured that they are being liberated.

Niebuhr, H.R., *Theology, History, and Culture*, 206.

My father's story came to an end, and the story of the remarkable generation of men and women with whom he worked and prayed—that came to an end, too. But their example taught me the obvious truth that the story of a prayer has no ending at all—it must continue into the future. The story of the Serenity Prayer has no final cadence.

Sifton, *Serenity Prayer,* **11.**

It was painful for Pa and his friends to observe their work being neglected or traduced. But my mother would remind me how wrong it was to try to calculate the value of a life or career by measuring whether or how much in it endured. It is not for us to make this accounting.

Sifton, *Serenity Prayer,* **346.**

"I have a dream..." by Jim Houston

Appendix

Brief Profiles of the Niebuhrs Employed in This Reader

GUSTAV NIEBUHR [JR.]

Born: July 30, 1955, Poughkeepsie, New York.

Son of Richard Reinhold Niebuhr (RRN), grand-nephew of Reinhold and Hulda, he has reflected on the place and import of his known family members, including honouring his paternal great-grandfather, his namesake (see Beyond Tolerance, cf. entry for 6/19). A working and teaching journalist—formerly New York Times, Washington Post, Wall Street Journal, and founder/presently Religion and Media, Syracuse University—Gustav comments on current events, delves into rich historical perspectives for the sake of interfaith social ethics, and to this end, his writings are thankfully noted and employed.

H. RICHARD NIEBUHR

Born: 1894, Wright City, Missouri; Died: July 5, 1962, Greenfield, Massachusetts.

The youngest of the Niebuhr brothers; the oldest, Walter, not a minister but following their father's sudden death assisted the family, enabling the mother, and two other brothers carry on.

Subject to depression, possibly induced by the silent treatment by his father, HRN was considered the wiser theologian (so affirmed by Reinhold and others) and published less but abides. Many of his writings and quotable morsels are employed herein. Several were edited and prefaced by his son, RRN or students (especially the late James M. Gustafson, blessed be their memories). He combined and integrated the disciplines of theology, sociology, philosophy, history, and church life and thought (ecclesiology).

HULDA NIEBUHR (CLARA AUGUSTA)

Born: March 9, 1889 (San Franciso, CA); Died: April 17, 1959 (one month before retirement).

The first of four children of Gustav [Sr.] and Lydia, Clara Augusta Hulda Niebuhr, was born in 1889. Unfortunately, although her father made plans for his sons, Pastor Niebuhr had rather conventional ideas about the education of his only daughter. Fortunately Hulda did not fit his image. It never occurred to him that a girl should or might be interested in advanced education.
. . . In 1945 the Presbyterian College of Education, associated with McCormick Theological Seminary in Chicago, recognized her experience and scholarly expertise and invited her to join the faculty as associate professor of religious education. In 1949 that school merged with McCormick and in 1953 Hulda Niebuhr became the first woman to hold the rank of full professor at McCormick Theological Seminary.

"Another Niebuhr" in Retrieving Women's Histories
http://d3n8a8pro7vhmx.cloudfront.net/unitedchurchofchrist/
legacy_url/13146/microsoft-word-rh-23-another-niebuhr-format-
ted-and-revised.pdf?1418439396#:~:text=Hulda%20Niebuhr%20
died%20at%20age,a%20creative%20and%20imaginative%20
scholar [accessed May 27, 2021].

Elizabeth Caldwell's biography of Hulda, A Mysterious Mantle, includes many morsels of her shorter writings.

LYDIA NIEBUHR (NEE: HOSTO)

Born: December 25, 1869, Illinois; Died: 1961, Lincoln, Illinois.

Given her children and their generational offspring, Lydia was known as "The Queen Bee of American Theologians," in a PhD dissertation, which also named her an "Evangelical Matriarch" (John Clifford Helt, Evanston,

BRIEF PROFILES OF THE NIEBUHRS   223

Illinois, June 1994). In his eulogy of Lydia, theologian Paul Lehmann added, ". . . in her own right a person of unforgettable gentleness, humane sensibility, humility and unreserved caring."

Also a "preacher's kid" and with musical talent, Lydia creatively and perhaps uncannily devoted herself (as one of 12 children) a whole life of dedication to her son Reinhold and daughter Hulda's personal, family and vocational lives. She is given credit for many mid-week, Sunday programs, and church school sessions. See Richard Fox's biography on Reinhold and especially Chapter 4, "A New Kind of Monasticism."

GUSTAV NIEBUHR (REV.) [SR.]

> Born: 1863; Died: April 21, 1913.

Gustav [Sr.] was patriarch of the family in which Reinhold, H. Richard, and Hulda were born and raised. The oldest sibling, Walter, practiced business and supported the family upon Gustav's early death. Gustav immersed his family in biblical literature including studies of Hebrew and Greek, with them retaining the spoken language of German. He was a church planter and minister with the former German Evangelical Synod, eventually absorbed by the present United Church of Christ. He also supported the organizing of a liberal arts college, Elmhurst, and theological seminary, Eden. Gustav apparently favoured Reinhold and drove Walter away, discouraged Hulda from academic pursuits, and alleged to have treated his wife as a combination of "unpaid co-pastor and domestic servant" (Michael Westmoreland-Whyte, "An Appreciation of the Niebuhr Family," https://levellers.wordpress.com/2009/11/22/an-appreciation-of-the-family-niebuhr/).

Nonetheless warts, disciplines, and all, apart from Gustav, none of the rest of the Niebuhr family could have been alive for us to meditate and contemplate. Hence: "To the memory of my Father who taught me that the critical faculty can be united with a reverent spirit," said Reinhold Niebuhr of Gustav Niebuhr [Sr.], an inscription in "Does Civilization Need Religion?" (cited in Chrystal, "A Man of the Hour and Time," 416, note 3).

(KARL PAUL) REINHOLD NIEBUHR

> Born: June 21, 1892, Wright City, Missouri; Died: June 1, 1971; Stockbridge, Massachusetts.

224   BRIEF PROFILES OF THE NIEBUHRS

Profiles and biographies abound as do Reinhold Niebuhr's own interpretative reminiscences and intellectual autobiographies. Much of this
is found in this daily reader, including Reinhold's belated disclosure that
his wife, Ursula, could take virtual co-responsibility and, thus, credit
for many of his ideas and reflections, especially in his later years. Also
notable are the supportive roles his mother and sister exercised in Reinhold's parish life and work rendering him a virtual "new monastic";
that is, he was virtually set free to travel, organize Christian and secular
networks for political thought and action, preach on regular weekend
circuit rides (chiefly campuses and theological schools) and research for
books, lecture series, and a full load as a social ethics teacher and mentor
(see Douglas John Hall's "Foreword"). The Journey Films' biography-
documentary, "Reinhold Niebuhr: An American Conscience for Our
Time" (see Doblmeier in the Bibliography) testifies to his long and wide
influences, including the late Rabbi Abraham Joshua Heschel who provided the eulogy at Reinhold Niebuhr's funeral.

In addition to founding and leading several serious social justice
fellowships (e.g., Fellowship of Socialist Christians, Frontier Fellowship,
and Christian Action along with their accompanying quarterly journals),
he founded the bi-weekly Christianity and Crisis (1941-1993). He also
helped to fund and support ventures like the East Harlem Protestant Parish, black and white sharecropper associations, and Americans for Democratic Action—as well as bringing Paul Tillich and Dietrich Bonhoeffer
to Union Theological Seminary at crucial times of their lives and country.

RICHARD REINHOLD NIEBUHR

Born: 1926, Chicago, ILL; Died: February 26, 2017, Middlebury,
Vermont.

Son of H. Richard Niebuhr, Richard Reinhold began teaching at Harvard
Divinity School in 1956 and retired as professor emeritus. A renowned
scholar and theologian, he was also an ordained minister in the United
Church of Christ. More like his father, H. Richard Niebuhr, and less
social justice active as his uncle (Reinhold Niebuhr), one finds morsels
here and there in his writings, including editing and contributing to his
father's posthumous writings. These have hopefully been done some justice in this daily reader. Missing however are samples of his sermons,
prayers, and memoir-like contributions. But an intellectual biography
could compensate, perhaps in the works by his journalist son, Gustav

BRIEF PROFILES OF THE NIEBUHRS   225

[Jr.]? In addition to fathering Gustav and Sarah, with his wife, Nancy, his legacy endures via the Harvard Divinity School's Richard Reinhold Niebuhr Chair of Divinity.

URSULA MARY NIEBUHR (NEE: KEPPEL-COMPTON)

> Born: 1908, Southampton, England; Died: 1997, Stockbridge, Massachusetts.

One of the first woman Anglican theologians, she met Reinhold when a young student at Union Theological Seminary. While child-rearing early in their marriage, she creatively supported her husband and then especially when he had several strokes. Traces of this are delightfully found in the letters of Reinhold and Ursula (Remembering Reinhold Niebuhr). It is important background to Reinhold's sermonic essays and prayers (Justice and Mercy), also studiously researched and edited by Ursula. Elisabeth Sifton's own reminiscences *enrich* her mother and their family life in the 1930s and 1940s, via her *The Serenity Prayer* and its instructive subtitle, *Faith and Politics in Times of War and Peace*. Nonetheless, Ursula found her own into and through academic life founding and presiding over Barnard College's Department of Religion.

(BARBARA) ELISABETH SIFTON (NEE: NIEBUHR)

> Born: January 13, 1939, New York City; Died: December 13, 2019, Manhattan, New York.

One of two children to Ursula and Reinhold, Christopher being the older son, Elisabeth cut her teeth in the literary world as a book editor and publisher, and certainly provided a legacy favor to her father by editing and publishing several of Reinhold's early writings including, invaluably, his many prayers (see the Bibliography). Her virtual memoir of her life and times when in the family's household informs the origins, deep themes, and popularization of the "Serenity Prayer," and her discernment on "grace" in the now-retrieved and sustained original prayer is utterly indispensable. Elisabeth also contributed to the Journey Films' fitting tribute to Reinhold Niebuhr via its "Reinhold Niebuhr: An American Conscience for Our Time" (see Doblmeier in the Bibliography). Unsurprisingly, Elisabeth co-authored her last book, No Ordinary Men, with her second husband, the late Fritz Stern.

For an informative 2015 interview with Elisabeth (and Serene Jones) especially noting her edited publication of *Reinhold Niebuhr: Major Works on Religion and Politics*, but also life in the Reinhold and Ursula Niebuhr family and Union Seminary body, see https://youtu.be/WhI9fM-mgAc.

Indexes

The indexes are listed via chief topics or Themes, Special Days (except for the many entries to "God," "grace," "faith," "love," "justice," "power," "mercy," "Jesus," "spirit," etc.), and Special Months. Each index item is listed under the month/date in which it appears.

THEME INDEX

Addiction, 3/2, 3/6, 3/13, 3/14, 3/18, 3/22, 3/23

Advent, 2/4, 5/26, 6/11, 12/1, 12/6

Art, role of as education/educator; cf. Imagination, 5/29, 6/18, 7/21, 8/15

Balance of Power, Preface, 2/24, 4/11, 8/2, 9/3, 9/15, 9/16; aka: equilibrium, 2/27, 4/10, 8/17, 8/18, 9/7

Broken/Brokenness, 1/19, 2/2, 2/10, 2/16, 2/20, 3/10, 3/21, 5/12, 5/22, 5/24, 6/7, 7/3, 7/5, 11/9, 11/28, 12/27

Courage, 1/13, 2/3, 2/4, 2/20, 5/27, 6/30 and more

Covenant, 2/28, 6/19, 7/5, and more

Cross, 1/5, 3/27, 3/29, 3/31, 4/4, 4/5, 4/6, 4/8, 4/11, 4/12, 4/14, 4/16, 4/25, 6/14, 8/12, 11/24, 11/28, 12/17, 12/31

Cynic/Cynicism, 1/10, 7/5, 8/30, 9/21, 10/18, 11/7, 11/13

Death, 1/27, 2/1, 2/2, 2/17, 3/31, 4/2, 4/4, 4/5, 4/6, 4/9, 4/20, 4/24, 4/25, 5/4, 5/16, 6/1, 6/21, 6/26, 6/29 and more

Demonic/Demonicry, 3/2, 3/15, 3/22, 5/13, 9/l1

Dogma/Dogmatic, 1/5, 1/12, 1/23, 2/18, 2/28, 4/13, 4/16, 4/19, 4/29, 5/6, 5/8, 5/18, 5/21, 7/9, 8/25, 10/25, ll/13, 12/15, 12/18, 12/20, 12/21

Emancipation Day or theme, 1/18, 6/19, 8/1

Eschatology, Preface, 12/13, 12/14, *cf. Fulfillment*

Evil, 1/1, 1/9, 1/10, 1/13, 1/24, 1/27, 1/28, 1/30, 2/2, 2/5, 2/11, 2/20, 3/5, 3/11, 3/12, 3/15, 3/20, 4/3, 4/4, 4/5, 4/11, 4/12, 4/14, 4/20, 4/30, 5/17, 6/13, 6/21, 6/23, 6/27 and more

Faith, 4/2, 4/4, 4/5, 4/11, 4/12, 4/14, 4/20, 4/30, 5/17, 6/13, 6/21, 6/23, 6/27, and many more

Fitting/Fittingness, 4/23, 4/24, 5/7, 10/21

Fulfillment, 1/5, 1/7, 1/12, 2/28, 4/13, 4/19, 4/29, 5/3, 5/9, 5/13, 5/18, 5/29, 11/30, 12/31

Healing, 5/12, 8/18, 10/10, 11/12

Heaven, 6/13, 7/25, 8/10, 8/16, 11/8, 12/3

Humor/Humour, 6/14, 9/5, 9/21

Idealism, 7/4, 7/13, 11/4, 11/6, 11/22

Imagination, 1/20, 1/29, 2/21, 2/25, 5/28, 5/29, 6/23/ 9/11, 9/26, 12/16

Integrity, 3/13, 3/15, 3/17, 4/27, 8/8, 9/8, 9/26, 10/7, 11/2

Labor/Labour, 2/29, 7/16, 9/8, 9/17, 9/25

Lie/Lies, 1/28, 3/12, 4/13, 4/30, 5/3, 10/2

Organize, 2/23, 3/22, 5/27, 6/16, 8/16, 10/30

Photography/ Photographer, 6/18, 8/15

Politics/Political, 1/29, 2/12, 3/13, 3/17, 4/8, 4/10, 5/23, 6/7, 6/23, 7/6, 7/23, 8/15, 8/18, 8/19, 8/26, 9/3, 9/13, 11/4, 12/17

Prayer(s), *General:* 2/1, 2/14, 2/22, 2/23, 3/18, 3/21, 3/22, 3/24, 5/22, 6/1, 6/2, 6/4, 6/6, 6/9, 6/14, 6/21, 6/28, 6/30, 7/8, 7/16, 8/27, 8/31, 9/1, 9/14, 9/6, 9/9, 9/17, 9/18, 9/10/9, 10/12, 10/17, 10/28, 11/8, 11/9. 11/10, 12/30; *grace-based Serenity Prayer:* 1/11, 2/2, 2/29, 3/16, 9/8, 9/20, 9/22, 9/24, 9/27, 9/28, 9/29, 10/17, 10/23, 10/24, 11/17, 11/18, 11/19, 11/20, 11/25, 12/3, 12/5, 12/6, 12/16, 12/26, 12/31

Realism, 8/30, 11/4, 12/7, plus citations to Christian Realism and Political Problems

INDEXES   229

Repentance, 1/10, 2/7, 3/16, 3/21, 4/12, 4/14, 5/10, 5/12, 5/16, 6/23

Saint(s), 3/24, 3/28, 10/10, 11/1

Sex, 3/18, 3/22, 3/23, 3/24, 3/26, 3/28, 7/11, 7/19, 7/28, 10/1, 10/10

Suffering, Cover, Preface, and: 1/5, 2/1, 2/14, 2/18, 3/21, 3/24, 3/30,
    4/2, 4/3, 4/5, 4/7, 4/11, 4/12, 4/13, 4/17, 5/6, 6/13, 8/13, 8/23, 9/17,
    11/2912/12, 12/23, 12/27

Temptation, Test/Testing, 1/10,2/1, 3/12, 4/20, 5/23, 5/24, 6/7, 7/8

Vital/Vitalities, 1/3, 3/2, 5/13, 5/23, 5/24, 6/8, 9/7, 9/15, 11/2, 11/6

Wisdom, 1/11, 2/9, 2/15, 2/24, 3/27, 3/28, 4/16, 5/8, 5/9, 5/10, 6/7,
    6/14, 6/30, 7/1, 7/4, 8/26, 9/9, 9/16, 9/20, 9/22, 9/23, 9/26, 9/27,
    11/9, 11/17, 12/5, 12/27, 12/28, 12/31; Cf. entries for "grace-based
    Serenity Prayer"

SPECIAL DAYS INDEX

Aboriginal Day, 6/21

Aboriginal Veterans Day (if Canada), 11/8

Aids World Day, 12/1

Allende, Salvador (Assassination of), 9/11

Canada Day, 7/1

D-Day, WWII, 6/6

Democracy, International Day of, 9/15

Dietrich Bonhoeffer, Execution, 4/9

Emancipation, 1/18, 6/19 (USA), 8/1 (Canada)

Family Day (USA), 9/26

Friendship, International Day of, 7/30

Grandparents, 7/27, 9/13

Happiness, 3/20

Hiroshima, 8/6

Holocaust Remembrance Day, 1/27

Housing Day and class conflicts, 11/22

Human Rights Day, 12/10

Independence Day, USA, 7/4

International Day of Midwife, 5/6

Islamophobia, Action Against, 1/29

July 26th Movement, precursor to 1959 Cuban Revolution, 7/26

Justice, 2/20, misc. and et al.

King, Jr., Martin Luther Day, 1/18

Kristallnacht . . . "Night of the Broken Glass," 11/9

Labour Day, 9/7 (if 1st Monday)

Lincoln Day, 2/12

Memory of Overdose Victims (incl. Eli Cooley-Morris), 3/18

Mental Health, 10/10

Merton and Barth's deaths, 12/10

Mother Earth Day, 4/22

National Day of Mourning for Work Deaths, 4/28

Niebuhr (nee: Keppel-Compton), Ursula, death of, 1/10, cf. 12/31

Niebuhr, Richard Reinhold, death of, 2/26

Niebuhr, Reinhold, death of, 6/1

Niebuhr, H. Richard, death of, 7/5

Niebuhr-Sifton, Elisabeth, death of, 12/13; cf. 12/31

Nine/eleven, 9/11

Non-Violence, International Day of, 10/2

Oscar Romero Feast Day, 3/24

Overdose Awareness Day, 8/31

Pardon Day, 9/8

Parkinson's, World Day of, 4/11

Poverty, Eradication of, 10/17

Racial Prejudice, Elimination of, 3/21

Reformation Sunday (if last of Oct), 10/31

Remembrance Day/Veterans Day (USA), 11/11

Safety & Health @ Work, 4/28

INDEXES 231

Saints (All), 11/1

Souls (All), 11/2

Thanksgiving Day, Canadian (if 2nd Monday), 10/12

Thanksgiving, USA (if 4th Thurs), 11/26

Vocations, Prayer for, 4/25

Women's Day, 3/18

Worker's Day, 5/11

SPECIAL MONTHS INDEX

January, National Mentoring Month, 1/1

February, Black History Month (USA and Canada), 2/1

March, Women's History Month, 3/1

April, Second Chance Month, 4/1

May, Mental Awareness Month, 5/1

June, National Indigenous History Month (Canada) and National Safety Month, 6/1

July, National Fragile X Awareness Month, 7/1

August, National Immunization Awareness Month (Canada and USA), 8/1

September, Gospel Music Heritage Month, 9/1

October, National Bullying Prevention Month, and Action, 10/1

November, National Family Caregivers Month (USA), 11/1

December, Month of the Advent Season, 12/1

Bibliography

Bingham, June. *Courage to Change: An Introduction to the Life and Thought of Reinhold Niebuhr.* New York: Charles Scribner's Sons, 1961.

Caldwell, Elizabeth. *A Mysterious Mantle: The Biography of Hulda Niebuhr.* Cleveland, OH: Pilgrim.

Chrystal, William G. *A Father's Mantle: The Legacy of Gustav Niebuhr.* New York: Pilgrim, 1982.

———. "A Man of the Hour and the Time": The Legacy of Gustav Niebuhr. *Church History* 49(4) (December 1980) 416-432.

Davis, H.R., and R. C. Good, eds. *Reinhold Niebuhr on Politics: His Political Philosophy and its Application to Our Age.* New York: Scribner's and Sons, 1960.

Diefenthaler, Jon. "H. Richard Niebuhr: A Fresh Look at His Early Years." In *Church History* 52 (January 1, 1983) 172-185. (Periodicals Archive Online)

Doblmeier, Martin, director, writer, narrator. "An American Conscience: The Reinhold Niebuhr Story," a biographical documentary. DVD. Alexandria, VA: Journey Films, 2017.

Fowler, James W. *To See the Kingdom: The Theological Vision of H. Richard Niebuhr.* Nashville, TN: Abingdon, 1974.

Fox, Richard W., *Reinhold Niebuhr: A Biography.* New York: Pantheon, 1985.

Littell, Franklin H. "'Reinhold Niebuhr and the Jewish People' given at the Niebuhr Lecture at Elmhurst College (1990-04-18)." Temple University Libraries Digital Collections. https://digital.library.temple.edu/digital/collection/p16002coll14/id/6360/rec/2 [accessed March 1, 2022].

Niebuhr, Gustav. (Jr.) *Beyond Tolerance: How People Across America Are Building Bridges Between Faiths.* New York: Viking Penguin, 2008.

———. "Las Vegas Journal; Feeding Spiritual Life Amid Pull of Casinos." *New York Times* 1 (January 30, 2000) 14. https://www.nytimes.com/2000/01/30/us/las-vegas-journal-feeding-spiritual-life-amid-pull-of-casinos.html [accessed January 15, 2022].

———. *Lincoln's Bishop: A President, A Priest, and the Fate of 300 Dakota Sioux Warriors.* NY: HarperCollins, 2014.

———. "Seeking Solace and Support in Meditation Books." *New York Times* A (June 29, 1994) 1. https://www.nytimes.com/1994/06/29/us/seeking-solace-and-support-in-meditation-books.html [accessed September 8, 2021].

Niebuhr, H. Richard. *Christ and Culture.* New York: Harper and Brothers, 1951.

———. *Faith on Earth: An Inquiry into the Structure of Human Faith*, edited by Richard R. Niebuhr. New Haven, CT: Yale University Press, 1989.

———. *The Meaning of Revelation*. New York: Macmillan, 1941.

———. et al. *The Purpose of the Church and Its Ministry: Reflections of the Aims of Theological Education*, 1-47, passim. New York: Harper and Brothers, 1956.

———. *Radical Monotheism and Western Culture*. New York: Harper Torchbooks, 1970.

———. *The Responsible Self: An Essay in Christian Moral Philosophy*. New York: Harper and Row, 1963.

———. "The Responsibility of the Church for Society" *and Other Essays*, edited by Kristine A. Culp. Louisville, KY: Westminster John Knox, 2008.

———. *Theology, History, and Culture*, edited by William Stacy Johnson. New Haven, CT: Yale University Press, 1996.

Niebuhr, H. Richard, and Martin E. Marty. *The Kingdom of God in America*. Middletown, CT: Wesleyan University Press, 1937/1988.

Niebuhr, Hulda. *The One Story*. Philadelphia: Westminster, 1949.

Niebuhr, Reinhold. "Advent Sermon in an Atomic Age." Audio Tape 8. *The Reinhold Niebuhr Audio Tape Collection*, Richmond, Virginia: Union Theological Seminary.

———. *Beyond Tragedy*. New York: Scribner's Sons, 1937.

———. "Chapel Talk on Romans 13:8." Audio Tape 26. *The Reinhold Niebuhr Audio Tape Collection*. Richmond, VA: Union Theological Seminary, 1979.

———. *The Children of Light and the Children of Darkness*. Chicago, IL: University of Chicago, 2011.

———. "Christian Faith and Social Action." In *Faith and Politics: A Commentary on Religious, Social and Political Thought in a Technological Age*, 119–37, edited by R. H. Stone. New York: George Braziller, 1968.

———. *Christianity and Power Politics*. Hamden, CT: Archon, 1969.

———. *Christian Realism and Political Problems*. Fairfield, NJ: Augustus Kelley, 1977.

———. "Development of a Social Ethic in the Ecumenical Movement." In *Faith and Politics: A Commentary on Religious, Social and Political Thought in a Technological Age*, 165–84, edited by R. H. Stone. New York: George Braziller, 1968.

———. *Discerning the Signs of the Times*. New York: Charles Scribner's Sons, 1946.

———. "Double Love Commandment." Audio Tape 3. In *The Reinhold Niebuhr Audio Tape Collection*. Richmond, Virginia: Union Theological Seminary, 1979.

———. *The Essential Reinhold Niebuhr: Selected Essays and Addresses*, edited by Robert McAfee Brown. New Haven, CT: Yale University Press, 1986.

———. *Essays in Applied Christianity*, edited by D. B. Robertson. New York: Meridian, 1959.

———. "Intellectual Autobiography." In *Reinhold Niebuhr: His Religious, Social and Political Thought*, 3–7, edited by C.W. Kegley and R. W. Bretall, Library of Living Theology, 11. New York: McMillan, 1961.

———. "Intellectual Autobiography." In *Reinhold Niebuhr: His Religious, Social and Political Thought*, 1–25, edited by Charles Kegley. New York: Pilgrim, 1984.

———. *An Interpretation of Christian Ethics*. New York: Harper and Brothers, 1935.

———. *An Interpretation of Christian Ethics*. New York: Meridian Books, 1956.

———. *The Irony of American History*. Chicago: University of Chicago, 1952.

———. *Justice and Mercy*, edited by Ursula Niebuhr. New York: Harper and Row, 1974.

———. "The King's Chapel and the King's Court." In *Ethics in the Present Tense: Readings from Christianity and Crisis 1966-1991*, 208-211, edited by L. Howell and V. Lindermayer. New York: Friendship, 1991.

———. *Leaves from the Notebook of a Tamed Cynic*. Chicago: Willett, Clark and Colby, 1929.

———. *Love and Justice: Selections from the Shorter Writings*, edited by D. B. Robertson. New York: Meridian, 1957.

———. *Moral Man and Immoral Society: A Study in Ethics and Politics*. Louisville, KY, 1932.

———. *The Nature and Destiny of Man, Volume 1: Human Nature*. New York: Scribner's Sons, 1964.

———. *The Nature and Destiny of Man, Volume 2: Human Destiny*. New York: Scribner's Sons, 1964.

———. *On Man's Nature and His Communities*. New York: Charles Scribner's Sons, 1965.

———. *Pious and Secular America*. Eugene, OR: Wipf and Stock, 2001.

———. *Reflections on the End of an Era*. New York: Charles Scribner's Sons, 1934.

———. *Reinhold Niebuhr: Major Works on Religion and Politics*. New York: Penguin Random House, 2015.

———. *The Reminiscences of Reinhold Niebuhr*. Microfilm. New York: Columbia Oral Research Project. 1957.

———. "Reply to Interpretation and Criticism." In *Reinhold Niebuhr: His Religious, Social, and Political Thought*, eds. Charles Kegley and R. Bretall, 429-52. New York: Pilgrim, 1956.

———. "Reply to Interpretation and Criticism." In *Reinhold Niebuhr: His Religious, Social, and Political Thought*, edited by Charles Kegley, 505-29. New York: Pilgrim, 1984.

———. *The Self and the Dramas of History*. New York: Charles Scribner's Sons, 1955.

———. "To America and Back," in *I Knew Dietrich Bonhoeffer*, edited by W.D. Zimmermann and R.G. Smith, translated by K.G. Smith. London, England: Collins, 1966.

———. "Toward New Intra-Christian Endeavors." In *Theological Crossings*, edited by A. Geyer and D. Peerman. Grand Rapids, MI: Eerdmans, 1971.

———. "A View from the Sidelines." In *The Essential Reinhold Niebuhr Selected Essays and Addresses*, 250-58, edited by Robert McAfee Brown. New Haven, CT: Yale University Press, 1987.

Niebuhr, Richard Reinhold. "The Creation of Belief." In *Cross Currents*, Summer 1990, 111ff.

———. *Experiential Religion*. New York: Harper and Row, 1972.

———. "Foreword." In *H. Richard Niebuhr: Theology, History and Culture*, edited by William Stacy Johnson. New Haven, CT: Yale University Press, 1996, vii-x.

———. "A Power and a Goodness," *Christian Century*, 80 (1965) 1472-75.

———. "Preface." In H. Richard Niebuhr. *Faith on Earth: An Inquiry into the Structure of Human Faith*, ix-xiii. New Haven, CT: Yale University Press, 1989.

———. "The Problem of Preaching at Easter." In *The Christian Century* (April 6, 1960) 410.

———. "The Widened Heart." *Harvard Theological Review* 62(2) (April 1969) 127-154.

BIBLIOGRAPHY

Niebuhr, Ursula, ed. "Introduction." In Reinhold Niebuhr, *Justice and Mercy*. New York: Harper and Row, 1974.

———. ed. *Remembering Reinhold Niebuhr: Letters of Reinhold and Ursula Niebuhr*. San Francisco: Harper, 1991.

Paeth, Scott R. *The Niebuhr Brothers for Armchair Theologians*. Louisville, KY: WJK, 2014.

Primeaux, Patrick. *Richard R. Niebuhr on Christ and Religion: The Four Stage Development of His Theology*. Toronto, Ontario: Edwin Mellen, 1981.

Sifton, Elisabeth (nee: Niebuhr). *The Serenity Prayer: Faith and Politics in Times of Peace and War*. New York: W. W. Norton, 2003.

———. interview by Serene Jones. "Reinhold Niebuhr and Union Theological Seminary: A Daughter's Reflection on His Life and Work," 2015, https://youtu.be/WhI9fM-mgAc [accessed February 14, 2022].

Sifton, Elisabeth, and Fritz Stern. *No Ordinary Men: Dietrich Bonhoeffer and Hans von Dohnanyi, Resisters Against Hitler in Church and State*. New York: New York Review, 2013.

Stone, Ronald. *Professor Reinhold Niebuhr: A Mentor to the Twentieth Century*. Louisville, KY: WJKP, 1992.

CPSIA information can be obtained
at www.ICGtesting.com
Printed in the USA
BVHW031107200622
639821BV00002B/2